Reconstructing Political Pluralism

SUNY Series in Political Theory:
Contemporary Issues

Philip Green, Editor

Reconstructing Political Pluralism

Avigail I. Eisenberg

State University of New York Press

Published by
State University of New York Press, Albany

© 1995 State University of New York

Printed in the United States of America

For information, address the State University of New York Press,
State University Plaza, Albany, NY 12246

Production by Bernadine Dawes • Marketing by Fran Keneston

Library of Congress Cataloging-in-Publication Data

Eisenberg, Avigail I., 1962–
    Reconstructing political pluralism / Avigail I. Eisenberg.
      p. cm. — (SUNY series in political theory. Contemporary issues)
    Includes bibliographical references (p. 193) and index.
    ISBN 0-7914-2561-4 (HC : acid-free). — ISBN 0-7914-2562-2 (PB : acid-free).
    1. Democracy. 2. Pluralism (Social sciences) I. Title. II. Series.
JC423.E37   1995
321.8 — dc20
                                                  94-49026
                                                      CIP

1 2 3 4 5 6 7 8 9 10

for Colin

Table
of Contents

Acknowledgments

I am grateful to my friends and colleagues at Queen's University, Cornell University, and the University of British Columbia who have read and commented on all or parts of this book and, in some cases, discussed at length with me the arguments developed in it. In particular, I would like to thank Don Blake, Dave Blatt, Matt James, Nadia Khalaf, Will Kymlicka, Jean Laponce, Cary Nederman, John Russell, Christine Sypnowich, and SUNY's reviewers for their helpful comments and encouragement. A special thanks is extended to Professor Jock Gunn, who supervised an earlier version of this project at Queen's University and who has taught me a great deal about scholarship and research. Finally, my deepest gratitude is extended to Colin Macleod, who helped me to develop many of the arguments and to express them clearly, and whose support and encouragement were tireless.

I
Reconstructing Political
Pluralism

In the 1990s, political theory has moved beyond the debate between liberalism and communitarianism to explore possibilities which can avoid the putative excesses of both positions. Many of these possibilities are built upon the recognition that contemporary liberal societies contain a plurality of groups, communities, and associations, and that political theory should not aim at overcoming this plurality but rather should strengthen it. In these theories, culture, difference, and identity are crucial. Indeed, the heterogeneity of most societies in these respects is now the central focus of analysis. It is viewed, at the same time, as furnishing a recipe for oppression and as providing a reason for celebration. The aim of this book is to retrieve and reconstruct a legacy of political pluralism that illuminates these developments and clarifies the type of challenges concerning pluralism that are central to contemporary politics.

Striking similarities exist between the new theories of difference and identity and a number of theories dating back to the turn of the century which comprise the tradition of political pluralism in liberal-democratic thought. Political pluralism is usually thought to consist of a set of ideas in postwar political science which held that democracy consists of interest-group competition. This conventional view is mistaken, and this book aims at broadening and deepening our understanding of political pluralism. It does so by examining the resources in the history of political pluralism that are usually given insufficient attention. The main argument is that political pluralism is comprised of two intertwined themes: the distribution of power amongst groups, and the group's power to direct individual development. At the center of the pluralist tradition are the analytical means to understand clearly, within the context of liberal-democratic politics, the political relation between individuals and groups or communities and the relation between a plurality of groups and the state. The tools supplied

1

by political pluralism allow political theory to move beyond the remnants of the liberal-communitarian debate and to approach the new theories of identity and community politics with deeper insight aided by historical hindsight.

Generally, what I mean by political pluralism are theories that seek to organize and conceptualize political phenomena on the basis of the plurality of groups to which individuals belong and by which individuals seek to advance and, more importantly, to develop, their interests. This definition emphasizes political, not metaphysical, philosophical, sociological, or psychological pluralism. However, pluralist theories are found at the crossroads of political studies and other disciplines. So, to a large degree, these other dimensions cannot be avoided when exploring political pluralism. Here, all the dimensions of pluralism which are relevant to understanding it as a political tradition are examined.

In order to capture accurately the nature of the tradition, the definition of pluralism that I propose is quite broad. It encompasses the work of some theorists who may not recognize, as many do not, the pluralist tradition in which their work fits. For reasons I shall explain, some theorists may even eschew the pluralist label and discourse in spite of the affinity of their theory to it. At the same time, the definition is not so broad that it includes any theory which is merely consistent with a pluralistic organization of politics and society. If it did, then any type of politics which protects the individual's freedom to associate might be called pluralist because individuals who are free to associate tend to form groups and associations.[1] Freedom of association is a necessary condition of political pluralism. But pluralist theories go beyond merely accepting the legitimacy of free association and, instead, view association and multiple group affiliations as the central elements of the liberal and democratic aspects of politics. Pluralism is not just tolerated; rather, it is the very life pulse of a healthy polity.

In many political theories, including theories of political pluralism, groups are the key to understanding and reconstructing liberal-democratic politics. There are three reasons for this. First, individuals, when given the freedom, tend to organize themselves into groups. Theories which ignore this fact are criticized for lacking sociological realism. Most significantly, this sociological fact has important implications because it indicates that a politics opposed to the group basis of society must be prepared to coerce individuals to abandon their chosen asso-

---

[1] For an interesting discussion of the relation between freedom of association and the pluralist tradition, see Horn, *Groups and the Constitution*, chapter 1.

ciative ties. All pluralists recognize that coercion is the only alternative to political pluralism.

Second, groups have a privileged place in liberal-democratic politics because they are the means to vindicating individual interests. If individuals are not driven to form groups in order to appease their instincts, then they do so in order to acquire the resources necessary to address their interests. These resources can be internal or external to the group. Internal resources might include skills or knowledge that group members teach each other and that then can be used to meet the interests of the members as individuals. The "tricks of the trade" are resources often gained in this way. External resources are usually the focus of political pluralism. In pluralism, groups are viewed as the means to acquiring political power. The internal resources which a group possesses are organized in order to capture external resources or power. This power is then used, for instance, to change a governmental policy in a way that advances the interests of the group's members. The idea here is that, whereas the individual is relatively powerless to challenge or change state policy, the aggregation of individuals in a group presents to the state a more formidable contender.

The third reason why groups are the key to liberal-democratic politics is that they help to construct individual identity and are the means to individual development. As communitarians have argued, self-development occurs in a social context. The individual's identity is inexorably tied to the individual's attachments to others or to contexts in which the individual is situated. The role that groups, communities, and associations play in self-development is central to political pluralism as well. The preciousness of groups inheres not simply in the instrumental role they play to advance individual interests. Groups are centers of human interaction, and interaction is the means by which individuals develop their personality or identity. Groups shape the individual's personality; they are the contexts in which different aspects of individual identity are nurtured. The political salience of this developmental process has two sides. On one hand, groups are the means to the sort of self-development often identified as the *raison d'être* of democracy.[2] On the other hand, groups can stifle and distort development through socialization processes that seek to control and oppress the individual. To understand the power and significance of groups requires that both these

---

[2] See Mill, *The Subjection of Women;* Macpherson, *The Life and Times of Liberal Democracy;* Kariel, *The Eclipse of Citizenship;* and Gould, *Rethinking Democracy,* amongst many others.

possibilities are considered and more — often groups protect and defend those aspects of the individual's personality that they have developed. In this sense, groups can develop or distort individual identity and, in either case, will seek to protect that aspect of identity which they have helped to create.

These three reasons — (1) that groups are part of the fabric of sociological reality, (2) that they are the means to political power and thus are instrumental in the pursuit of individual interests, and (3) that they are the means to individual development — partly explain why political pluralism places such importance on groups. But pluralism is not the same as group theory. The political significance of groups in pluralist theory is contained in two additional elements. The first element is that *many* groups coexist in society. The second element is that individuals have *multiple* affiliations and memberships.

For instance, with regards to the first element, pluralism grapples with the need to form groups in order to vindicate interests while insisting that power not be concentrated in one group. The centralized state, the notion of absolute sovereignty, the power elite, are all nemeses of political pluralism. Centralized political power, with its attendant risk of tyranny, is the problem that pluralism seeks to solve without abandoning the group. Historically, part of the pluralist challenge has been to develop the analytic means to distinguish the illegitimate use of power by a group to dominate other groups from the legitimate use of power by a group to vindicate the interests of its members. This challenge is met by adopting a broad view of power that includes both the resources groups can acquire and their influence in shaping the individual's personality. Pluralists insist that in liberal democracy both types of power must be shared by a plurality of groups.

Second, healthy individual development relies on a pluralist context and not simply a group context. Similar to the pluralistic understanding of political power, the critical tools for analyzing the politics of personal development are not found by merely understanding that individuals develop their identities in a social context. Nor is it sufficient to incorporate into one's political theory the mere observation that groups have the power to shape individuals in healthy and unhealthy ways, although in light of contemporary communitarian analysis, a reminder of this fact is entirely apropos. Pluralism holds that the individual requires a multiplicity of developmental contexts in order to enjoy healthy development. Each context develops part of the individual's identity, and together the social contexts provide a critical perspective from which the individual can scrutinize her relation to each context.

It is important to emphasize that, in the pluralist process, the individual is the only agent with legitimacy to negotiate and shape her identity. Pluralists have been unwilling to approach personal development with the disposition of a moral psychologist who is willing to pick and choose among the different facets of the individual's identity those parts which are healthy and those which are diseased. Moreover, to empower the state to make such judgments violates the pluralist program because the power over individual development that this would vest in the state would be so vast as to undermine a pluralistic distribution of power. In order for the individual to have the power to shape her own identity, she must enjoy many affiliations and, crucially, no single group or community may dominate and direct her development. Each group provides for the individual a different vantage from which she can critically assess her attachments to other groups. Reassessing one's attachments requires that a multiplicity of contexts be accessible to the individual. The individual need not be conceptualized as unencumbered by all attachments at once in order to understand how she is the author of her life and identity.

I argue that political pluralism offers the means to resolve the familiar tensions between political power and individual development, between individual autonomy and group membership, and thus between individualism and communitarianism. It focuses on the relation between political power and individual development and seeks to offer the analytic resources to distinguish between the empowerment and domination of groups in society and between the healthy development and social control of individuals. It accomplishes this by (1) insisting that group power not be centralized in society, (2) ensuring that individuals can effectively transform their associational ties, and (3) understanding the relation between group power and individual development.

The Historical Resources

The historical resources of political pluralism can be categorized into three episodes. The first episode occurs in the United States from the turn of the century until the 1920s and involves the work of John Dewey and William James. The second episode overlaps the first but addresses a distinct set of themes. It includes the work of J. N. Figgis, G. D. H. Cole, Harold J. Laski, and Mary Parker Follett and enjoyed significant attention in Britain and the United States mainly in the 1920s and 1930s. The third episode, again centered in the United States, involves a host of theorists but is chiefly captured here in the postwar pluralism of Robert Dahl.

These three episodes offer different ways in which various thinkers have explored the possibilities that political pluralism offers. They are not meant to represent an exhaustive survey of political pluralist thought. Rather, they have been chosen as vehicles by which to elucidate different ways in which the relation between the two central themes of political pluralism — (1) the distribution of political power to vindicate interests and, (2) the distribution of political power to facilitate individual development — has been conceptualized in political pluralism. Dividing the theories into three episodes is meant to distinguish theories that are historically and conceptually proximate with particular regard to their treatment of the two themes. The only theorist who is an exception to this general rule is Follett, who explicitly attempted to draw together the strengths of James's and Laski's pluralism. Her contribution bridges two episodes more clearly than it fits into either one.

In most cases, the pluralist thinkers examined here intellectually influenced each other. Part of the historical project which is pursued here traces these influences. It would be a mistake to suppose that these three episodes display an evolution of pluralist thought — particularly if by "evolution" one reads "improvement." The contributions of some pluralists, such as Laski and Dahl, have been chosen primarily because of the significant flaws found in their analyses. None of the thinkers examined in the context of the three episodes provides a theory of pluralism which is perfectly, or even nearly, suited to contemporary concerns. The claim here is that each of these three episodes and each theorist within a given episode offers a distinct perspective on the relation between political pluralism and democracy that is closely shaped by the political and philosophical preoccupations of their day. For example, Dewey's pluralism is born out of his pragmatic philosophy, while Dahl's pluralism is closely tied to behavioralism. Together, the episodes can be viewed as a tradition in which the two themes prevail despite other influences which distinguish the theories. They give rise to a critical perspective by which different theories of pluralism are seen as either sophisticated and clear or deficient and distorted accounts of the relation between the two themes.

For instance, Dewey found pluralism attractive partly because he saw in it an alternative to the absolutist conception of sovereignty. He also developed a political understanding of personal development in which, again, pluralism was key. But, his theory fails to trace the connection between these two elements and, as explained in chapter 2, leaves itself open to being misinterpreted as politically absolutist, or, in more contemporary exegesis, communitarian. In light of the seemingly contradictory rhetoric that Dewey used to explain his ideas in the intellectual circles of the 1920s, the key to discovering how to reconcile various aspects of his work is found in the pluralist dimension of his project.

In contrast, Laski's pluralism, while again containing at least a hint of both themes, neglects personal development and comes to reflect an obsessive preoccupation with the consequences of concentrated political power. The thinness of Laski's pluralism and the explanation for why he ultimately abandoned it in favor of a more Marxist approach to state power lay partly in his neglect of the developmental power that groups possess. Cole also ignored the developmental consequence of political pluralism. In contrast, Follett reintroduced the resources of pluralist personal development in criticizing Laski's theory. Figgis offered a developmental variant of pluralism, but one with holistic implications which the pluralists of his time sought to avoid.

The postwar theory of pluralism, which is explored here mostly through the work of Dahl, made prominent both elements of the pluralist equation. But, it was beholden to the standards of political behavioralism and, consequently, attempted to extract the normative dimension from these elements, from the pluralist theory that they comprised, and from democratic theory in general. While this postwar episode contains the pluralism that is most often referred to in contemporary understandings of the doctrine, it offers a distorted purview of the tradition. Nonetheless, the distortions reveal a great deal; the empirical bent of postwar pluralism placed maximal emphasis on the sociological realism and contextualism of pluralism. Existing practices and goods, including existing groups, pathways of socialization, associative ties, and cross-pressures (e.g., multiple affiliations) are legitimized by the functional explanation of democracy offered in postwar pluralism. Conversely, the tradition's radical resources to transform society and improve individual well-being through pluralistic personal development are stifled. In spite of the distortions, the central elements of this episode are those which persist in the other theories as well, namely, the pluralistic distribution of political power and the way in which groups shape individual identity.

The interconnection between the two themes of pluralism is the central focus here and provides the justification for both the choice of thinkers and the course by which pluralist thought shall be analyzed. The theorists chosen do not include all political pluralists, nor do I claim that they made the most important contributions to the pluralist thought

of their day, even though in most cases they are remembered as central
contributors. In some instances, the variants of pluralism explored are
ones in which important mistakes and deficiencies are evident. The purpose of doing so is, again, to trace the treatment of the two themes in
various pluralist theories and intellectual contexts in order to develop
historical hindsight. This hindsight is critical for the purpose of reconstructing political pluralism so that it can address contemporary questions regarding the political relations between individuals, groups, and
societies.

Contemporary Theory and the Resources of Political Pluralism

In addition to examining the historical resources and sketching the conceptual contours of political pluralism, this book addresses two additional needs in contemporary political theory. One need which has already been mentioned is to move beyond the liberal-communitarian
debate. Pluralism has the resources to accomplish this, but persuading
political theorists and political scientists that the resources discussed
here are pluralism's resources requires that several misunderstandings
about political pluralism be identified and that a broader historical understanding of the tradition replace the current one. The discourse of
pluralism has been poisoned by being typecast as a theory merely about
interest-group competition. So a second need, and one that must be addressed before the usefulness of political pluralism can be appreciated,
is to resurrect theories of pluralism and reconstruct the tradition on the
basis of a broader historical view.

Since it is significant to the historical perspective adopted in this
book that political pluralism has been misunderstood in contemporary
commentaries, some evidence of this misunderstanding should first be
offered. Most contemporary political theorists see pluralism solely as a
postwar doctrine about interest groups. Least surprisingly, this view
emerges in commentaries which examine the various theories of the
state and state power. Particularly when Marxist approaches are discussed, pluralism is introduced as the appropriate foil. Marxists were
successful in exposing postwar pluralism "as a naive and/or narrowly
ideological celebration of Western democracies."[3] In *Analyzing Marx*, for
example, Richard Miller launches his discussion of political power with
the pluralist thesis. "Pluralists believe that no social group or minority

---

[3] Held, *Models of Democracy*, 186.

coalition of social groups dominates government in the United States."[4] Throughout his discussion, Miller identifies only one pluralist theorist, namely Robert Dahl. Because Miller is interested in the postwar pluralist theory of state power to which Marxists offered such compelling critiques, one could argue that there is no need for him to give a full account of pluralism. Nonetheless, Miller does not explain to his readers that, by pluralism, he only refers to the postwar rendition.

Nor should he feel compelled to include such a proviso given how the doctrine is construed in the vast majority of current democratic theory. In David Held's *Models of Democracy*, an entire chapter is devoted to pluralist theory.[5] Here again, the postwar variant is taken as definitive of the tradition. "Classical pluralism," as Held calls it, is largely the construction of Dahl who is "one of the earliest and most prominent exponents of pluralism."[6] It is a theory about interest group competition and about the distribution of power within the state. Held discusses the Marxist challenge to pluralism. He identifies Charles Lindblom and the more current Dahl as "neo-pluralists" who attempt to meet Marxist and other challenges to the postwar doctrine. Unlike most other theorists, Held also ventures to make some observations about the historical antecedents of pluralism. But, in doing so, he only highlights the narrowness of his approach to the doctrine. The "intellectual ancestry of pluralism" is found in Schumpeter and Weber.[7] And its "intellectual terms of references" include Madisonian democracy and utilitarian concepts of interest satisfaction.[8] In each case, these antecedents are directly tied to the particular pluralist theories of Dahl and David Truman. The pluralist theories of Dewey, James, and Laski — including, for that matter, the traceable influence of these theorists on Dahl — are not mentioned by Held.

If one ventures outside the terms of reference set by those keen to investigate only theories of state power, the understanding of pluralism does not get any broader. One of the most significant examples is Carol Gould's extensive analysis of pluralist political theory and pluralist ontology in *Rethinking Democracy*. Schumpeter and Dahl are the key pluralists who, along with other advocates, take "politics as an arena of the conflicting interests of groups in a society."[9] Gould also under-

---

[4] Miller, *Analyzing Marx*, 152.

[5] Held, *Models of Democracy*, chapter 6, 186–220.

[6] Held, *Models of Democracy*, 187.

[7] Held, *Models of Democracy*, 186–87.

[8] Held, *Models of Democracy*, 187.

[9] Gould, *Rethinking Democracy*, 8.

stands pluralist doctrine as a whole to reflect only the themes found in the postwar variant of it. Moreover, as a description of the postwar variant, her interpretation emphasizes the weaknesses and faults of the doctrine, including faults that are questionably attributed even to postwar pluralism. For instance, Schumpeter is identified by Gould as a key proponent of pluralism whereas postwar pluralism is usually understood as the position which attempted to remedy the absence of intermediary groups in Schumpeter's conception of democracy.[10] Furthermore, contrary to the interpretation of postwar pluralism offered here, and most interpretations of Dewey's work, Gould contends that pluralism "eschews any notion of a common good as anything more than a political myth."[11] Like most contemporary commentators, she characterizes pluralism as though only the postwar variant counts, as a position which primarily entails elite competition for political power, and thus, as a doctrine that denigrates representation and participation.[12]

The narrowness of Gould's characterization would be no different from those offered in most democratic theory if it weren't for the fact that in introducing her discussion of pluralist ontology she cites the proponents of pluralism to include Madison, Dewey, Schumpeter, Dahl and Berelson. She goes outside the narrow postwar choices of pluralists, yet bases the description of pluralist ontology, like the previous discussion of pluralist theory, purely on interest-group competition and interest articulation, both of which dominate only the postwar understanding of pluralism. So, in addition to taking a narrow view of pluralism and thus reaffirming the view taken in most democratic theory, Gould mistakenly ascribes this narrow view to scholars such as Dewey who were pluralists but whose theories barely resemble that of Dahl (and certainly don't resemble that of Schumpeter!).

Gould, in particular, makes the task of retrieving a broad understanding of pluralism and its resources especially relevant because she identifies self-development as the central goal of an adequate democratic theory yet finds nothing in pluralism that is helpful to attaining this goal. In a sense, this is hardly surprising given that she takes pluralism to be a theory mainly about the distribution of political power and interest-group competition. Yet, even the postwar theories are replete with observations about how individuals are socialized through

---

[10] Held launches his chapter with precisely this contrast between Schumpeter and the post-war pluralists. See *Models of Democracy*, 186.

[11] Gould, *Rethinking Democracy*, 9.

[12] Gould, *Rethinking Democracy*, 9.

groups. Although, as I argue in the final chapter, socialization is distinct from self-development, Gould pays no attention to this facet of postwar pluralism nor, of course, to the theory of pluralist self-development in Dewey's work. On Gould's account, pluralism seems to have nothing to do with self-development.

One cannot help but suppose that pluralism occupies a central place in Gould's work, if only as a target of criticism, because she finds something attractive about the doctrine. Pluralism contains what she calls a "mixed ontology" based on individualism and holism.[13] The mixed ontology is attractive to her because the general aim of her book is to reconcile individual freedom and social equality. The reconciliation requires an ontological framework which can overcome the "traditional antithesis between the individual and society."[14] I argue that pluralist theorists have always aimed at overcoming this antithesis in developing their arguments. But given her view of pluralism, Gould finds the doctrine useless in this respect; "this theoretical model does not provide a ground for criticizing the inequitable relations of power and domination that may exist among individuals within a group, among groups and among individuals outside their group memberships."[15] With a broader view of the doctrine, Gould might find more use for political pluralism.

One additional example, also drawn from contemporary political theory, is Iris Marion Young's characterization of pluralism in *Justice and the Politics of Difference.* Young's book is an attempt to reorient theories of justice to address the oppression some groups experience which is caused by racism, sexism, homophobia, and the inequitable distribution of resources in society. The central challenge for Young is to construct a theory of political participation and representation that can include all groups in society while, at the same time, respecting their distinctive identities. Public deliberation, she argues, must take place in a diversity of groups and forums and from a variety of perspectives.[16] Her solution has a pluralist ring to it, which is strengthened when she identifies, as pluralists in the past have, the inadequate resources of both atomistic individualism and communitarian theories (which she calls, the "republican revival"). But Young strictly avoids the discourse of pluralism to characterize her own theory, although she mentions "interest-

---

[13] Gould, *Rethinking Democracy,* 99.
[14] Gould, *Rethinking Democracy,* 26.
[15] Gould, *Rethinking Democracy,* 100.
[16] Young, *Justice and the Politics of Difference,* 88.

group pluralism" mostly in order to dismiss the resources it offers as well. She describes pluralism as a theory based on the self-interested pursuit of policy objectives which uses the client-consumer relation to reconceptualize the citizen-state relation. The theory is said to fragment the "whole" citizen into various roles and interests. Moreover, because it views politics as the pursuit of private self-interest, it forestalls the emergence of public discussion and decision making. "The rules of interest-group pluralism do not require justifying one's interests as right, or compatible with social justice."[17] Pluralism appears to be completely inadequate for her purposes, since it stifles public deliberation and depoliticizes political processes.[18] Although Young does not identify any theorist who advances what she calls interest-group pluralism, the postwar political scientists appear to be the likely culprits if only because of the often-used label, *interest-group pluralism.*

As in the case of Gould, Young's book makes the job of retrieving a broader and more accurate understanding of political pluralism all the more important because she searches for resources that I argue are central to pluralism yet finds nothing useful in what she characterizes as pluralist theory. Her project is to find a means by which heterogeneous groups can engage in democratic politics without oppressing each other. As clearly as this is a project about pluralist politics of some sort, what she describes as pluralism is obviously deficient for her purposes. And this is the only pluralist theory at her disposal, I suggest, because this is nearly the only understanding of pluralism found in contemporary political theory.

While there are exceptions to the characterization sketched above, the view, that pluralism is an interest-group theory developed in the postwar period which has little to do with anything except competition and power politics, is represented in most contemporary political theory. I have mentioned four examples that together are exemplary of a broad range of contemporary theory: from Miller's contemporary Marxist theory, to Held's survey of democratic models, to new theories of democracy, such as those of Gould and Young, in which self-development and identity politics are central. Many more examples exist.[19] But these are sufficient to illustrate the nature and pervasiveness of the narrow caricature of political pluralism found in contemporary theory.

---

[17] Young, *Justice and the Politics of Difference*, 190.

[18] Young, *Justice and the Politics of Difference*, 72.

[19] For example, see Sunstien. "Beyond the Republican Revival"; Ward, "The Limits of Liberal Republicanism."

The Liberal-Communitarian Debate

Before exploring the richer alternative to this caricature, let me explain the second concern in contemporary political theory that this book addresses. In addition to improving our understanding of the historical legacy of political pluralism, a more complete understanding of pluralism's resources provides the means to move beyond the sharp disagreements between liberals and communitarians which dominated political theory in the 1980s.

Michael Sandel, Alasdair MacIntyre and Charles Taylor are the leading proponents of the communitarian critique of liberalism. Although the works of other communitarians are mentioned, I focus mainly on their influential contributions. The position of each of these communitarian theorists differs in some respects. But here their commonalities are of primary interest. What unites them is their broad diagnosis of the malaise suffered by contemporary liberal societies. In their view, the breakdown of a cohesive social fabric in Western democracies has been caused largely by the excessive individualism which pervades liberal philosophy and political practice. According to Sandel, who uses John Rawls as the exemplary liberal, liberalism crucially depends on a metaphysical notion of the self in which the self is conceptualized as isolated from all of its attachments and obligations. On this unrealistic basis, Rawls constructs an account of the requirements of justice. In a similar vein, Taylor argues that liberalism's fundamental premise is atomism. Atomism is a doctrine, most evidently displayed in the state-of-nature theories like those of Locke and Hobbes, that "affirms the self-sufficiency of man alone. . . ."[20] From these starting points, liberals construct the ideal of liberal society — a society that is suited to self-sufficient and unencumbered individuals. In the communitarian account, political practices, such as entrenched individual rights, secure a distance between the individual and the society or groups to which she is affiliated. Liberal rights are seen as supposing an extravagant notion of self-sufficiency, and they reinforce the individual's ability to challenge and resist the claims her society or community might otherwise make upon her.

For both Sandel and Taylor, the use of an asocial notion of individuals as a starting point is precisely the wrong way to conceptualize the contours of justice. To begin with, the idea that individuals are self-

---

[20] Taylor, *Philosophy and the Human Sciences,* 189.

sufficient, or that they can be imagined as separate from all their attachments to others, is unrealistic. In this respect, communitarian theories seem to have some affinity with feminist arguments which hold that liberal theory conceptualizes the individual as non-nurturing and childless; as a being who is reputed to be denuded of particular characteristics, yet nonetheless seems to prize autonomy over inclusion and individuation over sociality.[21] This conception of the individual is either completely unrealistic or, at least, it is cultural- and gender-specific. Communitarianism emphasizes the hazards of liberal individualism by highlighting the manifestly unrealistic conception of the individual at the heart of liberalism.

The second and more urgent problem for communitarians is that the atomistic or unencumbered individual of liberalism is the means by which liberals introduce values into their political theories that are inimical to the value of community. Liberal rights place strict limits on the pursuit by a community of shared communal ends. One need not be a communitarian to know that this is precisely what rights are supposed to do, especially those rights, such as freedom of speech, conscience, and religion, which have a historical legacy of protecting dissenters from their communities. Communitarians do not object explicitly to the right to dissent. Rather, they argue that the liberal culture of rights undermines the pursuit of the common good and is thereby self-defeating. Thus, the problem of liberal rights is presented in terms of the ideology of individual self-sufficiency that it promotes. Rights, according to Taylor, are intended to protect certain treasured human capacities. Yet, these capacities can only be developed within social contexts. Therefore, to be committed to the capacities, one must also be obligated to the social context in which the development of capacities is possible. Rights, which are thought to have primacy over community interests, accentuate the distance and separation of the individual from the social context in which valued capacities can be developed. The ideology of rights offers a portrait in which the individual is fully developed from the start, treasured capacities and all. All that rights need do is protect the fully developed, self-sufficient individual and her capacities from communal oppression. One central communitarian objection to the primacy of rights is that, in reality, individuals are not fully developed. As useful as rights might be to *protect* capacities, they are poor tools to *develop* these capacities. What is required for their development

---

[21] Friedman, "Feminism and Modern Friendship," 105. Others mentioned by Friedman include Dorothy Dinnerstein, Nancy Chodorow, and Carol Gilligan.

are healthy communal contexts and attachments, notions of common purposes and goods. Liberal political theory and practice, because it promotes individual self-sufficiency and autonomy, succeeds in distancing the individual from these means to her development. It undermines the development of those capacities it seeks to protect. According to communitarians, political theory needs to be refocused on the connection between the individual and her community or social context. For MacIntyre, the virtues of membership in community and the common good offer the key values of a better theory. Similarly, for Taylor and Sandel, those values consist of the shared ends and attachments that constitute our identity.

As provocative and compelling as communitarians have been, various problems seriously compromise the usefulness of their critiques. These problems are rooted in the fact that communitarian analysis and conclusions are ambiguous.[22] Communitarians are more forthcoming about their objections to the liberal conception of the self than about their alternative to it. On the basis of what is relatively clear in their analysis, two principal difficulties with communitarian politics merit special mention. First, communitarianism is undermined by its unrealistic understanding of individual development. Rosenblum argues that communitarians appear to have an affinity for a romantic conception of the self for which they search by focusing on the attachments that link individuals to the social context in which individuals are situated. The communitarian alternative promises to be more sociologically realistic than does the picture of the autonomous and self-sufficient individual that communitarians attribute to liberalism. But, in fact, the communitarian conception is beset with its own difficulties. First, communitarians seem dangerously disinterested in the possibility that the community's power to facilitate self-development also bestows on communities the means to social control. Second, the more expansive notion of selfhood that communitarians propose "lacks psychological realism" because it attempts to "float above the messy reality of pluralism."[23] Communitarians situate individuals in a community without recognizing that individuals have a plurality of attachments and that they may benefit from this pluralism.

A second limitation of communitarianism lies with its unsophisticated understanding of the nature of community. Communitarian theory harbors an unrealistic and naive notion of political power. For ex-

---

[22] See, for instance, Rosenblum, "Pluralism and Self-Defense," 216.
[23] Rosenblum, "Pluralism and Self-Defense," 220.

ample, communitarians argue that the latent traditions and shared meanings which liberal practices repress ought to be resurrected. They prescribe this resurrection without, for a moment, entertaining the possibility, noted by Rosenblum and others,[24] that "repression serves a crucial need and that what is unconscious is repressed because it is dark, dirty, or dangerous."[25] At its worst, communitarians require us to suspend our disbelief about the nasty side of political power which is exercised by communities.

Although communitarianism may have exposed weaknesses in liberal theory, it also displays some fatal flaws. Its lack of psychological realism about the plurality of attachments and contexts in which the individual finds herself is surprising given that attention to the requirements of self-development comprises such a central part of its project. Its lack of sociological acumen regarding the potential oppression found in community and the sexist and racist nature of many repressed or sadly unrepressed traditions is truly remarkable, since it is precisely this charge against liberalism, individualism, and state-of-nature theories that launches the communitarian critique.

Contemporary Strands of Pluralist Theory

One explanation for why communitarianism suffers from these problems is that, in constructing their arguments solely to address the weaknesses of liberalism, communitarians quickly lost sight of the problems that liberalism purports to solve. As a result, one way of addressing the challenges posed by communitarianism is to reinvigorate and tinker with liberal commitments. Most of the actual responses to the communitarian critique do exactly this. Throughout the 1980s, theorists explored the resources that liberalism contains to meet the communitarian challenge.[26] In some measure, this book contributes to this project of liberal renewal. After all, pluralism is one of the key resources of liberalism and, moreover, one that figures prominently in current thoughts about liberalism.[27] "Reasonable pluralism," Rawls argues, signifies a plurality of reasonable comprehensive doctrines that are "part of the work of free practical

---

[24] See Gutmann, "Communitarian Critics of Liberalism," 319.

[25] Rosenblum, "Pluralism and Self-Defense," 217.

[26] See, for instance, Galston, *Liberal Purposes;* Gutmann, "Communitarian Critics of Liberalism"; Kymlicka, *Liberalism, Community, and Culture;* Macedo, *Liberal Virtues.*

[27] Rawls, *Political Liberalism.*

reason within the framework of free institutions."[28] However, this work must be distinguished from other recent works in light of the special emphasis it places on the importance of mechanisms other than rights. In particular, pluralism, as a central value of liberal societies, contains the political resources to safeguard liberty and to facilitate self-development. By and large, recent liberal theory has not adequately recognized these resources and has, instead, depended heavily on liberal rights to perform these tasks. Even in Rawls's recent reflections, "reasonable pluralism" is not a tool. It is construed only as a sociological fact: the result of freedom, rather than the means to safeguard freedom.

There are a few theorists who have turned to a discourse in which pluralism, rather than liberal rights or liberal individualism, enjoys special recognition. Various theorists have found refuge from communitarian and liberal-individualist politics in something that looks like pluralism and, at times, is called pluralism by them. For example, Marilyn Friedman criticizes communitarianism for emphasizing the importance of only involuntary communities into which one is born or which one discovers. The potential oppressiveness of such communities, and the possible distortions of the identities that they help to create, is often revealed, according to Friedman, by communities of choice: ". . . some relations compete with others . . . provide standpoints from which others appear dangerous."[29] Friedman emphasizes, like so many pluralists do, that, realistically, the modern self belongs to a plurality of communities. And thus "[t]he problem is not simply to appreciate community per se but, rather, to reconcile the conflicting claims, demands, and identity-defining influences of the variety of communities of which one is a part."[30] Friedman seems to be searching for a pluralist discourse but her project does not provide, as this one does, an understanding of the historical roots of this discourse.[31]

Michael Walzer also places a type of pluralism at the center of his project. In *Spheres of Justice,* he argues for what might be called a pluralistic notion of distributive justice in which the distributive rules of fairness for different goods are said to depend on the good in question and the social context in which it is used. Walzer's pluralistic account of distributive justice is significantly different from the variety of pluralism discussed in this book. Nonetheless, there are points of common

---

[28] Rawls, *Political Liberalism,* 37.
[29] Friedman, "Feminism and Modern Friendship," 108.
[30] Friedman, "Feminism and Modern Friendship," 108.
[31] Another example of this sort is Macedo, *Liberal Virtues,* chapter 7.

concern. Many of the pluralist theories examined here require that power and thus authority be distributed pluralistically. By doing so, one might consequently be distributing to communities the authority to establish distinct rules of just distribution which are based on needs and practices particular to the community, as Walzer advocates. Walzer connects this notion of what he calls "complex equality" to the identity-constituting features of goods and practices to be distributed. The identity of a people is tied to the way they conceive, create, possess, and employ social goods.[32] From different identities there will arise different notions of just distribution. As in the reconstructed pluralism proposed here, ensuring that the identities of individuals can develop in a healthy manner is also linked by Walzer to dividing power pluralistically.

Throughout Walzer's work, the notion of pluralism is evident. In *Obligations*, Walzer discusses pluralistic association also in developmental terms. "Secondary associations" prepare individuals for citizenship by being forums in which one can learn how to rule and be ruled.[33] While writing about concerns very similar to those which animated British pluralism, Walzer argues that associations are forums whose size and scale are small enough to provide for meaningful participation. Groups can foster or challenge state loyalty and individual obligation to the state.[34] In a more recent essay, Walzer's idea of pluralism reemerges under the label of *critical associationalism*.[35] Critical associationalism holds that democratic politics and citizenship are dependent upon the "strength and vitality of our associations."[36] The state's role, under Walzer's formulation, is essential in both framing civil society and occupying space within it.[37] "It compels association members to think about a common good. . . ."[38] Because critical associationalism promotes small and more intimate forums for interaction, it is the means to efficacious political participation. It is the route to egalitarianism because it redistributes power and encourages the formation of groups for the purposes of empowerment. "Dominated and deprived individuals are likely to be disorganized as well as impoverished, whereas poor people with strong families, churches, unions, political parties and ethnic alliances are not likely to be dominated or deprived for

---

[32] Walzer, *Spheres of Justice*, 6–7.
[33] Walzer, *Obligations*, 219.
[34] Walzer, *Obligations*, 221–22.
[35] Walzer, "The Civil Society Argument."
[36] Walzer, "The Civil Society Argument," 98.
[37] Walzer, "The Civil Society Argument," 103.
[38] Walzer, "The Civil Society Argument," 103.

long."[39] And finally, a pluralized vision of civil society addresses the concerns of nationalism. The polarization of binational states can be prevented if nationalist politics and culture is pluralized.[40]

Many different aspects of pluralism appear in Walzer's work. The themes of self-development and political power are repeatedly mentioned. And associations are considered central to these themes as well as to participation, production, and cultural politics. So Walzer's view is helpful in constructing a new pluralist theory. But, it falls short of *being* such a theory largely because many of the relevant strands of pluralism which he discusses are never gathered together into a theory of pluralism. The connections between self-development and political power are not systematically traced. Nor does Walzer locate his pluralism in relation to other pluralistic arguments that have been entertained in political theory. Establishing such a location is central to the present project.

Part of what Walzer's vision entails has received a sophisticated elaboration in Paul Hirst's work on associational democracy. In an essay entitled, "Retrieving Pluralism," Hirst defends Dahl's position against criticisms of it levied mainly by Marxists. He argues, in ways similar to my argument, that pluralism has been misunderstood and that it is worth retrieving. But by "pluralism" Hirst seems to mean only the post-war variant. Nonetheless, he concludes that pluralism responds to a central weakness of Marxist theory, namely that Marxism lacks an account of why the ruling class is divided and how this affects its rule. Any attempt to explain this division will lead radicals to pluralist theory.[41] "[A]ccept that the 'ruling class' forms a large number, and the need, within Marxism, for a theory like pluralism becomes evident."[42] Hirst's understanding of what constitutes pluralism actually extends beyond Dahl's work and also includes the work of Laski, Cole, and Figgis. What Hirst calls *associational democracy* is a normative theory of society whose central claim is that "human welfare and liberty are both best served when as many of the affairs of society as possible are managed by voluntary and democratically self-governing associations."[43] As in Walzer's work, associations are said to empower the disempowered. They offer citizens greater control over their affairs, again, be-

---

[39] Walzer, "The Civil Society Argument," 100.
[40] Walzer, "The Civil Society Argument," 101.
[41] Hirst, "Retrieving Pluralism," 164.
[42] Hirst, "Retrieving Pluralism," 173.
[43] Hirst, "Associational Democracy," 112.

cause in them participation is more efficacious than it is in the modern state. Associations also empower the communities which they often represent and in which individuals can live by the shared common standards which they have chosen.[44] Associations are the means to empowerment in two senses. First, they are the route through which the politics of identity can strengthen a common political culture. A state that celebrates associationalism will provide groups with a reason to opt into, rather than out of, its political culture.[45] Second, associationalism also provides the route to economic democracy by forging the path between collective ownership and planning and unregulated market individualism.[46]

The richness of Hirst's analysis is compromised only by his insistence that the associations which ought to govern be voluntary ones. Associational relationships, he insists, must "arise from genuine cooperation . . . the idea of being *compelled* to join a voluntary association for any purpose is an absurdity. . . ."[47] While such an idea is absurd, his exclusive focus on voluntary associations allows Hirst to avoid some of the greater challenges of identity politics and self-development. Like Friedman, Hirst is primarily interested in communities that are chosen, whether they are economic or identity-based. With regards to identity politics, Hirst explains that "old and new identities are reshaped to be sources of social solidarity around *chosen* standards."[48] But it is an odd sense of choice that confronts women who fight against sexism or cultural minorities that fight against racism. The *absence* of choice in the construction of their identity partly shapes their efforts, and, to a large extent, it is the identities that they did not choose but that they nonetheless live with that they struggle against.[49] In this crucial respect, Hirst's retrieval of pluralism is incomplete. Although Hirst gathers together the strands of pluralism constructed by Dahl and by the British pluralists, his project does not provide a full reconstruction of a pluralist tradition in political thought.

Another contemporary attempt to reintroduce pluralism is found in the work of Kirstie McClure who explicitly seeks to reconstruct what

---

[44] Hirst, "Associational Democracy," 121.

[45] Hirst, "Associational Democracy," 119.

[46] Hirst, "Associational Democracy," 128. Another insightful attempt to resurrect British pluralism and the pluralist notion of economic democracy is found in Rainer Eisfeld, "Pluralism as Critical Political Theory."

[47] Hirst, "Associational Democracy," 131.

[48] Hirst, "Associational Democracy," 118.

[49] This argument is pursued in chapter 6.

she calls the pluralist tradition. She argues, as do I, that pluralist thought can be divided into three generations. According to McClure, the first generation consists of the work of Ernest Barker, Harold Laski, Arthur Bentley, and Mary Parker Follett. The second generation consists of Robert Dahl, David Truman, and Charles Lindblom, and the third generation includes the work of Michael Walzer, Chantal Mouffe, and Ernesto Laclau. All three generations oppose a unitary conception of state sovereignty, insist on the irreducible plurality of the social sphere, conceptualize the groups which arise in the social sphere as a product of dynamic struggles with each other, and view the individual as a site of multiple affiliations. The differences that McClure detects between these generations are many and varied, and they are partly affected by how she groups the generations. For example, Follett's theory of personal development escapes mention possibly because the significance of personal development as a pluralist theme is diminished in the company of Barker, Laski, and Bentley. Given McClure's categorizations and the curious omissions of many personal-development pluralists such as William James, John Dewey, and J. N. Figgis, personal development is not identified by her as a significant theme in pluralist thought.

But, what is fascinating about McClure's analysis is that she detects an evolution of the notion of politics which, she claims, pluralist theorists have facilitated. The first generation constructed a political theory that offered radicals an alternative to Marxism. They extended the purview of the public sphere by insisting on the inclusion of occupational groups and thus the extension of the political into the workplace. The notion of citizenship was also extended to include participation in the occupational group process. The second generation extended the notion of the public sphere still further. It rejected the strictures of political economy and redefined government as an arena in which *all* groups with articulated interests could compete and conflict with each other. The bounds of political identity, according to McClure, were widened in one sense by the second generation. But, the scope of identity politics was shored up again by the postwar insistence that the citizen was a rational actor who chose amongst her affiliations those interests she would formally express and that these interests were then expressed only through the political institutions of the state.[50]

The third generation seeks no such restrictions on the expression of identity in politics. The multiplicity of affiliations gives rise to a mul-

---

[50] McClure, "On the Subject of Rights," 119.

tiplicity of political sites and a corresponding expansion of the public sphere. Citizenship is expressed through participation and articulation in all the various new political spaces, and these new spaces, according to Laclau and Mouffe, are not just territorially bound or in the juridical institutions of the state. While the state remains an important site of political struggle and citizenship, the citizen now is seen to make political claims in her family, workplace, sexual relations and so on. Politics then "is not simply the projection of group 'interests' onto the screen of state policy, but indeed precedes this in the intricate processes of articulation through which such identities, representations, and rights claims are themselves contingently constructed."[51] The third generation of pluralism envisions "a politics which extends the terrain of political contestation to the everyday enactment of social practices and routine reiterations of cultural representation."[52]

The multiplicity of political sites that McClure finds in third generation pluralism might be the consequence of the pluralistic location of authority centers to which Rosenblum refers. "Certainly for women, the presence of state authority may be less imposing than male authority in settings like the family and work."[53] Rosenblum's notion of pluralism, like that of Hirst, connects pluralism to the themes of political power and self-development. And like that of McClure, it includes an historical purview of the tradition. But the history that Rosenblum surveys is not one of pluralism per se but rather of the romantic liberalism in which she argues pluralism was key. Rosenblum connects pluralism to a romantic longing that she identifies in the work of communitarians and some liberals. This longing appears to consist of finding an alternative to the sterile public sphere of liberalism — the meeting place for strangers and adversaries. For Rosenblum, the central element of any plausible alternative would consist of pluralism. Pluralism recognizes what Albert Hirschman called, the "shifting involvements" of the self amongst diverse spheres. John Stuart Mill also advocated a pluralist thesis in which the different spheres of life are seen as different arenas for self-development.[54] Shifting involvements, Rosenblum argues, are central to any accurate reflection on political freedom and theories of self. "[T]he context of moral and political practices is, on any description, pluralist; on any account of

---

[51] McClure, "On the Subject of Rights," 121.
[52] McClure, "On the Subject of Rights," 123.
[53] Rosenblum, "Studying Authority," 103.
[54] See Rosenblum, *Another Liberalism*, chapter 6.

personal development, the self is formed from an array of relations in diverse spheres."[55]

While Rosenblum's project does not explore the work of all the theorists identified here as pluralist, her argument has many similarities to mine. First, her project also views the standard portrayal of pluralism as a challenge to reconstituting a pluralist perspective. "For the past two decades or so," she argues, "[the pluralist alternative] has been submerged beneath a mountain of normative and analytical claims for pluralist politics as a way of making pubic policy."[56] Second, she also identifies as remarkable the lack of attention that pluralism receives in both liberal and communitarian traditions even though there have been the romantic liberals, such as Humboldt and Dewey, who found pluralism to be central to the liberal project. She finds fault particularly in communitarianism because many of its central elements such as attention to context and concern for individual development ought to lead its proponents to take pluralist arguments seriously. The communitarians stress an account of "thick" selves in which individual identities are constituted by their social environment. They argue for the need to resurrect latent traditions and shared meanings. But the community in which this reform shall take place is not imagined by them to be pluralistic. Instead, they offer examples of parochial groups such as tribes or Puritanical sects that cannot be taken as serious political alternatives. As Rosenblum notes, they "illustrate moral and psychological propositions about 'belonging,' not political ones."[57] As political options for self development, these are regressive and dangerous ones.

In the pluralist tradition one can find an alternative to the universal community of liberalism and the parochialism of communitarianism. Pluralism denotes, according to Rosenblum, "the existence of diverse centers of social influence and political power."[58] It emphasizes the shifting involvements through which the self develops and thus, one supposes, the ability to enter and exit associations and spheres.[59] The central political insight of pluralism is found in the shifting nature of involvements which is, for Rosenblum, a "self-defense." It allows the self to escape oppressive embeddedness while simultaneously seeking

---

[55] Rosenblum, "Pluralism as Self-Defense," 208.
[56] Rosenblum, "Pluralism as Self-Defense," 220.
[57] Rosenblum, "Pluralism as Self-Defense," 215.
[58] Rosenblum, "Pluralism as Self-Defense," 220.
[59] Rosenblum, "Pluralism as Self-Defense," 221.

community. It thus forges the connection between political power and self-development.

While Rosenblum is correct in emphasizing the need for associa- tion and the need to exit association as central to pluralism, her account is, as is much existing pluralist theory, irreconcilable with the fact that exit is not a realistic alternative in many cases of individual "belong- ing." The level of an individual's involvement in a political club differs greatly from her attachment to her culture or family specifically in terms of her agency to "shift" involvements. Associational ties are sometimes too deep to sever. Sometimes, they must be transformed through means other than exit. While Rosenblum recognizes the messy nature of plu- ralistic membership, she does not see the political ramifications of dif- fering depths of attachment. She forces all attachments to assume a vol- untary guise; pluralism is a liberal perspective which emphasizes the voluntary nature of association through the ability of individuals to shift involvements. "This . . . requires," she argues, "open groups which are denied guaranteed populations, with the result that a wide range of rights and claims are individual and not attached to collective identi- ty."[60] A fuller account of pluralism must also grapple with the political consequences of nonvoluntary and involuntary associations.

The works of these theorists — Friedman, Walzer, Hirst, McClure, and Rosenblum — consist of what might be a fourth episode of plural- ism. Some of these pluralists do not recognize the historical tradition of pluralism in which their work fits. Walzer's arguments fall into this cat- egory. The others recognize traditions which are slightly or significantly different from the one which shall be examined here. There is a plural- ity of perspectives within the pluralist tradition itself. The aim of this book is not to argue that only one correct construction of the tradition exists (namely, the one proposed here). The influences of political the- ory can and do travel in many directions. Those who have reconstruct- ed the pluralist tradition differently from how it is constructed here have done so in order to emphasize different themes. The themes that I shall emphasize differ significantly from the notions of politics and citizen- ship which comprise McClure's and Walzer's interest. Hirst and Rosen- blum focus on themes which are central to my project as well, but their historical projects differ from my own. Hirst is not interested in recon- structing a pluralist tradition as much as he wants to use pluralist ar- guments to solve contemporary political crises. And, while Rosenblum reconstructs a tradition, it is not a pluralist tradition per se but rather a

---

[60] Rosenblum, "Pluralism as Self-Defense," 221.

tradition of liberal romanticism, in which pluralism is key. Moreover, in the work of Rosenblum, Hirst, and many other pluralists, individual attachments are presumed to be voluntary. In casting associations only as voluntary, contemporary pluralists risk distancing their theories from the central challenges to democratic politics of culture and identity. Moreover, by doing so they ignore the potential oppression and distorted development which may occur through the socialization facilitated by groups, communities, and cultures. This particular problem is one that I shall examine and hope to solve in the last chapter.

The political pluralism found in each of the three sets of theories examined here recognizes a variety of groups and a variety of ways in which one can belong to a group. They each view pluralism as an alternative, on one hand, to excessive and implausible individualism and, on the other hand, to overly simplistic holistic notions of community. Together their theories provide a perspective from which one can analytically and practically distinguish political empowerment from domination and self-development from social control.

The first half of this book consists of two chapters. Chapter 2 examines the pluralist theory of John Dewey and briefly looks at William James's influence on Dewey's thinking about personal development. Chapter 3 starts by examining pluralistic notions of power and then compares the pluralist theories of J. N. Figgis, G. D. H. Cole, Harold Laski, and Mary Parker Follett. The second half of the book also consists of two chapters. Chapter 4 examines the group theories of Bentley and Truman and the behavioral theories which played a prominent role in postwar pluralism. The analytic focus of this chapter is the individualism that one finds in group theories and in the behavioral approach. Chapter 5 focuses on Dahl's pluralism and the notion of community and individualism found within it. Chapter 6 attempts to bring together some of the resources identified in the pluralist traditions discussed in earlier chapters in order to tackle the question of how pluralism can be reconstructed so that it addresses the sort of groups central to contemporary politics.

It is perhaps wise to warn readers about what the project does not entail. First, this examination is not meant to be an exhaustive survey of all theorists who might be classified as pluralists. Nor is it merely a survey of literature by and about the chosen pluralists. The intent is to reveal the contributions that a suitably reconstructed pluralism can make to understanding the relation between individuals and communities. Second, it is not a conceptual analysis which seeks to trace the etymology of the word *pluralism*. Particular theorists have been chosen in order to find specific resources of political pluralism, especially the resources appropriate to analyzing the relation between political power and personal development. This means that I do not investigate the moral pluralism to which Isaiah Berlin,[61] Joshua Cohen,[62] or Stephen Macedo[63] ascribe, the ontological pluralism to which Gould refers, or the metaphysical pluralism to which Dewey was drawn.

Finally, I do not intend to adhere strictly to the methods of an intellectual historian. I attempt to understand the theories according to the historical contexts in which they were fashioned. Moreover, I show how misinterpretations of some works (particularly, those of Dewey and Dahl) are the result of neglecting the intellectual context in which these scholars wrote. Nonetheless, I shall also be analyzing these theories according to standards and concerns relevant to contemporary politics.

---

[61] See Berlin, *The Hedgehog and the Fox.*
[62] See Cohen, "Moral Pluralism and Political Consensus."
[63] Macedo, *Liberal Virtues.*

II
John Dewey and the
Roots of Political Pluralism

The central insight of Dewey's political pluralism is that the fragmentation of political power facilitates individual development. The values which Dewey's theory privileges are individual development and community which he combined with the more familiar pluralist concern that power not be concentrated in the hands of one group.

Recently, there has been a reemergence of interest in Dewey's metaphysical and political theories. However, in these current reexaminations of his work, scant attention is paid to his pluralism. One gets glimpses of a Dewey who disdained idealist metaphysics,[1] who embraced empirical methods,[2] who criticized individualism,[3] and who characterized democracy as a "way of life." By focusing only on these elements and ignoring his commitment to pluralism, Dewey's theory of democracy has been mischaracterized as either unintentionally absolutist and thus antidemocratic, or as communitarian. These characterizations depend upon exaggerating some aspects of his theory — either his vision of the Great Community or the positivism of his pragmatic methods — and ignoring the significance of other elements. What is ignored (and in some cases denied) is the political and social pluralism that Dewey thought was necessary for democracy and for healthy individual development.[4] Without the pluralist element, Dewey's interpreters can only offer partial accounts that distort his theory and also misplace it in traditions of thought where its pluralist elements are sure to be forgotten.

---

[1] Rorty, "Post-Modernist Bourgeois Liberalism," 583–89.

[2] Kaufman-Osborn, "John Dewey and the Liberal Science of Community"; Metz, "Democracy and the Scientific Method in the Philosophy of John Dewey."

[3] Bellah et al., *The Good Society*, 164–65.

[4] An important exception to this is Westbrook's *John Dewey and American Democracy*. Westbrook acknowledges Dewey's pluralism intermittently throughout his analysis. See particularly, 244–47.

Here I retrieve Dewey's pluralism and, at the same time, explain why the absolutist and communitarian interpretations of Dewey are inaccurate. First, I examine the intellectual context in which Dewey developed his arguments. Second, I turn to the absolutist thesis, developed in the work of William Metz and T. V. Kaufman-Osborn, which focuses on the role of scientific methods in Dewey's political analysis. These commentators suggest that Dewey's methodological commitments propel his theory towards an absolutism in which diversity of opinion need not be tolerated. Third, I explore Dewey's methods and show how, contrary to the absolutist interpretation, they gave rise to his notion of political pluralism. Fourth, I examine Dewey's understanding of the Great Community in the context of claims made by Robert Bellah et al., William Sullivan, Benjamin Barber, and others, that Dewey is a communitarian of an earlier age. The communitarian interpretation, though mistaken, is inviting because both Dewey and contemporary communitarians develop their political theories around the observation that the self develops in the context of community. Dewey's commitment to pluralism distinguishes him from communitarians. Communitarianism fails to recognize what Dewey emphasized, namely, that precisely because groups play an important role in developing individuals, their power over individuals must be limited and fragmented.

The Metaphysics of Pluralism

The dominant thrust of American political theory at the turn of the century was to discredit classical liberalism, specifically the way in which liberalism treated the individual. From Hobbes to Mill, the "old liberalism" was condemned for juxtaposing liberty to social action. It was purported that liberals portrayed the individual as "a Newtonian atom having only external time and space relations to other individuals, save that each social atom was equipped with inherent freedom."[5] Even John Stuart Mill, who is known to have departed from traditional individualism in order to develop a theory that depended on social context,[6] was

---

[5] Dewey, "The Future of Liberalism," 696.

[6] Gaus, *The Modern Liberal Theory of Man*, 7, 16. Gaus explores the manner in which many of the writers at the turn of the century were interested in reconciling individuality with sociability. In *The New Liberalism*, Freeden also illustrates how collectivist and organic concepts had a great influence on turn-of-the-century liberalism, forcing theorists of that time to reconcile individuality with notions of social welfare and sociability.

regarded as just another classical liberal. While perhaps Mill's liberalism is socially sensitive compared to that of Hobbes or Kant, his critics had their own very high standards of social sensitivity with which they assessed his theory. For example, Leslie Stephen argued that Mill's distinction between self- and other-regarding actions violates the condition of mutual dependence that exists between society and the individual and belies the "excessive individualism" of Mill's position in which society is portrayed as an aggregate of individual "atoms" rather than as an organic whole.[7]

Neo-Hegelian idealists, such as T. H. Green, Bernard Bosanquet, and Josiah Royce, also rejected the notion that individuals are self-sufficient units. Bosanquet denounced the "negative individuality" of Mill because it encouraged individuals to become "absorbed in their exclusiveness." He argued that, for Mill, "[t]he dim recesses of incommunicable feeling are the true shrine of our selfhood."[8] For similar reasons, he criticized liberal theories of psychology. "Associationism" was considered by the critics to be typical of liberal explanation because it requires that the whole be analyzed by looking at the parts. It held that states of consciousness or experiences are constructed by the association of "mental atoms" or "idea elements." When liberals analyze society, they look to individuals and see separate units and finite selves who alone cannot possess "ultimate reality" or "Real Value."[9] Conversely, idealists understood the parts in terms of the whole. Only collectively could individuals come close to Reality or perfection — to understanding the nature of the Mind that informs their nature. Human nature, the neo-Hegelian idealists argued, is revealed only at the level of humanity and has little to do with the individuality of people.[10]

One central interest of this idealist school was to discover how best the individual is able to develop distinctively human capacities. After rejecting associationist psychology, they opted for a theory with greater social substance. They argued that, since all higher interests relating to "humanness" are inherently social, the individual's association with others is the only vehicle to human development of any sort. Only within the context of society can individuals come to understand their natures. This sort of theory, while successful in introducing a social element to the notion of personal development, was criticized for

---

[7] Stephen, *The English Utilitarians*, 289–94.

[8] Bosanquet, *The Value and Destiny of the Individual*, 36.

[9] Bosanquet, *The Value and Destiny of the Individual*, 69, 104–5.

[10] Gaus, *The Modern Liberal Theory of Man*, 45.

compromising individuality and individual autonomy. Particularly, Bosanquet's theory implied that interests relating to one's humanness were to be set independently of securing acknowledgment or agreement from individual citizens. Although the idealists claimed that their position did not completely preclude the possibility of individual choice, the choices individuals could make would be limited by a concept of "the Good" that can only exist at the societal level. In other words, these idealists believed that the Good defines individuals rather than being defined by them. Therefore, unlike Millian liberals, who regarded individual development as the primary goal of politics, idealists such as Bosanquet understood personal development to be the means to unraveling Goodness or Truth.

William James's Pluralist Metaphysics

To many political and psychological theorists, idealism offered a novel perspective on personal development and politics, but not one that was any more plausible than the liberal formulation. Theorists, like William James, who were disenchanted with both idealist and liberal notions, attempted to construct a third alternative that borrowed elements from each tradition.

In his *Principles of Psychology*, published in 1890, James resituated psychological inquiry from its traditional place in philosophy to what he considered to be a more scientific context. His central complaint was that psychological theories ignore even minimal scientific standards and that both associationist and idealist theories could not be considered scientific because they were unverifiable.[11] His alternative was a pragmatic approach or what he called "radical empiricism" which insists that truth be dependent on verification and knowledge be dependent on experience.[12]

James's theory of psychology is far more positivistic than the idealists' theories. However, he and many scholars whom he influenced, including Dewey, were in no sense rigid positivists or empiricists.[13]

---

[11] See James, *Principles of Psychology*, 332–41 for critiques of Mill, Hume, and associationist psychology; 341–50 for critiques of Hegel, Kant, and Green and the idealists' notion of self.

[12] Moore, *American Pragmatism*, 135–80.

[13] Wahl, *Pluralist Philosophies of England and America*, 153, and Moore both label James's work as positivist and empiricist. Because James and particularly Dewey have been held to rigid standards of positivistic science by some interpreters, various inconsistencies, which will be explored below, have been mistakenly attributed to their arguments.

Pragmatism is probably the more suitable label for his radical empiricism because the methods he advocated strive to serve the practical purposes to which his theories are directed. Pragmatism meant concentrating on phenomena which are central to psychological reality though perhaps not, strictly speaking, quantifiable. For instance, he insisted that relations between individuals are objects of the senses in the same way as individuals are and that dynamic values such as development, maturation, and growth must be made central to psychological theory. These values, he argued, reflected psychological reality more than do either the stagnant concept of an all-inclusive Mind or the mechanistic ideals of associationism.[14]

In 1904 and 1908, James published *A Pluralistic Universe* which is partly devoted to analyzing critically the metaphysics of Hegel, Kant, and Leibniz. According to James, the central component of idealist metaphysics is monism in which everything in the universe is somehow the product of the same value. Depending on the theory, that value is either Goodness or Truth or the Mind. James argued that monism cannot be taken seriously because the existence of an Absolute is unverifiable. Yet, the available alternative — atomism — was no more plausible, since it holds that there are no connections between aspects of the universe.[15] According to James, between these extremes, the actual universe exists, and it contains a plurality of values. Not everything is part of the same "kingdom" or infused with the same transcendent Mind. Nor is reality captured by a metaphysics of atoms wherein compounds or bundles are mysteriously linked.[16] The universe, according to James, is pluralistic in the sense that aspects of the universe are connected in some ways, while in other ways they are not connected; "the pluralistic world is therefore more like a federal republic than like an empire or kingdom."[17] Furthermore, the connections that exist can be *observed*. Unlike monism and atomism, pluralism is verified by pragmatism. Pragmatism holds that

---

[14] For further analysis of how James viewed his ideas as distinct from idealism and associationism, see Bernstein's "Introduction" in William James, *A Pluralist Universe*, xv, and Scheffler, *Four Pragmatists*, 113.

[15] James, *Radical Empiricism and the Pluralistic Universe*, 51.

[16] James noted that Mill is an important exception among the associationists. According to James, Mill disclaimed the argument that a "nonphenomenal" binding agent cements thoughts together even though he claimed to support associationism. James contended that, in order to explain the stability of self-identity over time from an associationist perspective, Mill had to ascribe to this or a similar view. See James, *Principles of Psychology*, 340.

[17] James, *Radical Empiricism and the Pluralistic Universe*, 322.

truth is based on experience. Truth about the nature of reality reveals that reality is varied, as is the nature of individual experiences.[18]

From these metaphysical conclusions, James applied pluralism to psychological theory. I shall discuss James's pluralist theory of personal development and its influence on Dewey below. For now, what is important to note is that the intellectual atmosphere in which Dewey was situated was one in which a heightened sensitivity existed regarding the individualistic and holistic implications of political theories. It would be surprising to find a theorist in this context who unintentionally endorses either excessive individualism or holism. Moreover, James and possibly those like Dewey, whom he influenced,[19] were searching for an alternative way, from that proposed by liberals and neo-Hegelian idealists, to conceptualize the individual's relation to the social whole.

The Absolutist Thesis

Like James, Dewey was enthusiastically attracted to the scientific approaches taken to problem solving, and he used these approaches as models for reconstructing social inquiry. At the turn of the century, he rejected the abstract theorizing characteristic of neo-Hegelian idealism and searched for methods which relied on scientific standards. The pragmatic approach, which James had pioneered, offered him the alternative he sought. Pragmatism entailed seeking knowledge through experience and experiment. It required that ideas be verified and that the problems of philosophy be directly connected to the "problems of men." It was the path, for Dewey, to discovering "the laws of the phenomena of society."

In describing and developing these improved methods, Dewey embraced the positivistic language of the physical sciences. Here lies the first reason why his theory is misinterpreted as absolutist. Dewey's methodological ambitions have been interpreted alongside those of Hobbes, Durkheim, and Weber to belong to the "scientific rationality school of social science" in which the authority of science demolishes alternative sources of shared value.[20] According to Kaufman-Osborn, sci-

---

[18] Wahl, *Pluralist Philosophies of England and America*, 155–56.

[19] James's influence on Dewey is reflected in Dewey's dedication to James of his *Studies in Logic*. James's influence is also well documented throughout Westbrook, *John Dewey and American Democracy*.

[20] Kaufman-Osborn, "John Dewey and the Liberal Science of Community," 1163.

ence for Dewey was a type of language that revealed to everyone who applied it a common perception of social problems and their solutions.[21] The dissemination of scientific standards constructed a community in which the political virtue of all participants entailed understanding and applying the scientific method to problems confronting the community. The common perspective disclosed by correct application of the method would replace the role that individual opinion and perspective have usually assumed in democratic politics.[22]

The absolutist thesis focuses on the tyrannous potential of community rather than its potential assets. According to Kaufman-Osborn, Dewey implied that a correct answer exists to every social and political problem and that this answer emerges by applying scientific methods. Therefore, the methods would justify dispensing with political opinion and political parties along with public participation and democracy. As Kaufman-Osborn explains, "[t]he very existence of parties presupposes the arbitrary conflict of opinion that is to be overcome when genuinely scientific solutions to social problems reveal to all the harmony of interest that lies beneath present partisan discord."[23] So, Dewey's community is potentially one of perfect consensus rather than one of diversity and pluralism. The successful application of science to social concerns means that differences of opinion no longer divide the citizenry because the correct answer to any problem can be determined by applying the right methods.

Metz agrees with Kaufman-Osborn that, in Dewey's theory, the scientific method is the authoritative standard and sole legitimate means of judgment. But, Metz argues that, rather than forcing consensus, as Kaufman-Osborn claims, Dewey's methods will lead to government by scientific experts. If, as Dewey claimed, social problems can be solved scientifically, why solicit participation from the citizenry in political decision making? Because he emphasized scientific problem solving, Dewey's conception of democracy is one in which decisions are best made by experts rather than through maximal participation of the citizenry. While Dewey realized the potential danger of government by experts and technicians alone, his theory putatively fails to show how members of the community will have sufficient knowledge of the method to check the experts.[24] Metz

[21] Kaufman-Osborn, "John Dewey and the Liberal Science of Community," 1152.
[22] Kaufman-Osborn, "John Dewey and the Liberal Science of Community," 1152.
[23] Kaufman-Osborn, "John Dewey and the Politics of Method," 189.
[24] Metz, "Democracy and the Scientific Method in the Philosophy of John Dewey," 257.

concludes that "the formation of intelligent public opinion based on scientific method — however potentially valuable in a genuine democracy
— remains an obscure and futuristic goal within Dewey's theory."[25] Kaufman-Osborn concludes likewise that Dewey's attempt to eliminate all reconstructed opinion and interest from a scientific democracy is decided-
ly "undemocratic and anti-political."[26]

Dewey's Methods

The absolutist thesis holds that Dewey's conception of scientific inquiry
and its role in politics commits him to a technocratic authoritarian vision
of political organization. This interpretation also leads to a characterization of Dewey's notion of the Great Community in which the community is constructed out of the common language, standards, and
sense that shared scientific methods of inquiry cultivate. I shall set aside
the character of the Great Community for now and first consider the
argument based on methods. The argument consists of two parts: 1)
that Dewey's methods were scientific in nature, and 2) that these methods effectively replaced democratic politics and eliminated pluralism.
    Indisputably, scientific methods were used by Dewey as standards
for developing pragmatism. Pragmatism entailed forming "working hypotheses," "experimentation" and "operational reasoning." But, Dewey's
interpreters have exaggerated the identity between pragmatism and positivistic science and attributed to Dewey a rigid positivism that is not exhibited by his writing.[27] Dewey unequivocally argued that pragmatism em-
ulated only the *logic* of scientific argument; the pragmatic approach
"expressly disclaims any effort to reduce the statement of matters of conduct to forms comparable with those of physical science. But it also expressly proclaims an identity of logical procedure in the two cases."[28]
When he explains the sense in which social inquiry ought to be experimental, Dewey reiterates the distinction between his methods and those
of the physical sciences: "[w]hen we say that thinking and beliefs should

---

[25] Metz, "Democracy and the Scientific Method in the Philosophy of John Dewey,"
258.

[26] Kaufman-Osborn, "John Dewey and the Politics of Method," 293.

[27] Westbrook agrees. ". . . by giving such terms [i.e., scientific intelligence, social control, and adaptation] meanings Dewey never intended, some interpreters of his work
have managed to burden him with positions he explicitly rejected," *John Dewey and American Democracy*, xiii.

[28] Dewey, *The Problems of Men*, 214.

[29] Dewey, *The Public and Its Problems*, 202.

be experimental, not absolutistic, we have then in mind a certain logic of method, not, primarily, the carrying on of experimentation like that of laboratories."[29] Again, in the context of making clear his intentions, Dewey promoted scientific procedures by pointing out that experience ought to be considered the basis of an experimental method whereby ideas about the social world are tested. When analytical efforts are considered in experimental terms, the process of theorizing is understood as confirming or disproving a "hypothesis"; "[i]f we exclude acting upon a hypothesis, no conceivable amount of intellectual procedure can confirm or refute the validity of an idea."[30] Moreover, reasoning processes are "operationalized" or, as he also claimed, made "reflective" by nothing more dramatic than carefully thinking through a problem. Sidney Morgenbesser's description of Dewey's notion of operational reasoning reflects this characterization:

> [w]e start to inquire when we encounter a problem we cannot resolve simply by relying on our current beliefs; we acquire knowledge as a result of inquiry; and we use that knowledge to make sense out of what we experience or to act on now warranted belief . . . — getting to know, knowing, using knowledge — and arguing for the view that we get to know by acting in order to confirm hypotheses and to resolve problems encountered.[31]

There is little that is particularly positivistic about this form of reasoning beyond the rhetoric that it employs. Yet, the standards upon which Dewey insisted differed significantly from those that, he argued, characterized classical liberalism and neo-Hegelian idealism. The monism and absolutism of Hegelian abstractions and the unverified universalism of liberal prescriptions were repeatedly used by Dewey as foils to his efforts. One did not have to go as far as adopting rigid positivism to formalize analysis in a way that appeared scientific when compared to these alternatives. It is more plausible to view Dewey's insistence on greater methodological rigor as a response to the nebulous and elusive Hegelian and liberal doctrines rather than a wholesale, uncritical endorsement of positivism.

But, in addition to exaggerating Dewey's affinity to positivism, the absolutist thesis relies on caricaturing scientific methods as a whole.

---

[30] Dewey, "Essay in Experimental Logic," 944.
[31] Morgenbesser, *Dewey and His Critics*, xiii–xiv.

Although the prospect of certain knowledge seems to accompany the discovery of physical laws of nature, scientific inquiry is also sensitive to context, it displays flexibility about what approaches to inquiry may be fruitful, and, in recognition of fallibility, it often draws conclusions tentatively. These standards of science get short shrift in the absolutist interpretation. Yet, these were the values that Dewey argued were most useful when pragmatism was applied to politics. For example, he argued that pragmatism could instill in analysis the flexibility and attention to circumstances which scientific procedures brought with them. "Policies and proposals for social action [ought to be treated] . . . as working hypotheses, not as programs to be rigidly adhered to and executed."[32] He also argued that by applying operational reasoning, including experimentation and hypothesis testing, ideas can grow and change character.[33] The pragmatic method elucidates the active and changing nature of knowledge because, in casting proposals for social action as working hypotheses, it encourages those who apply it to be active in solving social problems. Hypotheses are confirmed or refuted only through testing. Testing an hypothesis means attempting to solve the problem at hand. Applying one hypothesis after another, in the process of testing each, enhances the probability of actually solving social problems. Moreover, viewing the enterprise in experimental terms — "in the sense that [hypotheses] will be entertained subject to constant and well-equipped observation of the consequences they entail when acted upon, and subject to ready and flexible revision in the light of observed consequences"[34] — would incorporate the perfect amount of flexibility into the process. The scientific posture of the approach introduces into social inquiry a sensitivity to context, a motivation to put ideas to work solving problems, and an acute awareness of the consequences of solutions.

The sense in which Dewey's methods drew upon scientific standards is also reflected in his understanding of how they were to apply to the analysis and practice of democratic politics. In practice, the methods were clearly *not* supposed to get rid of diversity of opinion as the absolutist thesis suggests: "Differences of opinion in the sense of differences of judgment as to the course which it is best to follow, the policy which it is best to try out, will still exist."[35] Dewey's objective, again, was to

---

[32] Dewey, *The Public and Its Problems*, 202–3.
[33] Dewey, *The Quest for Certainty*, 161.
[34] Dewey, *The Public and Its Problems*, 203.
[35] Dewey, *The Public and Its Problems*, 203.

reform reasoning employed in politics in a far less rigid sense than positivism demands. He emphasized the need to *reduce* ungrounded or unsupported differences in view, not to eliminate diversity of opinion per se. Once pragmatism was adopted, he hoped that "opinion in the sense of beliefs formed and held in the absence of evidence will be reduced in quantity and importance."[36] The position he opposes is not the diversity and pluralism fostered by deliberation and reflected in differences of opinion but rather the "views generated in view of special situations [that are] frozen into absolute standards and [that] masquerade as eternal truths."[37] Dewey argued that reconstructed opinion, which is held tentatively and which is based on good reasons, will allay the derogatory connotations that "mere opinion" has acquired in the political sphere.[38] So, opinion is not eliminated from democratic politics. To the contrary, pragmatism rescues and revitalizes opinion for democratic politics.

Dewey's Pluralistic State

One final reason to conclude that the absolutist thesis mischaracterizes the nature and implications of Dewey's methodological commitments is that Dewey believed that pragmatism provided grounds for pluralism rather than absolutism. Pragmatism required that practical definitions of political and social concepts be adopted. The most significant of these concepts for Dewey were the public-private distinction and the notion of state sovereignty. Rather than being attached to some obscure concept of the Absolute, as the neo-Hegelians advocated, the public becomes a concrete, empirical entity defined on the basis of observable transactions and consequences. A public is a group motivated to act by an issue that arises as a result of the indirect consequences of a transaction that takes place within society. It "consists of all who are affected by the indirect consequences of transactions to such an extent that it is deemed necessary to have those consequences systematically cared for."[39] This definition was intended to provide a practical means of distinguishing the public from the private.[40] Whereas matters of public concern are transactions that produce indirect consequences, matters of private concern are transactions with no indirect consequences or at least none that

---

[36] Dewey, *The Public and Its Problems,* 203.

[37] Dewey, *The Public and Its Problems,* 203.

[38] Dewey, *The Public and Its Problems,* 202–3.

[39] Dewey, *The Public and Its Problems,* 15–16.

[40] See Meyer, *Public Good and Political Authority.*

affect others adversely. For example, economic transactions are firmly within the public, not the private, sphere because the market clearly produces numerous indirect consequences, many of which are significant enough to merit public attention.[41]

Just as more than one issue generates indirect consequences at one time and therefore finds itself in the public domain, more than one group counts as "a public" at any given time. The problem of participation in democratic politics, according to Dewey, is not caused by the absence of common interest. "It is not that there is no public, no large body of persons having a common interest in the consequences of social transactions."[42] Rather, there are many publics.[43] Each public arises in order to control the "[i]ndirect, extensive, enduring and serious consequences of conjoint and interacting behavior."[44] So, the publics conflict with one another as they strive to use the state's machinery to curtail the indirect effects of the transactions which gave rise to their joint activity in the first place. Moreover, his definition of the public allows different issues at different times to be considered public ones depending upon whether from them there arise indirect consequences of significance to some group of individuals. In this way, his method provides a way of conceptualizing the public that is flexible and sensitive to changing circumstances.[45]

This flexibility is also apparent in his reconceptualization of the state and state sovereignty. The state, Dewey argued, is the machinery that regulates public transactions. The state is neither all-inclusive, applying to all that goes on in society — as some idealists argued — nor strictly limited to regulating prespecified activities — as liberals insisted. The state's domain is the public domain, according to Dewey. So, transactions and associations that have no indirect consequences of any import are private transactions and are outside the ambit of the state. Conversely, if all associations and transactions are of public concern, that is, if all associations and transactions produce indirect consequences of enough import, the state becomes all-inclusive. But this is not the all-inclusive state of absolutism, as some interpretations sup-

---

[41] Even though Dewey's definition led to social-democratic conclusions, he viewed his definitions as ideologically neutral, since circumstances could arise in which what was once considered public would become a private matter.

[42] Dewey, *The Public and Its Problems*, 137.

[43] Dewey, *The Public and Its Problems*, 137.

[44] Dewey, *The Public and Its Problems*, 126.

[45] For the ambiguities that affect Dewey's use of the term public see Westbrook, *John Dewey and American Democracy*, 305–6.

pose,[46] because state machinery is never controlled by a single group. Even if all transactions counted as public ones and therefore were controlled by state machinery, no one public would control the state machinery. Rather, each public would employ a small part of the state machinery to control the consequences of transactions which activated that public.[47]

Conflict is inevitable in this pluralist society even if, as explained below, it was not considered ideal. The existence of numerous transactions and their numerous indirect and unintended consequences activate many associations, each of which wants to use state resources for its own purposes. Conflicts will inevitably arise when pluralism is promoted under a condition of scarce resources. Since Dewey assumed that scarce resources would prevail, he did not expect that political conflict would disappear. He sought to prevent conflicts in which certain groups could gain only by disadvantaging others. He hoped that society would develop methods for determining which interests ought to be given priority when conflicts arise and how all groups could be given the opportunity to develop.[48]

Aside from superficial positivistic rhetoric, the evidence does not support the absolutist thesis. I have identified four lines of argument that show the absolutist thesis to be mistaken. First, Dewey explicitly distinguished his methods from those used in the physical sciences. He did not simply import the methods of physics into political analysis. Second, he emphasized that the characteristics of scientific inquiry most useful for political analysis were attention to context, flexibility, argument based on good reasons and evidence, the experimental disposition, and an openness to error — all of which are hardly absolutist in their effect. The effect of the methods on political analysis initially entailed concept clarification which he deemed necessary in light the overly abstract

---

[46] Metz, "Democracy and the Scientific Method in the Philosophy of John Dewey," 254.

[47] Joseph Metz argues that because Dewey allows the state to be potentially all-inclusive his theory is antipluralistic. Metz uses the pluralism of Harold Laski and G. D. H. Cole, which is primarily based on dividing and fragmenting sovereignty, as the model of pluralism against which to assess Dewey's theory. He supplies no evidence to suggest that Dewey was apprised of the work of Laski and Cole. Nor does he explain why the work of the British pluralists should be understood as definitive of pluralism. Moreover, his notion of all-inclusiveness confuses 1) that which controls the state (i.e., a single person or group) and 2) that which is controlled by the state. Dewey's theory remains pluralistic in the first sense.

[48] Westbrook, *John Dewey and American Democracy*, 245–46.

notions he attributed to neo-Hegelian idealism and classical liberalism. Third, the intellectual context against which Dewey constructed his own theory steered him away from endorsing absolutist conceptions. Absolutism in one form or another was part of what he found so problematic about Kantian and neo-Hegelian theories. And finally, the result of applying his methods to politics would not eliminate differences of opinion nor, as he clearly stated, was it aimed at doing so. Rather, the methods rescued opinion and, in the course of doing so, revealed a pluralistic configuration of publics.

The Communitarian Thesis

In *The Public and Its Problems,* published in 1927, Dewey illustrates how his pragmatic methods apply to social and political problems. The political theory that emerges is one in which the ambit of state sovereignty depends on the activity of a plurality of publics which vie for state resources in order to control the indirect consequences of transactions. The pluralism of publics, which I place at the center of Dewey's theory, is the starting point, rather than the conclusion, of his democratic theory. Democracy fully developed, he argued, is the Great Community. The development and dissemination of pragmatic methods helped to create this community. In turn, the community facilitated individual self-development and harmonized the relations between the many publics.

The centrality of community in Dewey's theory has led contemporary theorists to find in it the roots of modern communitarianism. Three strong similarities exist between communitarianism and Dewey's democratic theory. First, both agree that the context which community provides is essential in order to endow human pursuits with meaning. Second, and more specifically, both argue that, without community, politics cannot be democratic and is apt to be corrupt. And third, both stress that individuals require community in order to develop their personality and capacities. There is, however, a crucial difference between Dewey's democratic theory and communitarianism. Unlike communitarianism, Dewey's theory relies on pluralism, particularly for the purpose of self-development. This difference helps to expose a serious flaw in contemporary communitarian politics. The concern with communitarianism is that the notion of a single, united community puts at risk individual diversity and difference. A community which is too homogeneous may impair rather than facilitate self-development. Dewey's pluralism provides a way in which this tension within the communitarian ideal can be avoided.

The first similarity, that community provides a context which imbues human pursuits with meaning, is where Dewey's theory of community and his enthusiasm for disseminating pragmatic methods meet. The Great Community, though utopian, is supposed to be the outcome of realistic processes whereby the publics, while retaining separate interests, increasingly interact harmoniously with each other. The harmonious interaction between groups in society is directly tied to the development of pragmatic methods of inquiry. Once such methods are disseminated, they would, in the words of one interpreter, generate a "shared fund of accumulated meaning" by stripping objects of social inquiry of those elements whose "singularity hinders their democratic apprehension."[49] The methods create a shared understanding of the social world and are the basis upon which a new language about the social and political world would evolve. This is the language of community. It is a vehicle of communication that reflects and sustains a pattern of shared activity.[50] Dewey believed that once people saw problems in the same light, they would opt for the same solutions, and, as long as they were flexible, they would agree on which problems ought to be given priority.

According to contemporary communitarians, one reason why community is essential for human pursuits to flourish is because community is the site at which shared standards, particularly moral standards, are constructed. MacIntyre expresses the argument plainly: "Detached from my community I will be apt to lose my hold upon all genuine standards of judgment."[51] Furthermore, he explains, "all morality is always to some degree tied to the socially local and particular and . . . the aspirations of the morality of modernity to a universality freed from all particularity is an illusion."[52] Because individuals are constituted as moral agents by others,[53] the recognition and sustenance of their moral qualities depend upon the standards and circumstances of their communities. William Sullivan makes the same point: "the protection of human dignity depends upon the moral quality of social relationships and . . . this is finally a public and political concern."[54]

---

[49] Kaufman-Osborn, "John Dewey and the Liberal Science of Community," 1150–52.
[50] Kaufman-Osborn, "John Dewey and the Liberal Science of Community," 1148.
[51] MacIntyre, "Is Patriotism a Virtue?" 11.
[52] MacIntyre, *After Virtue*, 126–27.
[53] MacIntyre, "Is Patriotism a Virtue?" 10.
[54] Sullivan, *Reconstructing Public Philosophy*, 22.

Few political theorists — communitarian or not — would disagree with Sullivan's statement. But, according to communitarians, liberalism is a theory that fails to give recognition to the crucial concept of community. For Barber, liberalism is driven by a quest for an Archimedean point from which values that transcend social and political contingencies — that transcend community — can be apprehended. This quest, which Barber identifies with Descartes, and MacIntyre finds throughout the Enlightenment project, has uncovered only the elusiveness of truth. In the absence of Truth, each individual is left to apply a personal truth to human relations.[55] Liberal tolerance has led to the presumption that each person's truth or opinion is equally close to or distant from the Truth. So, there is no point to participating in politics, let alone expending much energy participating, when no means exist either to contrive common truths or to determine which side has opinions that are closer to the Truth. On this interpretation, liberalism encourages a politics of passivity[56] because, using its epistemological standards, no right answers can be discovered. The best liberal politics can do is reveal which opinions are the most popular.

The quest for elusive, transcendent values is the flaw of liberalism consistently identified by communitarians. For communitarians, it provides proof of the liberal disparagement of community because it indicates how liberals ignore community as a source of grounding values. If the absolutist account of Dewey's theory was correct, his theory would be subject to a similar criticism because it celebrates scientific methods that purportedly intend to "strip objects of the particularities that hindered their democratic apprehension." But, as already shown, the absolutist thesis misapprehends the values of science that Dewey intended to apply to political theory. And as Barber notes, Dewey was amongst those theorists of his time highly critical of the "quest for certainty" that was identified with classical liberalism.[57]

The relation between the existence of community and the existence of political, moral, or scientific standards is central to Dewey's theory. His pragmatic methods linked the truth of speculations to the particular context in which they could be tested. This first meant that morality was context dependent, a point that Dewey repeatedly made when contrasting his position to that of liberalism.[58] Moral standards, he argued,

---

[55] Barber, *Strong Democracy*, 66.

[56] Barber, *Strong Democracy*, 62.

[57] Barber, *Strong Democracy*, chapter 3. Also see Dewey's *The Quest for Certainty*.

[58] See Dewey, *Liberalism and Social Action*, 34; Dewey, *Reconstruction in Philosophy*, 176.

ought to be viewed in light of the specific historical and cultural community in which they arise. Second, Dewey argued that knowledge itself requires community. The primary ingredients of community, which include custom, tradition, and habit, are the means by which activity is socially shared and by which social and cultural communication is possible. Since "knowledge is a function of association and communication," it depends upon community; "it depends upon tradition, upon tools and methods socially transmitted, developed and sanctioned."[59] "Faculties of effectual observation, reflection and desire," Dewey argued, "are habits acquired under the influence of the culture and institutions of society, not ready-made inherent powers."[60] In the absence of community, knowledge could not be shared widely because the means — the customs, traditions, and habits — by which knowledge is transmitted would not exist.

Societies which lack these ingredients of community and thus lack the means by which knowledge is shared will be those in which knowledge is monopolized by an elite class. These are societies which are either governed by experts who monopolize knowledge or by a poorly informed citizenry whose opinions and political organizations are unable to sustain the democratic way of life. Both possibilities reveal that, without shared standards of knowledge, democracy becomes untenable. So, according to Dewey, shared standards stave off absolutism and authoritarianism. They also shield societies from political corruption. Customary loyalties are the means by which communities protect themselves from the political manipulation of ambitious individuals who pursue political power for private ends. Unless the standards of truth are communally shared and transmitted, politics will operate without the help of shared knowledge and methods. And, without standards to judge which opinions are better than others, society is open to the manipulation of individuals whose positions are self-serving and whose politics is thereby corrupt.[61]

The connection between the presence of community and the absence of political corruption is the second similarity between Dewey's theory and communitarianism. Barber argues that the absence of shared standards characteristic of liberal societies keeps individuals apart and this leads to tyranny. "Totalitarianism thrives in the political vacuum left by skepticism."[62] MacIntyre explains further that, without community,

---

[59] Dewey, *The Public and Its Problems*, 168.
[60] Dewey, *The Public and Its Problems*, 168.
[61] Dewey, *The Public and Its Problems*, 158–63.
[62] Barber, *Strong Democracy*, 112, and see 96.

politics can only be based on manipulation rather than persuasion.[63] Manipulative behavior treats people as means rather than ends in themselves. A politics based on persuading individuals to do X or not to do X requires a shared conception of the good and therefore a shared basis on which to formulate good reasons to behave in certain ways or to hold certain beliefs. Without community, people do not share good reasons and therefore politics cannot be based on persuasion. Instead, it will be based on manipulation, coercion, or both. In Barber's words, a society without shared standards will practice a politics of zoo-keeping rather than of democracy.

So far, two similarities have been identified between communitarianism and Dewey's theory. First, both find community to be the locus of knowledge. Both argue that, in order to be recognized as such, knowledge requires standards and, in order for standards to have meaning, they must be shared. Communitarians try to identify the ways in which liberalism has severed the means by which sharing occurs. The second similarity is that, in the absence of shared standards, all of these theorists observe that democracy is impossible and political corruption is inevitable. For Dewey, communities in which loyalties, habits, and knowledge are shared are resistant to the manipulation of potential oppressors. The same reasoning underlies MacIntyre's conclusion; when standards for what counts as a good reason are shared, politics depends on persuasion rather than manipulation.

The third thematic similarity is that both Dewey and the communitarians maintain that individuals require community in order to develop their selves and their capacities. Again, Dewey orients his argument in opposition to a form of liberalism which inaccurately views the individual "in terms of liberties of thought and action already possessed by him in some mysterious ready-made fashion, and which it was the sole business of the state to safeguard."[64] Notwithstanding these flaws, Dewey embraces the core of liberalism, namely the value it places on each individual as "expressed through the possibility of educating and developing each."[65] The notion of liberty which liberals celebrate, he argued, is unable to serve this development. If liberty is going to serve self-development, then it must entail more than merely removing external restrictions on the individual imposed by the

---

[63] See MacIntrye, *After Virtue*, chapter 4.
[64] Dewey, *Liberalism and Social Action*, 5.
[65] Dewey, *Liberalism and Social Action*, 56–57.

state or society.[66] Personal development requires the "release and fulfillment of personal potentialities which take place only in rich manifold association with others. . . ."[67] Therefore, liberty must be understood communally. It must be reconceptualized to reflect that individual development takes place through association. Because liberalism conceptualizes the individual in isolation, it denies this factor and robs the individual of the possibility of recognizing and developing her potential.

The similarity between the way in which communitarians and Dewey view the liberal conception of self is striking. Like Dewey, Taylor locates the central flaw of liberalism in the presumption and promotion of individual isolation. The claim, central to liberalism, that individual rights have primacy over communal goods, putatively rests on atomism. Atomism is also the target of Dewey's and James's criticisms of liberal metaphysics.[68] According to Taylor, atomism "affirms the self-sufficiency of man alone," outside community or society.[69] By giving primacy to rights, liberals presuppose that individuals can enjoy rights separately from a certain type of community or context. If liberals would recognize — as they do not — that context is essential to the enjoyment of rights, they would also recognize that primacy belongs to creating a community of a certain sort. As for Dewey, the problem that Taylor identifies in liberalism has less to do with the values that liberals ascribe to individuals than the means by which they propose to actualize those values. Taylor recognizes that those individual capacities which command our respect ought to be recognized.[70] But, he disputes that rights offer the best protection.

To respect these capacities requires that a social context conducive to protecting and developing these capacities is sustained; "the identity of the autonomous, self-determining individual requires a social matrix. . . ."[71] Assigning primacy to individual rights rather than to obligations that sustain this context undercuts the possibility of meeting the goal liberalism has set for itself — that is, of developing certain human

---

[66] The circumstances of the 17th century, Dewey argued, led early liberals to an individualistic conception of liberty that was hostile to social action. See *Liberalism and Social Action*, 90.

[67] Dewey, *The Public and Its Problems*, 150.

[68] See Dewey, "The Future of Liberalism." Also see James, *Radical Empiricism and the Pluralistic Universe*, 51.

[69] Taylor, *Philosophy and the Human Sciences*, 189.

[70] Taylor, *Philosophy and the Human Sciences*, 192.

[71] Taylor, *Philosophy and the Human Sciences*, 209.

capacities and potentialities. As in Dewey's argument, the mistake of liberalism for Taylor is that it conceptualizes the individual in isolation and therefore neglects the primary means — for example, the community — by which her development is facilitated.

The place of personal development is a central and recurring theme of communitarianism. "The self," MacIntyre insists, "has to find its moral identity in and through its membership. . . ."[72] Sandel argues that the liberal self, as described through Rawls's notion of the original position, is a self that exists separately from its ends and attachments.[73] The unencumbered self of liberalism is a being incapable of attachments that are deep enough to be constitutive. The self is neither ideally free nor rational, Sandel argues, but rather, is "a person wholly without character, without moral depth."[74] Because the liberal self lacks constitutive aims and attachments, she is "[d]enied the expansive self-understandings that could shape a common life" and "is left to lurch between detachment on the one hand, and entanglement on the other."[75] Against the liberal self, Sandel argues for a conception in which our attachments are able "to reach beyond our values and sentiments to engage our identity itself."[76] The alternative self is one that is inseparable from its attachments — in his words, a self that is thick with these attachments and associations to the point that they "define the person I am."[77]

The striking similarity between the communitarian conception of the self and that of Dewey is perhaps best approached by examining James's pluralist psychology. James argued that the self "is the sum total of all that he can call his, not only his body and his psyche powers, but his clothes and his house, his wife and children, his ancestors and friends, his reputation and works, his lands and horses, and yacht and bank account."[78] The self is constituted, at least in part, by its observable possessions and attachments. These attachments comprise three general categories of self: the spiritual self, the social self, and the physical self. Within each category, the potential for having many different selves exists. The existence of each self depends upon each being recognized first by the individual and then by the outside world. Recog-

---

[72] MacIntyre, *After Virtue*, 221.

[73] Sandel, *Liberalism and the Limits of Justice*, 179.

[74] Sandel, "The Procedural Republic and the Unencumbered Self," 90.

[75] Sandel, "The Procedural Republic and the Unencumbered Self," 91.

[76] Sandel, "The Procedural Republic and the Unencumbered Self," 62.

[77] Sandel, "The Procedural Republic and the Unencumbered Self," 90.

[78] James, *Principles of Psychology*, 279.

nition by a community or group is particularly important for the social selves. Because each self depends for its practical existence upon recognition by the individual or by society, the individual can have as many selves as she has involvements with distinct groups that recognize different selves.[79]

James's understanding of personal development is similar to the idealists' understanding in the sense that, for him, the self relies on social recognition to the point that some selves will cease to exist without recognition. Some selves will be denied reality and "discarded" if their development conflicts with the requirements of other selves.[80] Therefore, the identity of the individual is always in the process of developing because some selves are being nurtured while others are being discarded.

The self consists of a plurality of selves, but this plurality, James argued, is not without limits. Each self is nurtured insofar as its development does not conflict with the development of other selves. In cases of conflict, one or more selves can be denied recognition and thus discarded. When deciding which self to discard, the individual's psychological processes give priority to either the self that is more central to the personality or to the one that is most beneficial to the individual's survival in the context of all her other selves and thus all her other attachments. The one self that cannot be discarded, according to James, is the innermost self which reflects on the sensations. "Compared with this element . . . the other parts, even of the subjective life, seem transient external possessions, of which each in turn can be disowned, whilst that which disowns them remains."[81] While the individual's identity is bound to her attachments up to the point that different attachments cause the emergence of a different, integrated self, the innermost self is able to reexamine and discard these attachments when they no longer fit with the other selves. The innermost self is not transient, yet neither is it definitive of whole self. Rather, the integrated self determines the individual's personality.

Dewey makes a similar argument. Individuality is formed through association. Each facet of the individual's personality is the product of some type of association and contains within it capacities that are dormant until developed by associating with others. The whole, integrated individual is a distinctive product of a combination of various associations. As Dewey describes the process:

---

[79] James, *Principles of Psychology,* 282.
[80] James, *Principles of Psychology,* 295–96.
[81] James, *Principles of Psychology,* 285.

> Any human being is in one respect an association, consist-
> ing of a multitude of cells each living its own life. And as
> the activity of each cell is conditioned and directed by those
> with which it interacts, so the human being whom we fasten
> upon as individual "par excellence" is moved and regulat-
> ed by his associations with others; what he does and what the
> consequences of his behavior are, what his experience con-
> sists of, cannot even be described, much less accounted for,
> in isolation.[82]

The roots of this notion of the self are found in Dewey's early works
which reflected his interest in Hegel and organic notions of democracy.[83]
But, he brought this notion of self-development along with him when he
abandoned Hegel and developed pluralism. Each dimension of the individual's personality was seen as the product of association. As James
argued, the individual has as many selves as she has involvements with
distinct groups that recognize different selves.[84] The more associations
the individual has, the greater are her chances to develop a variety of capacities. The fewer associations she has, the more likely that her capacities will be undernourished within her psyche.

Crucial to this pluralist self-development are the social and political factors that distort development. Both James and Dewey argued that,
in two ways, the power that groups have to develop the capacities of individuals may also be used to distort individual development. First, associations may cultivate individual characteristics that conflict with characteristics cultivated in other groups. In one sense, this sort of conflict is
inevitable, and it need not lead, according to either theorist, to the distortion of individual development. According to James, distortion is
avoided when some selves, whose development conflicts with the requirements of other selves, are "discarded"[85] and when the individual's
psychological processes give priority to either the self that is more central to the personality[86] or to the one that is most beneficial to the individual's survival in the context of all her other selves and thus all her
other attachments. According to Dewey, conflicts between different parts

---

[82] Dewey, *The Public and Its Problems*, 188.
[83] See Dewey, "Ethics of Democracy." Also see Westbrook, *John Dewey and American Democracy*, 38–42.
[84] James, *Principles of Psychology*, 282.
[85] James, *Principles of Psychology*, 295–96.
[86] James, *Principles of Psychology*, 285.

of the personality are resolved as the individual seeks to integrate the different parts of her personality. She will encourage flexibility and compromise between groups in order to facilitate this integration. She may also abandon her commitment to certain groups when inconsistencies arise. She discards attachments in order to avoid disharmonious self-development. But if she opts for neither of these routes, she risks distorting her development each time she associates with inflexible and incompatible groups. Individuals become maladjusted when their capacities are not developed in a healthy (i.e., flexible and integrative) manner. Dewey illustrated what he meant using an example of an inflexible group:

> [a] member of a robber band may express his powers in a way consonant with belonging to that group and be directed by the interest common to its members. But he does so only at the cost of repression of those of his potentialities which can be realized only through membership in other groups. The robber band cannot interact flexibly with other groups; it can act only through isolating itself. It must prevent the operation of all interests save those which circumscribe it in its separateness.[87]

So, the individual's identity is bound to her attachments, and the process of forging and dissolving associations with others is bound to personal development. Different attachments cause the emergence of a different, integrated self.

The individual will become antisocial when she associates with incompatible and inflexible groups. As groups may corrupt and deform the individual, in turn, they will become corrupted if they are comprised of maladjusted individuals. Moreover, since groups comprise society, corrupted groups means a corrupted society. Therefore, the process of self-development is significant to the political relations in society. Its political resonance is perhaps clearest when group domination occurs. Groups corrupt development when they dominate individuals to the exclusion of other groups. "Life has been impoverished," Dewey argued, "not by a predominance of "society" in general over individuality, but by a domination of one form of association, the family, clan, church, economic institutions, over other actual and possible forms."[88] Political and social domination penetrate the psychological development of individuals. The domination of one association over all

---

[87] Dewey, *The Public and Its Problems*, 148.
[88] Dewey, *The Public and Its Problems*, 194.

others and over the individual leads to inflexible single- or narrow-mindedness. Individuals become maladjusted when one group dominates, and societies suffer when they are comprised of maladjusted citizens. Politically, such domination creates an illiberal and oppressive atmosphere that, later in the century, was labeled by pluralists to be "totalitarian." The primary objective of Dewey's pragmatic methods was to diagnose such domination and reveal the means "for bringing the interests of all groups of a society into adjustment."[89]

The communitarian understanding of personal development complements Dewey's and James's theory in two respects. First, each contends that the development of capacities and personality occur within a social context. For this reason, the political organization of society is attached in both accounts to the psychological development of the individual. Second, in each view, the individual's identity is constituted by its attachments and memberships — a point particularly salient for Sandel, who distinguishes the liberal view from his own on this basis.

But Sandel drives his analysis too far away from the values underlying individualism. In his rendition of liberalism, the self can be imagined in Rawls's original position as unencumbered by its attachments, commitments, and ends; "deontology insists that we view ourselves as independent selves . . . in the sense that our identity is never tied to our aims and attachments."[90] His alternative, thick conception of the self is presumably an improvement because it offers no such distance between the individual and her attachments; a self with moral depth and character is one for whom these attachments are not easily or plausibly severed. The contrast with Rawls's position is dramatic. Either we have no sustaining commitments or we have ones which we cannot sever. As Kymlicka points out, Sandel is mistaken to suppose that the original position requires that individuals imagine themselves with no commitments or attachments whatsoever. Rather, the original position is a means by which the self reexamines its present ends by imagining itself with different ends[91]; "we understand our selves to be prior to our ends, *in the sense that no end or goal is exempt from possible re-examination.*"[92]

James's and Dewey's pluralist notion of the self is designed to facilitate just this sort of reexamination while nonetheless adhering to a

---

[89] Dewey, *Lectures in China*, 71; cited in Westbrook, *John Dewey and American Democracy*, 246.

[90] Sandel, *Liberalism and the Limits of Justice*, 179.

[91] Kymlicka, "Liberalism and Communitarianism," 190.

[92] Kymlicka, *Liberalism, Community and Culture*, 52.

thick notion of the self. The whole self is comprised of a plurality of selves and thus, as an integrated unit, can reexamine any single self. So, the individual is never completely unencumbered, although she could sever any particular attachment. In fact, healthy development requires just this. It requires that the individual reflect on any single attachment and discard those that are incompatible with others or destructive. Within the pluralist psychology, the attachments of the self are constitutive while also being ever-changing. Over time, individuals cultivate certain attachments and distance themselves from others. Their identity is always in the process of changing because some selves are being nurtured while others are being discarded. So attachments constitute the self, yet no single attachment or commitment can be wholly constitutive. To the contrary, when a single attachment dominates, the individual's development is distorted. The domination of one attachment robs the individual of the means to reflect critically on that which dominates.

Sandel's alternative to the liberal self does not offer the distance and flexibility that Kymlicka identifies as essential to leading one's life "from the inside" and that Dewey places at the center of his theory. Although Sandel does not indicate just how constitutive are the individual's attachments, his argument provides no means to reexamine these attachments. Both he and Taylor fail to account for the implication of their central insight — that community provides the means to individual development. The power that communities have over individual development is precisely the reason why they have the potential to dominate and oppress. Politically what is required is a context in which a plurality of associations can flourish but where none is able to dominate. As Dewey recognized, outside of a community in which social and political pluralism are encouraged and celebrated, the individual cannot reexamine her attachments and her development will be distorted.

The communitarian project parts from that of Dewey primarily where pluralism is introduced. But this need not be because all communitarianism is antipluralistic. Although MacIntyre is hostile to pluralism because it celebrates the diversity of standpoints and opinions that divide community, Bellah et al. explicitly express the compatibility of pluralism and their theory of community. Yet, in both cases, no account of what pluralism entails is offered. And in most cases, specifically that of Sandel and Taylor, there is no mention of pluralism nor any discussion of the need to limit the power of any single community. The virtue of pluralism as a means to dividing power is not considered, and its implications for self-development are rejected by communitarians.

Defenders of contemporary liberalism fail to appreciate the centrality of political pluralism to the success of their theories as well. Although Kymlicka's understanding of liberalism is compatible with pluralism, his theory, as well as that of Rawls, relies, to a large degree, on liberal rights to preserve for the individual the means to escape unhealthy associations. Political pluralism, though not hostile to rights, stresses the importance of a plurality of associations which facilitate self-development and provide both the critical perspective and the power to discard unhealthy or incompatible associations. Associations tie the individual to the context in which her identity can be developed. They contain the standards by which the individual's world has meaning.

At the psychological level, Dewey hoped that, at least, the various facets of the individual's personality will not interfere with one another, and, at most, that each will help in developing the others; ". . . a good citizen finds his conduct as a member of a political group enriching and enriched by his participation in family life, industry, scientific and artistic associations."[93] Ideally, group interests will complement each other, and groups will be flexible towards one another's interests and values. Democracy

> demands liberation of the potentialities of members of a group in harmony with the interests and goods which are common. Since every individual is a member of many groups, this specification cannot be fulfilled except when different groups interact flexibly and fully in connection with other groups.[94]

Like the different facets of the individual's personality, Dewey hoped that "the pulls and responses of different groups [will] reinforce one another and their values [will] accord," making social harmony a realistic possibility.[95] Social harmony and integration represented the values of the Great Community which Dewey referred to as an unattainable utopia, useful only in order to orient the direction of growth; "[n]ot perfection as a final goal, but the ever-enduring process of perfecting, maturing, refining is the aim of living."[96] But even if this utopia were attained, it would include pluralism. Just as the integrated personality consists of the flexible interaction of a plurality of selves wherein no

---

[93] Dewey, *The Public and Its Problems,* 148.
[94] Dewey, *The Public and Its Problems,* 147.
[95] Dewey, *Liberalism and Social Action,* 79.
[96] Dewey, *The Public and Its Problems,* 177. Also see 148.

single self dominates, the Great Community is one in which harmony is not secured at the price of domination. Instead, a plurality of associations must flexibly interact with each other while simultaneously providing a context for individual development and a critical perspective by which the individual can reexamine the worth of her other attachments.

Conclusion

Dewey's political pluralism is lost when his theory is characterized as either unintentionally absolutist or as communitarian. Nor does the Hegelian-liberal label[97] do justice to his scholarship which is so clearly born out of a rejection of both neo-Hegelianism and classical liberalism. Pluralism was an attempt for Dewey, as it was for James, to find an alternative to these traditions. So, in addition to the mistakes of liberalism — atomism, isolated individualism, and a narrow understanding of liberty — he was also wary of the absolutism, monism, and potential oppressiveness of the Hegelian alternative.

Dewey's pluralist alternative also ought not to be confused with the postwar variant of this tradition, although, again, similarities can be detected. Dewey was not captivated by the "behavioral revolution" or the "fact-value distinction" as was postwar American political science, and thus his pluralism was not fashioned by these standards. In their place, his theory privileged individual development and community alongside the familiar pluralist concern that power not be concentrated in the hands of one group. But the primary reason that he concluded that power ought to be held by a plurality of groups is unfamiliar to postwar pluralism. Healthy individual development required the fragmentation of power. A central feature of his political theory was that self-development only takes place within a social context. In this respect, his argument is strikingly similar to a major theme that informs contemporary communitarianism. Yet, again, the pluralist element of his theory clearly distinguishes his solution from those of contemporary communitarians.

---

[97] The label is used by Kymlicka to refer to Rorty's characterization of Dewey's theory. See "Liberalism and Communitarianism," 191. Rorty uses Dewey's pragmatic metaphysics as a springboard from which he constructs a political theory that does not resemble Dewey's vision and, according to Richard Bernstein, "distorts and betrays Dewey's legacy." See Bernstein, "One step forward, two steps back," 541. Rorty replies in "Thugs and theorists." Rorty's thought on Dewey is analyzed by Wain in "Strong Poets and Utopia."

III
Pluralism
to Limit
State Sovereignty

One key reason why communitarianism fails to offer a plausible political alternative to liberalism is that it does not deal critically with the fact and the effects of domination.[1] The strong suit of communitarianism is, instead, its criticism that liberalism disempowers community. Liberal politics is condemned for perpetuating barriers between people in political society primarily in two ways: by aggrandizing individual rights which guarantee, as Ronald Dworkin puts it, an individual "trump" against community[2] and by ensuring a neutral state which does not embrace a notion of the good by which it justifies its policies.[3] Purportedly, liberal politics empowers only the individual through her rights and gives to her exclusive power to choose a notion of the good with which to guide her life plans. No communal good exists in the liberal state. Nor can a liberal community legitimately trump individual rights. Liberal practices and ideology disempower communal power in order to protect individuality. The consequence of pursuing the liberal strategy is that goods which are only attainable through a united community and a common conception of the good may be unobtainable under liberal regimes. The sacrifice of these goods, which include, according to communitarians, the possibility of healthy individual development, is too high a price to pay in order to protect the individual from the potential of communal tyranny. Moreover, liberal rights and state neutrality fail to attain their promised protection of the individual. Communitarians insist that liberal politics foments tyranny and political corruption by isolating individuals from their communities through the promotion of the primacy of individual rights and

---

[1] Okin, *Justice, Gender and the Family*, 44.
[2] Dworkin, *Taking Rights Seriously*, chapter 7.
[3] Kymlicka, "Liberal Individualism and Liberal Neutrality," 165–85.

by fragmenting communal values. In this way, liberalism is said to sabotage its own purposes with respect to the individual's well-being.

Even if these criticisms are compelling, no clear alternative to the liberal approach is offered by communitarians. Nonetheless, their criticisms arouse expectations. One expects that if what Taylor, MacIntyre, or Sandel has in mind is a politics distinct from the empty liberalism of modern society, it shows its difference in not relying on those practices that disempower community. Thus, communitarian politics would not rely upon liberal rights and liberal neutrality. The problem is that, without these practices and protections, the scheme of social organization proposed by communitarianism appears to be colossally naive with regards to its understanding of political power. It needs to provide alternative methods for dealing with domination. And, as critics of communitarianism have been quick to point out, such methods have not been found. Amy Gutmann sums it up best when she writes, "[t]he enforcement of liberal rights, not the absence of settled community, stands between the Moral Majority and the contemporary equivalent of witch hunting."[4]

To be sure, the communitarian alternative is supposed to be democratic. But, by minimizing the importance of those liberal practices which prevent democracy from turning into domination, communitarianism cannot offer a convincing alternative to liberalism. In theory, a unified public might tap into those communal values that are thought to be central to human well-being. But in practice, a unified public is bound, as Young states, to "exclude or silence some groups."[5] One wonders how communal unity or a single notion of the common good can be promoted otherwise.

So, it seems, on the one hand, that a unified community is attractive because it allows individuals to live their lives through the substantive values that they share with others. In order to ensure that these substantive values are deeply shared in a communal context, practices such as individual rights must be strictly limited in their scope of application, and liberal neutrality must be abandoned. On the other hand, by abandoning rights and neutrality, the likelihood of communal oppression increases. And to minimize the likelihood of oppression would lead right back to practices that empower the individual at the expense of community. The choice is a dilemma between empowering the individual and risking a weak community or empowering the community and risking the domination and oppression of individuals by groups.

---

[4] Gutmann, "Communitarian Critics of Liberalism," 319.
[5] Young, *Justice and the Politics of Difference*, 183. See also 183–91.

Political pluralism provides a way to resolve this dilemma. Just as Dewey and James thought pluralism to be the third alternative in metaphysics to atomism and monism, political pluralism contains the resources needed to construct an alternative to liberal individualist and communitarian ways of organizing power. The analysis of pluralism and power which follows illustrates in two parts how this is possible. First, the analytical relation between pluralism and the problem of political power is examined. A distinction is drawn between two types of power — aggregative and developmental — and I show how a pluralistic vision of community addresses each type.

In the second part, the analysis turns to the ways in which power was configured in the pluralist theories of J. N. Figgis, G. D. H. Cole, Harold Laski, and Mary Parker Follett. Examining these theories serves two purposes. First, their work is key to reconstructing the pluralist tradition in political theory which started with the work of James and Dewey. Secondly, because these theorists conceived of pluralism primarily as a means to limit state sovereignty, their theories reflect the difference between better and worse understandings of the relation between pluralism and power. Specifically, they provide a means to illustrate that pluralist theories which do not consider the power ramifications of the group's role in self-development will not only contain a deficient notion of political power but will also fail to provide a convincing rationale for the pluralist aspect of their theories.

Political Pluralism and Power

While the focus below is on prewar theories, the critics of postwar pluralism provide useful arguments with which to start this discussion. Postwar pluralists, such as Dahl, attempted to prove that power is pluralistically shared in the United States and not, as some critics claimed, monopolized by an elite. To test this claim, Dahl and others sought to identify whose preferences prevailed in concrete decision-making processes and to quantify this information. They found that the pattern of preference satisfaction disproved elite theories and instead confirmed that power was pluralistically distributed. The conception of power which guided the postwar pluralist analyses came under attack by critics such as Peter Bachrach, Morton Baratz, and Steven Lukes for reasons that are relevant to all pluralist theories. Bachrach and Baratz argued that ascertaining the amount of power possessed by any individual or group must go beyond merely noting whose preferences win in concrete decision making processes.[6] Power is also exercised by controlling the agenda, determining which issues shall receive priority and which shall be excluded from discussion. The system's biases to include or exclude particular policy issues are an important source of power that may be consciously or unconsciously used by individuals or groups but, in any case, will not be detected by studies that focus only on the outcomes of concrete instances of decision making. Postwar theories were purportedly incapable of accounting for this second "face" of power. They were blind to the biases inherent in different systems because of their strict focus on quantifiable behavior and concrete instances of decision making.

The sort of power conceptualized by the postwar pluralists is here called *aggregative* power. Possessing power, which in this case led to preference satisfaction, depended on aggregating the most resources. Aggregation occurs, for example, when individuals band together in groups to pursue their interests and also when groups form coalitions for the same reason. But, it also includes the sort of resources which Bachrach and Baratz identified as a second face of power. In addition to votes and dollars, knowing how to exploit the system's biases or how to capture the agenda are both resources that certain groups possessed and others tried to acquire. The problem that Bachrach and Baratz identified was that the postwar analysis had neglected to consider this dimension of aggregative power.

However, recently, Iris Young has tried to identify institutional biases as a source of power which cannot be distributed and thus, one assumes, cannot be aggregated. Young argues that justice is not satisfied merely by ensuring that resources are distributed equitably. One source of power not captured by the distributive paradigm, she argues, is found in institutional structures. "The predominant focus on the distribution of wealth, income and positions . . . ignores and tends to obscure the institutional context within which those distributions take place."[7] The institutional context "includes any structures or practices, the rules and norms that guide them, and the language and symbols that mediate social interactions within them, in the institutions of state, family, and civil society, as well as the workplace."[8] So, it includes what Bachrach and Baratz called the mobilization biases of the system.

[6] Bachrach and Baratz, "Two Faces of Power," 947–52.

[7] Young, *Justice and the Politics of Difference*, 21–22.

[8] Young, *Justice and the Politics of Difference*, 22.

Now, these biases may not be amenable to equitable distribution in the way that dollars or votes are. And, in large part, this is Young's point. Along with Gould, she argues that theories of justice, such as that of Rawls, "rarely . . . take such structures as an explicit focus."[9] Young may be right about the *focus* of theories of justice. But, her argument suggests further that the conceptual scheme of distributive justice cannot capture the injustice caused by structural bias because these structures cannot be considered *resources* that are *distributed*. For example, she states that "[c]onceptualizing power in distributive terms means implicitly or explicitly conceiving power as a kind of stuff possessed by individual agents in greater or lesser amounts. . . . A distributive understanding of power, which treats power as some kind of stuff that can be traded, exchanged, and distributed, misses the *structural phenomena* of domination"[10] (emphasis added).

This argument seems mistaken because it needlessly mystifies what usually counts as a political resource. There seems no good reason not to count advantageous goods, such as structural biases, as resources just because, once one group possesses them, they may not be available to any other group. For example, the structure of the parliamentary agenda may not be a resource that can be divvied up among groups. If it confers special advantages on one group, other groups must mobilize different kinds of resources, such as public sympathy or anger, to compete successfully. But, there is a sense, which is plain enough, in which the advantages to a group that flow from the structure of parliamentary procedure count as political resources for that group. Part of the critique that Bachrach and Baratz offer is that, had the postwar theorists viewed these structures and biases as resources, they would have been less complacent about their conclusion that power was distributed pluralistically. No mysterious, nonresource theory of power need be adopted to understand their conclusion. Theories either have comprehensive or deficient understandings of what counts in politics as a resource. If, as Young suggests, theories of distributive justice have failed to scrutinize institutional structures when constructing a model of just political organization, they will be found deficient, not because such structures cannot be treated as conferring resources. Rather, they will be inadequate for the simple reason that they have a naive or curiously circumscribed conception of what political resources are.

---

[9] Gould, *Rethinking Democracy*, 133–34; as cited by Young, *Justice and the Politics of Difference*, 23.

[10] Young, *Justice and the Politics of Difference*, 31.

So, in constructing an account of political power, it is crucial to recognize that the biases of institutional structures can generate important resources for different groups. The supposition that all institutional structures are neutral between groups is simply untenable. Ideally, one might argue, the institutional context should strive for neutrality among competing groups. But, given the sheer diversity, in terms of culture, gender, race, class, and other characteristics of groups, it is unrealistic to suppose that neutrality can be maintained. Therefore, without condoning sexist, racist, or classist biases within societal institutions, it may be nonetheless mistaken to identify an institutional context as unjust simply because its structures are not neutral in every possible way. Certain structures may favor certain types of interests over others. In terms of aggregative power, groups will try their best to utilize the resources open to them, although some resources will be more difficult to capture than others for certain groups. For example, in a competition between secular and religious groups over religious education, secular groups do not have access to religious networks and congregation-contexts in order to lobby for their interests. Nor should fairness require that such access be provided. Injustice will not occur merely because any given structure is more receptive to one type of interest than to another. Instead, structural injustice exists when *systematic* biases characterize the institutional structures taken together, so that certain groups or sets of interests are bound to win consistently over others. The point here is that the unfair element of aggregative power associated with institutional bias is not exhibited merely in departures from institutional neutrality. Rather, a group derives unfair advantages if institutional structures systematically or consistently privilege its interests.

The notion of aggregative power can capture a large array of different sorts of resources that groups can utilize to advance their interests. But what is not captured under this category is the second type of power. In addition to ignoring the power found within the system's biases, Lukes argued that both the pluralists and critics such as Bachrach and Baratz were blind to perhaps the most important aspect of power. The dimension of power noted by Lukes is the power that groups exercise over individuals through socialization. Groups shape individual attitudes, beliefs, and preferences. Power is exercised over individuals

> by shaping their perceptions, cognitions, and preferences in such a way that they accept their role in the existing order of things, either because they can see or imagine no alternative

to it, or because they see it as natural and unchangeable, or because they value it as divinely ordained and beneficial.[11]

This dimension of power plays an important role in what I call personal development, and it has been identified as a key component of Dewey's and James's theories. Because the personalities of individuals are partly, if not wholly, formed within the context of groups, groups potentially have the power to advance their interests by socializing certain attitudes into the individual's personality. In the quotation above, Lukes describes unhealthy development; the individual is being inculcated with perceptions that obscure her opportunities and choices rather than clarify them. His intention is to expose the insidiousness of this feature of power in paving the way to group domination. Power is used to form the individual's personality to suit the needs of the group or to secure established standards and traditions by directing the individual to lead one sort of life (consistent with the aims of the group) rather than another.

That socialization is a central source of political power is not new to political theory, even though, as many critics observed, it was absent from the postwar pluralist conception of power. Marxists and feminists have well understood the force of socialization. For both perspectives, "false consciousness" placates and reproduces the oppressed in precisely the manner that Lukes describes. This type of power is not captured by the "aggregative" conception. Groups don't *aggregate* resources through socialization. Rather, they *create* resources which then can be aggregated. So, what Lukes identifies is a different type of power which here is called "developmental." Developmental power is the power to create resources by socializing individuals to hold certain attitudes or to behave in certain ways.

The problematic relation between these types of power and politics is due to the fact that each type can play a beneficial or destructive role. Power is used for good and for ill. For this reason, power has to be controlled rather than extinguished; it has to be available to serve good purposes and restricted from serving base ones. Understanding this requires that politics contains mechanisms that protect against the abuse of both aggregative and developmental power.

Political pluralism was conceptualized to be such a mechanism. For some of the pluralists examined below, pluralism was a tool that identified the difference between the use and abuse of aggregative power. *Aggregative* power is beneficial when it allows individuals,

---

[11] Lukes, *Power: A Radical View*, 24.

through groups, to pursue and vindicate their interests. Put in prescriptive terms, political pluralism holds that groups ought to have resources so that they can vindicate the individual interests for which they are formed. This role is based on the observation, central to the pluralist theories examined below, that the individual is relatively powerless when she stands alone against the state. Individuals need groups and group power in order to actualize their interests.

Under pluralism, *aggregative* power is abused when one group dominates all others. Single-group dominance means that the interests of one group consistently assume a privileged position over those of all others. Elite theorists of democracy, who postwar pluralists sought to disprove, argued that a single elite dominated American society and politics. In the prewar theories examined below, a similar argument was made. The dominating group was the state and, for the British pluralists, the concept of "state sovereignty" served as an ideological vindication of the state's all-encompassing power over resources and over other groups. The pluralist theories of Figgis, Cole, and Laski were intended to expose the factual and ethical flaws of this notion of sovereignty.

Pluralism also distinguishes between the use and abuse of developmental power. Under pluralism, especially, though not exclusively, that of James and Dewey, *developmental* power is used beneficially to facilitate healthy development of the individual's personality. Groups empower individuals through educating them to understand their potentialities. Groups form a context of meaning for the individual, providing her with structures, standards, and traditions which imbue her life with meaning. Pluralism is a means of tapping individual potential by promoting diversity. Moreover, pluralism cultivates individual autonomy; it allows the individual to sever or alter her connections to any group while remaining associated to all the other groups to which she belongs.

Again, the abuse of this sort of power occurs under single-group dominance. Single-group dominance hinders the individual from exploring options inconsistent with the dominating group's interests. It narrows the individual's options and thus limits the development of her potentialities. It perverts her personality. Single-group dominance is oppressive partly because it does not allow individuals to escape the standards, values and interests held by the single group that dominates. And moreover, in the absence of pluralism, any escape that might be imagined is an exit to nowhere. Since no other group figures into the individual's development, she is either dominated by one group or left to nothingness.

In sum then, pluralism provides a means to conceptualize both types of power and to identify when either type is being abused. First, with regards to aggregative power, pluralists argue that groups provide the resources through which individuals can vindicate their interests. Second, this power is abused when a single group monopolizes all the resources. Pluralism protects against this sort of monopolization. Third, with regards to developmental power, pluralism recognizes that groups facilitate individual development. And fourth, this power is abused when a single group dominates all others. Without pluralism, the individual's personality is cut off from diversity, and the possibility of autonomy is extinguished.

Although pluralism contains the resources to identify these four roles of power, most pluralist theories fail to do so. Often, the groups supposed to be typical of pluralist theories are "voluntary" associations that seem more like Dahl's interest groups than like Taylor's communities of self-development. When voluntary associations are the sole model for individual-group relations, pluralism will fail to provide an adequate account of democratic politics. It will not be able to account for the fact that groups help to create the identities of their members. Nor can it recognize that exiting a group is often more complicated than stopping to attend evening meetings or not paying one's annual dues. Taken only as a theory of voluntary interest groups, pluralism cannot consider the power that groups have as a result of their contribution to personal development. It cannot incorporate into its program one of the key insights of communitarianism — that it is difficult, realistically, to distance ourselves from our communities and attachments. Without tracing the significance of developmental power, pluralism will presume that all the associations to which individuals belong are voluntary when they are not. Such a presumption ignores and excludes from analysis groups which form on the basis of culture and gender or, more likely, treats these groups as if they were like all other interest groups. To be made more convincing, political pluralism must account for developmental power.[12] Otherwise, it will either remain a narrow interest-group theory whose relevance to contemporary politics is limited or it will offer a false analysis.

In the next section I shall examine the notion of power constructed by four prewar pluralists in order to illustrate that, the more these roles and the interplay between them are recognized by a theorist, the more sophisticated the pluralist theory becomes. Pluralist theories which fail to take into account the power that groups have in developing the in-

---

[12] In chapter 6, I examine the implications of pluralist theory for contemporary politics which involves voluntary, involuntary, and nonvoluntary associations.

dividual's personality or identity are unable to explain why power is or ought to be distributed to groups rather than to individuals. An adequate theory of pluralist politics must account for both the power that groups gain through the resources they have to advance their interests in the political arena and the power that they have through their developmental influence on the identities and personalities of their members. Without accounting for both types of power, pluralist theories will fail to offer an accurate and useful means to understand contemporary liberal-democratic politics. The more pluralism is able to recognize both the aggregative and developmental power that groups have, and the more that it can trace the interplay between these types of power, the more evident it will be why pluralism must be central to an adequate account of democratic politics.

The Intellectual Atmosphere

Four aspects of the intellectual atmosphere in the 1910s and 1920s help to locate the contributions of Figgis, Cole, Laski, and Follett. The first aspect is the large number of books and articles published in the United States and Britain affirming or criticizing a pluralist perspective. For example, in 1919 the *Philosophical Review* devoted its November issue to pluralism and drew together articles on pluralist metaphysics, psychology, and politics.[13] The *American Political Science Review* continued this trend in the 1920s by publishing articles on pluralism by Francis Coker,[14] E. D. Ellis[15] and W. Y. Elliot.[16] Early in the century, pluralism was a topic central to political analysis, and by the 1920s it was displacing the conventional conception of the state.[17] Its multi-dimensional approach incorporated analyses from sociology, philosophy, and psychology, and, in doing so, it led some to wonder whether or not political science could survive as a distinctive discipline.[18]

Second, this was also an atmosphere in which the pluralist theories of James and Dewey figured prominently in intellectual debate.

---

[13] The articles included: Urban, "The Nature of the Community"; Laski, "The Pluralistic State"; Follett, "Community is Process"; Tufts, "The Community and Economic Groups."

[14] Coker, "Technique of the Pluralist State," 2.

[15] Ellis, "The Pluralistic State," 3.

[16] Elliot "The Pragmatic Politics of Mr. H. J. Laski," 2.

[17] Gunnell, *The Descent of Political Theory*, 105.

[18] Gunnell, *The Descent of Political Theory*, 108.

Their influence is particularly evident in the work of Laski and Follett. Laski, who developed much of his pluralist theory while visiting Harvard from 1914–20, admitted an intellectual debt to James and Dewey.[19] He was described by at least one of his critics as "professedly a disciple of William James"[20] and as committing mistakes similar to those of Dewey.[21] Follett also claimed to be highly influenced by the metaphysical and psychological pluralism she found in James's work. She was critical of Laski for failing to utilize sufficiently the resources that James offered.[22]

Despite this influence, the pluralist perspective developed by this second set of theorists departed from the concerns upon which James and Dewey focused. Nevertheless, their work shared two themes, both of which stem from the influence of political idealism. First, in both sets of theories, one finds idealist notions regarding the pervasiveness of group influence on the individual. Second, both sets (with the possible exception of Figgis) clearly reject of the sort of abstract theorizing that idealism was purported to have encouraged. Both argued that pluralism offers a more realistic picture of liberal-democratic politics and that pluralism is driven by a sociological reality. People organize themselves into groups because individuals think and act through the groups to which they belong. But, despite these similarities, Laski, Cole, Figgis, and, to a lesser extent, Follett popularized a pluralist approach that was primarily designed to assess and manage the power relations between groups.

The third aspect of the intellectual atmosphere was the pervasive focus on the concept of "sovereignty."[23] For the pluralists, the sovereign of Hobbes, Bodin, or Austin is conceptualized as having power far beyond what is realistic or desirable. In their introductory pages, both Figgis and Cole use the conventional notion of sovereignty as the point from which they launch their pluralist critiques. In *Churches in the Modern State*, Figgis charges that

> this exaltation of the Austinian sovereign has led to the depreciation not only of religion and morality, but of all State action save that of the purest Machiavellianism, and would,

[19] Laski, "The Sovereignty of the State," 10.

[20] Elliot, "The Pragmatic Politics of Mr. H. J. Laski," 252.

[21] Elliot, "The Pragmatic Politics of Mr. H. J. Laski," 253. Also see Gunnell, *The Descent of Political Theory*, 107.

[22] Follett, *The New State*, 264–67.

[23] In 1915, Ernest Barker commented on the prevalence of this interest in his article entitled "The Discredited State."

if logically employed, have justified the worst excesses of barbarism.[24]

Similarly, in *Social Theory*, Cole describes John Austin's sovereign state as "the 'determinate superior,' having in its hands not only the majesty of law, but the ultimate weapon of physical compulsion." He continues by implying that the state's superiority is arbitrary: it "has been singled out and set on a pedestal apart from all other forms of associations, and treated as *the* social institution *par excellence*, beside which all other associations are merely corporate or quasi-corporate individuals, . . ."[25] These theories, in addition to that of Laski, attack the notion of sovereignty because it allows one group — namely, the state — to dominate all the rest.

The fourth, and perhaps most important, intellectual influence on the British pluralists was the theories of association, concession, and group personality found in the work of Otto Gierke and his translator F. W. Maitland. Gierke and Maitland argued that the state possessed the power to deny to various groups legal recognition and that it exercised this power in order to counteract challenges to its own rule. Gierke traced this notion of state sovereignty to the "concession theory" in Roman law. The concession theory holds that "associations or groups were brought into being and existed at the sufferance of the state."[26] The theory was employed frequently, especially in times of state instability when "[i]t was feared that . . . a corporate organization would become the centre of political agitation."[27] By prohibiting associations from functioning without the sovereign's permission, the state could prevent the formation of groups that would challenge its authority. Related to the concession theory is the "fiction and group personality theory" in which the legal status or "personality" of an association is considered to be a "fiction" created by positive law. The fictitious personality of groups is a legal means of asserting the sovereign's control over all associations in society. For example,

> the group's "real" life was dependent upon an act of papal concession without which it could not exist. If a group or even an individual aroused the Pope's displeasure, he could,

---

[24] Figgis, *Churches in the Modern State*, 13–14.
[25] Cole, *Social Theory*, 6.
[26] Heiman, "Introduction" in Gierke's *Associations and Law*, 19.
[27] Heiman, "Introduction" in Gierke's *Associations and Law*, 30.

in theory, withdraw his concession to the group or excom-
municate the individual. He thereby divested the person of
his juristic, rightful status.[28]

The concession and fiction theories were often used by the absolutist
sovereigns emerging in the postmedieval period to restrict the right of
assembly and the right to associate.[29] For this reason, the theories carried
with them the hangover of absolutism because they made a group's status dependent on the sovereign's recognition and approval.

    According to Gierke, by requiring sovereign approval, these the-
ories violated the historical understanding of group personality found
in German thought which held that groups are real, living things. As
Barker described Gierke's position: "groups were real persons — real
'unitary' persons, existing over and above the multiple individual persons of which they were composed."[30] While in association, the wills of
individuals combine to produce a group will. The group's will, along
with its laws and language, he argued, are irreducible to the wills and
characteristics of individuals. Consequently, groups possess real personalities. The legal claim which follows, which is the more important
one in the context of British pluralism, is that all groups, including voluntary associations, have the "right" to their legal personality because,
like individuals, they possess "real" personalities.[31]

    Other advocates of the group personality doctrine were more re-
strained when employing the metaphor and argued for the legal recognition of groups because of how this would contribute to individual
welfare. Maitland explored the historical roots of the concept "group
personality" and, like Gierke, found that the independent standing of
groups is undermined by the fiction theory which ties the legal status of
associations to positive law.[32] Unlike Gierke, Maitland had no interest in
preserving the group's personality for its own sake. Yet, without as-

---

[28] Heiman, "Introduction" in Gierke's *Associations and Law*, 32.
[29] Heiman, "Introduction" in Gierke's *Associations and Law*, 32.
[30] Barker, "Introduction" in Gierke's *Natural Law and the Theory of Sovereignty*, xxix.
[31] Although one of Gierke's translators, Ernest Barker, argued that Gierke did not
intend to suggest that groups are real persons, as opposed to being "like" real persons, it
is clear from much of what Gierke wrote and from how his critics understood him that he
was willing to take the analogy up to the point of physical likeness. In both his "Introduction" to Gierke's *Natural Law and the Theory of Sovereignty* and in "The Discredited
State," Barker clearly argued against the position that groups have personalities in the
same sense as individuals do.
[32] Maitland, "Moral Personality and Legal Personality."

cribing moral personality to groups, he had to offer an alternative to the concession and fiction theories. His strategy was to argue, first, that there are good reasons to suspect the state's motives in denying legal recognition to groups since, traditionally, groups are denied legal personality by the state in order to restrict any challenges to state authority. Secondly, under the fiction theory, all associations not authorized by the sovereign become illegal, and, increasingly, the individual comes to stand alone in relation to the sovereign.[33] Association serves the interests of individuals by empowering them. Therefore, the legal status of groups serves the interests of individuals. According to Maitland, even if groups do not possess moral personalities,[34] they ought to be treated by the state as if they do, not because of the benefits this offers groups themselves, but because recognizing the legal status of groups contributes to individual well-being.

Although individual well-being is a feature of both accounts, only Maitland identified it as primarily important. However, unlike Dewey, Maitland approaches the individual's position vis-à-vis groups and the state purely in terms of power and not in terms of personal development: that is, groups were seen as the means to vindicating individual interests rather than to creating or shaping these interests. Gierke, on the other hand, avoided discussing the individual's well-being at all. The little he wrote about individuals indicates that, as in Maitland's theory, group life is valued because it provides individuals with power. In addition, groups help to satisfy an associative instinct that individuals possess.[35] The predominant issues for Gierke were sovereignty and personality — but not the individual's personality. His main concern was that the group's personal development suffers as a result of an omnipotent sovereign.

Gierke and Maitland set the terms by which the British pluralists developed their theories, and, therefore, some of the debates between Gierke and his critics were replicated amongst those interested in pluralism. But the spark that led, particularly, Cole and Laski to use the resources Gierke offered consisted of controversies that arose in Britain due to the growing influence and power of trade unions. Arguments about group personality and the concession theory fit in well with the

---

[33] For an elaboration of connections between the legal recognition of group personalities and politics, see a collection of essays edited by Webb, *Legal Personality and Political Pluralism*.

[34] Maitland, "Moral Personality and Legal Personality," 233–35.

[35] Heiman, "Introduction" in Gierke's *Associations and Law*, 14.

attempts by the British state to undermine union status and power. Those who were critical of the overarching power of the state, such as the pluralists, as well as those who were sympathetic with trade unions, such as the Fabian socialists, were attracted to the group-personality argument in order to legitimize their position.

To sum up, the four aspects of the intellectual atmosphere pertinent to the development of the second episode of pluralism are, first, the popularity of pluralist theory; second, the influence of James's and Dewey's brand of pluralism; third, the focus on theories of state and sovereignty; and fourth, the influence of ideas regarding group personality and concession theory. From the start, this episode was bound to be distinct from the first episode specifically in the way that its proponents viewed the state. Rather than the state being a set of neutral instruments, as it was for Dewey, the British pluralists argued that the state is, in some sense, another of society's groups. But, it is a group with the power to dominate all the other groups — a power which it frequently exercises.

J. N. Figgis

Figgis's contribution reveals clearly how Gierke's ideas fit into pluralist theory. Figgis was interested in the status of the Catholic church in the state. In addition to criticizing the view of sovereignty, which, he claimed, presented the state as "larger than life," his pluralist analysis is, like that of James and Dewey, highly critical of liberalism. The liberal view, that individuals are found in a "sand-heap," "all equal and undifferentiated, unrelated except to the State, . . ."[36] is false; "[i]n the real world, the isolated individual does not exist. . . ."[37] Moreover, this vision ignores the crucial and obvious fact that societies are organized by "an ascending hierarchy of groups, family, school, town, county, union, Church, etc. etc."[38]

More clearly than the other British pluralists, Figgis connected the associative aspect of social and political life to the manner by which the individual personality develops. Individuals, Figgis insisted, are most realistically viewed as members of the groups to which they belong.

---

[36] Figgis, *Churches in the Modern State*, 87.
[37] Figgis, *Churches in the Modern State*, 88.
[38] Figgis, *Churches in the Modern State*, 87.

[The individual] begins always as a member of something, and . . . his personality can develop only in society, . . . I do not mean to deny the distinctness of individual life, but this distinction can function only inside a society. Membership in a social union means a direction of personality, which interpenetrates it, and, according to your predilection, you may call either an extension or a narrowing; it is, in truth, both.[39]

Figgis also seemed to recognize the danger posed by the group's role in self-development. Groups "penetrate your imagination and your thought and alter not only what you do but what you want to do."[40] But he did not turn this observation, as Dewey did, into an argument for limiting the power of groups over individuals. Like Gierke, he did not see individual development as the ethical end that motivated the pursuit of pluralist politics. In fact, individual welfare and the relation between the individual and the association are barely mentioned in his work.[41] And when they are mentioned, they are clearly of secondary importance to group welfare. For example, the central reason that he gives for why toleration is a worthy value for the state and for all associations, particularly the Catholic Church, is because it strengthens *the group* by intensifying the conviction of its members.[42] So, even though Figgis introduced a promising thesis about the individual's relation to associations, he failed to examine the implications of developmental power.

His primary concern was the power of groups vis-à-vis each other, in particular the status of the Church vis-à-vis the state. In theoretical terms, he asked whether smaller communities have an existence of their own or whether they are the "mere creatures of the sovereign."[43] Drawing from Gierke's work, he argued that the state has consistently employed its power to limit the power of the Church by denying it legal status. Such actions were "false to the facts of social existence"; to deny recognition to the Church's personality, "is of the same nature as the

---

[39] Figgis, *Churches in the Modern State*, 88–89.

[40] Figgis, *Churches in the Modern State*, 89.

[41] Figgis, *Churches in the Modern State*, 87–93. Henry Magid argues to the contrary that Figgis's pluralism is an attempt to justify "freedom of association" by invoking the requirements of self-development. This is inconsistent with 1) the scant attention Figgis pays to the relation between individuals and associations; and 2) Figgis's enthusiasm for Gierke's ideas, which also marginalize individual welfare. See Magid, *English Political Pluralism*, 11.

[42] Figgis, *Churches in the Modern State*, 115–16.

[43] Figgis, *Churches in the Modern State*, 8.

denial of human personality which we call slavery, and is always in its nature unjust and tyrannical."[44] As the possessors of moral personality, groups have a right, similar to that of individuals, to be recognized by the state. Like individuals, group activity ought to be regulated. But the state has no authority to regulate all group activities nor to determine whether or not a group exists for legal purposes. Allowing the state this power extends to it the means to fashion the group's personality.

Rather than viewing pluralism as a means to individual development, Figgis viewed it as the last refuge for a community, namely the Church, that was being challenged on all sides. The defensiveness of his theory is clear; "[a]ll we can claim, all we can hope for, is freedom for ourselves as one society among many."[45] He viewed pluralism as a means to conceptualize power — including, in some senses, developmental power. But the development whose abuse concerned him most was that of groups or the group personality. The explanation for his focus seems to lie partly in the type of association upon which he concentrated. The Church is a multifaceted community which embodies traditions and world views. It has a history — one surpassing that of the state — and a future. It is closer to a dynamic, living force than nearly any other type of substate community. Moreover, the Church is often viewed not simply as a community whose purpose was to serve the interests of individuals. Rather, it and its members were supposed to serve the interests of God. For these reasons, the notions of Gierke and the amorphous abstractions such as the group personality served Figgis's purposes well. Individual welfare would be achieved, according to Figgis, though only if the welfare of groups such as the Church was first served.

In the end, Figgis's contributions to the analysis of power are disappointing. In terms of aggregative power, he could have argued, as did Maitland, that associations are the source of collective power by which otherwise impotent individuals can challenge the coercive state. In terms of developmental power, he could have recognized the need to balance the power of all groups in society because of the influence groups have over individual development. Both arguments would link the notion of group autonomy to individual well-being. But he made neither argument, even though he recognized the encompassing influence of groups.

---

[44] Figgis, *Churches in the Modern State*, 42.
[45] Figgis, *Churches in the Modern State*, 120.

Cole's Pluralism of Functional Associations

Cole's pluralism posed a stark contrast to that of Figgis. He rejected the significance of philosophical theories, such as those of Gierke and Maitland, that were central to the interests of Figgis, Laski, and Follett. His objective was to develop a pluralist scheme for a socialist society as an alternative to centralized or state socialism which placed all power in the hands of the state.[46] Like Figgis, his starting point was the traditional view of sovereignty (this time one attributed to John Austin), which he attacked for being contrary to political and social reality. He then grounded his theory in the individual. Society is held together, he argued, because of the motivating wills of citizens rather than because of "force of power in the Austinian sense." If the wills of citizens were ascribed the importance they are due, the actions of the state would appear "as of the same nature with the actions of any other association in which men are joined together for a common purpose."[47] The state would become one amongst many associations within society.

Cole's pluralism was strictly individualistic in the sense that groups derive *all* of their legitimacy from the function they perform for their individual members.[48] He repeatedly emphasized his individualism partly to distinguish his position from those, such as Gierke, who treated the state as the "embodiment and representative of social consciousness" and who believed that associations are like individuals — "although it is perfectly plain that they are not."[49] Associations are formed as a result of coordinated attempts to satisfy common wants and, in terms of action, for the execution of common purposes.[50] They arise on the basis of the function that individuals want them to serve, and this function entails the aggregation of power to vindicate individual interests. Two rules of pluralism followed. First, the internal government and administration of associations must operate according to democratic and representative mechanisms.[51] And second, associations must act only according to those goals "which affect all its members more or less equally and in the same way."[52]

---

[46] See Coker, "The Technique of the Pluralist State," 203–8 for a discussion of Cole's guild socialism.

[47] Cole, *Social Theory*, 7.

[48] Cole, *Social Theory*, 96.

[49] Cole, *Social Theory*, 6.

[50] Cole, *Social Theory*, 39.

[51] Cole, *Social Theory*, 183.

[52] Cole, *Social Theory*, 96.

These two criteria also apply, Cole argued, to the state, which is, after all, merely another association. The state "ignores the differences between men because it is concerned not with their differences but with their identity, and its function and interest are concerned with men's identity and not with their differences."[53] All associations, Cole argued, legitimately operate only within the spheres clearly demarcated by their function. And for the state, this meant precluding it from regulating economic activities or any other activity which does not "affect every individual equally and in the same way."[54] According to Cole, only in regulating political activities, including deciding whether personal relations ought to be publicly regulated or not, can the state legitimately act.

The sort of pluralism Cole envisages consists of numerous associations which are far from the multifaceted communities Figgis presupposed and, instead, are strictly limited by functional criteria. Each association pursues its function, and all group activities are coordinated by a council of essential associations. The state is merely another association whose function is to deal with matters which involve an "identity of interests" amongst the citizenry.

Although Cole viewed associations as primarily the means by which individual interests are vindicated, he observed that the nature of associations will also be shaped by their interaction with each other. Each association, he argued, must consider its purposes in the context of purposes that are being pursued by other associations. For instance, a new association "enters into the structure of Society, and in doing so both modifies Society as a whole and is itself modified."[55] In recognizing that the autonomy of each association over its external activities is delimited by the natures and functions of other associations, his theory is similar to Dewey's understanding of community harmony wherein the community becomes integrated by the complementary relations between associations. Yet, for Cole,

> the new organization [may act] as a disruptive force in Society, and may, if it is strong enough, end by tearing the social structure asunder, and compelling a fundamental reconstruction. Or, on the other hand, it may be itself destroyed, even if it is performing a useful function in Society.[56]

---

[53] Cole, *Social Theory*, 96.
[54] Cole, *Social Theory*, 135.
[55] Cole, *Social Theory*, 206.
[56] Cole, *Social Theory*, 205.

He repeatedly insisted that associations will be unable to accomplish their goals until harmony is established amongst them.

The problem with harmony, or, in Dewey's case, integration, is that, as a political value, each concept has an inertia which renders new groups, interests, and values as disruptive of the status quo. Cole recognized the power of this inertia. "Atrophied associations," as Cole called them, continued to have power because they inculcated in their membership a strong force of habit that sustained them. "Some Medieval Guilds still linger on in the atrophied form of Livery Companies, and, when Capitalism has ceased to exist . . . atrophied survivals of capitalist association will continue in existence."[57] Capitalist associations were, for Cole, the primary obstacles to the new pluralist society in which trade unions would become the producers and distributors of commodities. If harmony excludes groups that one supports, as capitalism did for Cole, then disruptive influences and disharmony will be favored. While Cole clearly favored the disruptive influence that trade unions were having on the British state, his theory provides no means of distinguishing beneficial disruptions from destructive ones. Moreover, he provided no reasons to suppose that the harmony of interests in the postcapitalist society will be any more inclusive of diversity.

The drawbacks of insisting upon associational harmony would have become apparent to Cole had he been more sensitive to the developmental power of associations. Yet, as careful as he was to notice that the social context shapes the character of each group, he was surprisingly insensitive to the possibility that the individual's relation to any group would change the individual.[58] Rather than approaching pluralism in terms of personality and development, Cole assumed that individuals come complete with interests and needs intact. In fact, his pluralism relies on the fact that individuals are already fully developed and know their needs. The "essential aspect of human organization" — the association — arises from individual needs that already exist and wills that are already formed.

---

[57] Cole, *Social Theory*, 198–99.

[58] Magid contends that, behind Cole's notion of "true" democracy, there is a view of the human personality as complex and diverse: "Cole held that no human personality can be represented as whole and still remain free." (Magid, *English Political Pluralism*, 35). While this particular position is not inconsistent with anything that Cole argued, Magid emphasizes this point in a way that is inconsistent with what Cole is preoccupied with in *Social Theory*. Moreover, Magid gives no indication as to where Cole referred to the personality in this way.

The result of ignoring the developmental power of associations is that Cole's network of associations, will consistently struggle against associations that arise which are new but which, nonetheless, may facilitate self-development. Given the clearly demarcated spheres in which separate functions are performed and the requirement of harmony, Cole's system of functional associations poses many obstacles to those associations, i.e., those needs that have yet to arise. New associations struggle to fit into the context of other associations and sometimes must struggle, as trade unions do, to replace associations whose function they share. In light of the fact that the associations are supposed to be semi-sovereign and that they have the power to cultivate a strong "force of habit," this system is sure to discourage the sort of change that might occur as a result of self-development.

Cole's theory helps to illustrate that the primary difficulty with any pluralist theory which strives for harmony or integration is that an incentive always exists for existing associations to exclude new groups from legitimately vying for resources. In terms of aggregative power, this means that new needs which arise will not be easily vindicated. In terms of developmental power, it potentially means that the influence of new groups on individual personality may be perceived as antisocial or disruptive.

Since Cole's motivation in using pluralist ideas was to find an alternative to state socialism, his primary concern was to avoid the concentration of state power. His theory accomplishes this by distributing power amongst groups according to their function. Attending to the individual's need for personal development was not part of Cole's pluralist problematic. However, by leaving self-development out of the formula, Cole's pluralism was less comprehensive as a democratic theory than was Dewey's theory. Dewey emphasized that pluralist society provides for self-development while guaranteeing and delimiting individual liberty by encouraging individuals to enjoy membership in many diverse associations. The problem for Cole was that he saw the virtue of harmony but failed to understand the need for diversity. He did not see the significance of the mere fact of diverse associations. The pluralistic nature of society presented itself as a problem that had to be addressed without recreating the state, rather than an attribute of society that ought to be cultivated.

Harold Laski's Mixture of Pluralisms

Like Dewey, Laski had a very lengthy academic career. Over the years, his thought underwent as many as four transformations, each of which led to a significantly different and more radical political program.[59] During the early part of his pluralist period, Laski thought about groups in terms of their personalities. The importance of the legal-personality argument in Britain at the beginning of the century stems largely from the application of this argument in the *Taff Vale* case of 1901.[60] The judgment, confirmed by the House of Lords, held that, even though the *Trades Unions Act* of 1875 denied unions the full legal status of corporations (that is, legal personality), they could nonetheless be treated as corporations for the purposes of being sued or otherwise being held responsible for tortuous acts of their members. According to Figgis, this judgment confirmed that group personality is a natural phenomenon.[61] But amongst the social democrats, Laski was alone in agreeing with the judgment in *Taff Vale*. He supported trade union responsibility and the recognition of group personality because he thought this would lead to the recognition of a more extensive set of rights and duties for unions in law.[62] Like Figgis, he claimed that a group's personality is distinct from the personalities of its members. "Just as we have been compelled by the stern exigencies of events to recognize that the corporation is distinct from its members, so too, we have to recognize that its mind is distinct from their minds."[63]

---

[59] Deane, *The Political Ideas of Harold Laski*. According to Deane, Laski's career can be divided into five stages. In the first stage, from 1914–24, Laski was a Fabian socialist and was primarily interested in attacking state sovereignty. In the second phase of his career, from 1925–31, he continued to develop his socialist ideals but was far less hostile to the state. His Marxist sentiments dominated the last three stages, from 1932–39; 1940–45; and 1946–50. In the third phase, he abandoned pluralism and adopted a conventionally Marxist assessment of the state and state reform. In the fourth stage, he became preoccupied with fascism as a stage of capitalism and advocated the violent overthrow of the capitalist system. In the last stage of his career, he was less zealous about revolution and instead focused on criticizing the United States for its overblown individualism and hostility towards collectivism.

[60] A. C., 426.

[61] Figgis, *Churches in the Modern State*, 64.

[62] Laski, *Foundations of Sovereignty and Other Essays*, 165. In *Groups and the Constitution*, chapter 1, Robert Horn provides a brief account of the sort of privileges granted to corporations once their personality is recognized. Essentially, groups gain autonomy in governing their internal affairs.

[63] Laski, *Foundations of Sovereignty and Other Essays*, 155–56.

Laski did not adamantly defend the notion of group personality for very long,[64] and, even initially, he was unwilling to take the analogy as far as Figgis or Gierke took it. Rather than arguing that groups resembled individuals, Laski maintained that group personality "simply means that we encounter a unified activity which comes from the coalescence of the thoughts and wills of divers men."[65] What followed was that, in a democracy, groups should be given the legal and political status commensurate with the recognition that individuals give to them through participating and sharing in their goals. Decisions as to which groups should be recognized in law (which should be given rights and obligations), and where sovereign power can be found, should be made according to whether a group actually possesses political power rather than whether it has received the sovereign's approval.

At first, Laski challenged the conventional approach to sovereignty by juxtaposing to it a more sociological approach. The conventional approach located political power in institutions on the basis of how the constitution formally or conventionally distributed power. Again, Austin's theory of law exemplifies this tradition for, in it, law is defined as the command of the sovereign, and the sovereign is defined as the determinate authority, habitually obeyed and itself beyond the reach of authority. This positivistic definition, according to Laski, denies that inconsistencies could arise between sovereign law and democratic consent, legal obligation, or other "reciprocal relations of government and citizens." According to Laski, the boldness of Austin's definitions is purchased at the price of accuracy. How can Austin's sovereign be reconciled with the political and social reality of the sovereign's problems?: "[a]s a matter of law [the] government may possess unlimited power; in actual fact there will always be a system of conditions it dare not attempt to transgress."[66] Catholic dissent shaped the state's authority in the

---

[64] Given that two of his critics focus on his use of the notion, one would think it was more central to his theory. (See Cohen, *Reason and Nature*, 396–98; and Elliot, "The Pragmatic Politics of Mr. H. J. Laski," 259, 271.) In a July 22, 1916, letter to Justice Holmes, Laski hardly defends the use of the the term personality at all against Holmes's charge that he draws "doubtful conclusions from it." Laski responds: "I take your comment on 'pushing personality too hard' to heart and mind. I wonder though if the kind of polyarchy it politically represents isn't as a fact the real salvation for democracy. It seems to me that groups — even if we have later to read them in a state context — are simply basic and I am human enough to read sovereignty in terms of their consent." See Holmes-Laski, *The Correspondence of Mr. Justice Holmes and Harold J. Laski*, 7.

[65] Laski, *Foundations of Sovereignty and Other Essays*, 67.

[66] Laski, *Foundations of Sovereignty and Other Essays*, 22.

area of religion just as defiant trade unionists led the state to reconsider its attitude towards picketing and strikes.[67]

In response, Laski's critics argued that he had created a straw man by characterizing the Austinian sovereign as immune from challenges to its authority.[68] Elliot argued that the penal system is evidence that the state expects challenges to its authority. It is not defiance alone, but rather, defiance without penalty that would put the idea of sovereignty in jeopardy.[69] Responding to a similar point made by Justice Oliver Wendell Holmes, Laski clarifies his position: "Of course the sovereign usually does make you obey; the trouble is that often when it does it is hopelessly wrong."[70] The conventional approach robs one of the means to draw this type of normative conclusion. Its one-dimensional quality discourages one from looking beyond legal institutions to social and political conditions that shape and limit sovereign power. The conventional approach cannot go beyond the sovereign's will to explain why the law has the shape and character that it has.

In addition to the sociological thrust of his approach, there are four additional aspects of Laski's pluralist theory of the state worth noting. First, like Cole, Laski thought the state was no different from any other association. When viewed in terms of individual loyalties, the state is no more than a successful political party, and, far from encompassing some universal aspect of the individual, the state ought to be viewed as the servant of the particular interests of the group that dominates government.[71]

Second and relatedly, Laski argued that associations do not function in a cooperative manner, each contributing one small part to the harmony of the political system as a whole. "Whatever theory may say, an analysis of the modern state reveals it as a complex of interests between which there is no necessary or even predominant harmony."[72] Many groups have antithetical purposes and irreconcilable differences.

---

[67] Laski, *Studies in the Problems of Sovereignty,* 136–37.

[68] See Ellis, "The Pluralistic State," 397–98, 400–2; Elliot, "The Pragmatic Politics of Mr. H. J. Laski," 261–63; and Coker, "The Technique of the Pluralist State," 193–95. Also see Holmes' September 15, 1916, letter to Laski in Holmes-Laski, *The Correspondence,* 21.

[69] Elliot, "The Pragmatic Politics of Mr. H. J. Laski," 257.

[70] Holmes-Laski, *The Correspondence,* 23. The letter is dated September 16, 1916.

[71] Laski, *Foundations of Sovereignty,* 29. Also see Deane, *The Political Ideas of Harold Laski,* 16. This argument brought the charge from Ellis in "The Pluralistic State," 402–3, that Laski confused the state and the government. Yet, it seems clear that he did not confuse the concepts, but rather, rejected the distinction often drawn between them.

[72] Laski, *Foundations of Sovereignty and Other Essays,* 228–29.

"We cannot . . . find the basis of enduring collaboration between trade unions aiming at the control of industry through the destruction of capitalistic organization and the upholders of capitalism."[73] Unlike the pluralism of Cole, Dewey, or James, Laski argued that each group in society actively promotes its own vision of the good life by competing with other groups, each of which is also promoting a distinct interpretation of the good life, "and what they mean by 'good' is, for the most part, the preservation of their own interests."[74]

The third aspect of Laski's pluralist theory of the state which is also a central ambiguity in the theory is the nature of the groups in which Laski located sovereign power. On one hand, Laski wrote about a pluralism of functionally and territorially limited associations to which power would be distributed.[75] In this way, his theory seemed consistent with that of Cole. On the other hand, the idea of group personality invoked an image of a multifunctional and multidimensional community, as did the categories of "capital" and "labor." Particularly in "The Pluralistic State," the groups that comprise society represent entire conceptions of the Good in the way that religions do or in a manner that is characteristic of some political movements.

The fourth and possibly most important aspect of Laski's pluralism — an aspect that also generates a serious ambiguity — is Laski's recognition that pluralism safeguards individual liberty. Unlike Cole, who viewed federalism as the best way by which separate needs can be met, Laski claimed that, regardless of its success in meeting its members' needs, the structure of a federal system is to be prized because it is a safeguard of liberty:

> [f]or where the creative impulses of men are given full play, there is bound to be diversity, and diversity provokes, in its presence, a decentralized organization to support it. That is why the secret of liberty is the division of power. But that political system in which a division of power is most securely maintained is a federal system; and, indeed, there is a close connection between the idea of federalism and the idea of liberty.[76]

---

[73] Laski, "The Pluralistic State," 566.
[74] Laski, "The Pluralistic State," 566.
[75] In particular, see Laski, *Studies in the Problems of Sovereignty.*
[76] Laski, *The Foundations of Sovereignty and Other Essays*, 86–87.

The idea of liberty in Laski's pluralist theory raises the question of what view he held regarding the individual's relation to the group. Did Laski see the group as a context for individual development, or was it merely a vindicator of individual interests?

On one hand, the individual in Laski's theory is left behind in the course of justifying the real personality of groups. In "The Personality of Associations," individuals seem to lose any distinctive standing in the theory. Individuals do not participate in the construction of their own identity, but rather are mere products of the groups to which they happen to belong. Indeed, in this work, Laski refers to individuals as merely "bundles of hyphens" whose natures are largely determined by their associative ties.[77] Pluralism is not a vehicle for individual development. Instead, it responds to the needs and putatively real personalities of groups.

Notwithstanding these nonindividualist directions, Laski seems to have been dedicated to preserving the importance and standing of the individual in most of his writings. Although groups had personalities, they could not have interests that were distinct from the interests of their individual members, nor was their well-being captured other than through the well-being of their members. One of the central virtues of federalism, according to Laski, is that the diversity it promotes gives full play to the "creative impulses of men."[78] Similarly, multiple-group membership is prized because it is a means of bettering individuals by curing them of "undue localism."[79] Groups are the "organs of genuine citizenship" and the means by which individual rights will not be ignored.

> If you ask what guarantee exists against their [i.e., rights] destruction in a state where power is distributed, the answer, I think, is that only in such a state have the masses of men the opportunity to understand what is meant by their denial. It is surely, for example, significant that the movement for the revival of what we broadly term natural law should derive its main strength from organized trade unionism.[80]

The importance of a plurality of groups rests on the role that groups play in preserving individual liberty and protecting individual rights.

---

[77] Laski, *The Foundations of Sovereignty and Other Essays,* 170.
[78] Laski, *The Foundations of Sovereignty and Other Essays,* 86.
[79] Laski, "The Pluralistic State," 573.
[80] Laski, "The Pluralistic State," 573.

Laski's individualism distinguishes his theory from that of other political pluralists. Although Laski seemed, at times, aware of the influence of groups on self-development, he did not develop the implications
of this socially sensitive observation, and, as we shall see, he did not appear to be very committed to this social thesis in most of his pluralist
writings. More often, Laski stressed the need for individual freedom
from the constraints of any dominating association, and he advocated
the use of individual rights to protect individual liberty from the state.[81]
Rights were also to be used to protect the uniqueness of each individual
"for in any system of rights, the ultimate uniqueness, and, therefore, isolation of the individual, is the basic starting-point."[82] Although he tried
to portray rights as serving a social function, Laski emphasized that
rights are directly useful in separating the individual from the group by
". . . safeguard[ing] our uniqueness in the vast pressure of social forces."[83]

The need for isolation in order to protect individual uniqueness is
also emphasized in Laski's discussion of consent. He argued that individuals should judge for themselves the legitimacy of the demands
placed on them by the associations to which they belong, including the
demands of the state. They must be free to reject the demands that their
experience and judgment deem unreasonable: "[i]t is, in the first place,
clear that there are no demands upon our allegiance except the demands
of what we deem right conduct."[84]

Laski's notion of individual liberty is too excessive to be consistent
with the notion of personal development to which other pluralists adhered. This is especially evident in his writings at the end of his pluralist phase. The possibility of piecing together a theory of personal development that situates individuals within groups is completely
undermined by Laski's drive to secure for the individual freedom from
the group. In *Liberty in the Modern State,* Laski ignored the problems associated with linking personal development to group membership and,
instead, argued that the individual's "true self is the self that is isolated
from his fellows . . ."[85] While he goes on to state that, "an individual ab-

[81] Laski, *Grammar of Politics,* 91.
[82] Laski, *Grammar of Politics,* 95.
[83] Laski, *Grammar of Politics,* 94.
[84] Laski, "The Pluralistic State," 572. In *Grammar of Politics,* Laski argued that the individual should not be free to act antisocially. He might then argue that antisocial disobedience constitutes adequate grounds for punishment. Yet, it is unclear what type of civil
disobedience would not be considered antisocial in some way or by some segment of the
population.
[85] Laski, *Liberty in the Modern State,* 25.

stracted from society . . . is devoid of meaning,"[86] the dominant theme of these writings is inconsistent with a sensitivity to the importance of groups to self-development displayed here. As both Magid and Deane argue, Laski separated the individual from the group and from society by arguing that "man's true self is his isolated and non-social self"[87] and that "not only can no single association absorb the whole of human personality but also that all associations together cannot."[88]

Furthermore, Laski contended that the political conditions under which the individual personality flourishes have little to do with the social meaning imparted to individuals through the groups to which they belong. Liberty, Laski argued, is simply the absence of restraint.[89] Thus, pluralism is prized because it divides and decentralizes power. Its virtue is in what it guards against or how it facilitates separation from the community rather than because it provides a viable context for development.

To view individuals as unrestrained, creative, and unique beings is significantly different from viewing them as bundles of hyphens. Juxtaposing these views is the source of a serious confusion in Laski's work. But more problematically, the dominance of an extreme form of individualism in Laski's theory undermines the basis for pluralism in it. If the ends to which his theory are directed are individualistic, and if the means are also primarily individualistic (i.e., requiring individual consent, respecting individual rights, and protecting individual liberty), why did Laski need pluralism? Even though Laski admitted that some limitations to freedom are essential to happiness, he failed to indicate why pluralism was needed in order to enhance the well-being of individuals. In his theory, personal development is facilitated primarily through the absence of restraint or the absence of single-group dominance. Pluralism is attractive because it removes or weakens restraints on the individual by weakening the power of any one group over the individual. Although removing or weakening restraints on individual liberty is central to all variations of pluralism examined so far, this characteristic alone does not make a theory pluralistic. One can advocate that restraints on individuals be weakened without the help of political pluralism. Moreover, pluralism is not the most direct means of dealing with these restraints. A more direct route is simply to protect the individual from any sort of group dominance. Laski could not maintain

---

[86] Laski, *Liberty in the Modern State*, 12.
[87] Deane, *The Political Ideas of Harold Laski*, 105.
[88] Magid, *English Political Pluralism*, 62.
[89] Laski, *Liberty in the Modern State*, 12–13; and *Grammar of Politics*, preface.

that pluralism is the only or the best way of accomplishing his goals. A broad reliance on individual rights, which protect the individual from actual and potential forms of dominance, is a more direct expression of the sort of individual liberty Laski sought to guarantee. Yet, if rights alone would accomplish these goals, the question arises as to whether Laski's theory has any distinctive commitment to pluralism.

Two elements of Laski's theory might be invoked to designate his theory as genuinely pluralistic. The first is the notion of a group personality which entails the decentralization of power along pluralist lines. However, as already indicated, Laski rarely invoked the idea of group personality even though he explicitly supported it in one of his more renowned works, "The Personality of Associations." Group personality is not the centerpiece of his pluralism nor the starting place from which he criticized traditional conceptions of sovereignty. While Laski was attracted to the notion, he used it only when it was convenient to substantiate his arguments for decentralizing the power of the state. Furthermore, he did not attempt to reconcile it with his more individualistic arguments. And, finally, he abandoned the notion of group personality by 1925. While still advocating a pluralist political theory, he denied "the existence of any group will over and above the organized wills of the members of the group."[90]

The second element of Laski's theory which is potentially pluralistic might be found in a certain interpretation of his claim that "man is so essentially an associative animal that his nature is largely determined by the relationships thus formed."[91] Here, Laski might be interpreted as recognizing that self-development is facilitated by an individual's association with a plurality of groups. Yet, Laski never developed this line of argument, and it seems to stand in stark contrast to his view of the priority of individual liberty which is outlined above. So, Laski's views on individual liberty suggest that his theory only indirectly relies on pluralism. By widely dispersing power, pluralism might be one means of ensuring the absence of constraints on individual liberty. However, the traditional liberal devices of legal rights are more direct means of securing such liberty.

Without a commitment to group personality, or a view of individual development which requires association and social interaction, there is little normative justification for Laski to insist on a pluralist or federalist division of sovereign power. Of course, there are good reasons

[90] Deane, *The Political Ideas of Harold Laski,* 91.
[91] Laski, *The Foundations of Sovereignty and Other Essays,* 130.

to agree with Laski that individuals organize themselves in groups and that a division of powers provides security for individual rights. Yet, Laski does not provide strong reasons to suppose that pluralistic society is better than all others at securing legal rights. If one's sole aim is to protect individual liberty from groups, one does not need pluralism. If one is not concerned about groups as vehicles for personal development at all, then legal rights which leave the individual untouched by commitments or obligations to any group are sufficient to protect liberty. While Laski's vision of what is realistic pulls individuals into groups, his vision of individual liberty pulls them out, isolating and protecting them from social forces.

Mary Parker Follett

Mary Parker Follett came closer than any other proponent or critic of Laski's style of pluralism to recognizing that the problem in pluralist theories was a failure to balance personal development and political power. Follett attempted to combine these elements in her own rendition of pluralism. For the personal-development side of the equation, she drew upon the social psychology of James. For an understanding of power relations and group personality, she turned to the pluralism of Laski and Cole.

Consistent with most of the other pluralists of this era, Follett rejected atomistic renditions of individualism and society. She argued that a collective will emerges out of "a harmonizing and coming together of individuals." Within society, which she described as a "psychic process," the individual is not a unit but rather is "a centre of forces." "This conception," she argued, "must replace the old and wholly erroneous idea of society as a collection of units, and the later and only less misleading theory of society as an organism."[92] The mistake of "social atomism," she argued, was its reliance on the idea that developed individuals exist before coming together to form society. She argued that organicism was no more realistic in depicting individuals in society as functionally related like cells are related in an organism. Unlike cells, Follett argued, "minds *blend*."[93]

As Follett's choice of words reveals, she greatly admired the writings of Hegel despite her rejection of organicism. One of her central crit-

---

[92] Follett, *The New State,* 75.
[93] Follett, *The New State,* 75.

icisms of Laski and Cole was that they failed to recognize the usefulness of Hegel's arguments. The political pluralists, she argued, are fighting a misunderstood Hegelianism. They adopt the crudely popular conception of the Hegelian state as something "above and beyond" men, as a separate entity virtually independent of men. Such a conception is fundamentally wrong and wholly against the spirit of Hegel.[94] The real Hegel, according to Follett, had much in common with James in that he understood that, in some senses, the members of the state form a single collective experience. In Follett's words:

> [a]s for James the related parts and their relations appear simultaneously and with equal reality, so in Hegel's total relativity: the members of the state in their right relation to one another appear in all the different degrees of reality together as one whole total relativity — never sundered, never warring against the true Self, the Whole.[95]

Like Hegel, James recognized that political and social processes are governed by the behavior and actions of individuals in groups. James recognized that individuals require multiple associations to give expression to their multiple natures. So, according to Follett, pluralism captured the means to self-development for precisely the reasons that James identified. "Man discovers his true nature, gains his true freedom only through the group."[96]

> We *find* the individual through the group, we *use* him always as the true individual — the undivided one — who, living link of living group, is yet never embedded in the meshes but is forever free for every new possibility of a forever unfolding life.[97]

While it is unclear whether or not Follett thought Hegel's theory could be interpreted to endorse pluralism, Hegel certainly recognized what Follett emphasized, that individual freedom and self-realization was found through the group.

---

[94] Follett, *The New State*, 266.
[95] Follett, *The New State*, 266–67.
[96] Follett, *The New State*, 6.
[97] Follett, *The New State*, 295.

A theory of personal development would be a valuable asset to Laski's political pluralism, Follett argued, partly because personal development reveals clearly why harmony between groups must be secured. Society, as Follett described it, is a "self-unifying activity." And pluralists, such as Laski, have too quickly dismissed the importance of harmony and context.

> It is the pluralists themselves who are always saying, when they oppose crowd-sovereignty, that atomism means anarchy. Agreed, but atomism in any form of groups as well as individuals, means anarchy, and this they do not always seem to realize.[98]

According to Follett, the aspects of James's understanding of personal development that emphasize unity provide the means by which the anarchical tendencies of the pluralist theory of consent could be overcome.

In addition to offering a strange mix of Hegelianism and pluralism with regards to personal development, Follett also embraced idealist rhetoric while advocating that pluralists adopt the scientific methods upon which James built his social psychology. She argued that these methods provide a scientific and pragmatic guide by which to understand political and social processes. Such a guide would be useful to Barker, Cole, and especially Laski, she argued, because they rightly place a high premium on concrete theorizing even though they fail to consider all the lessons that the pragmatic school offers to them.[99]

Follett's project of integrating Laski's insights regarding political power and groups with James's insights regarding pragmatism and social psychology tapped into the most important democratic potentiality of pluralist theory, namely, establishing a link in theory and practice between the political power of groups and the self-development of individuals. Yet, it failed to have a significant impact on pluralist theory at the time because of the Hegelian rhetoric she adopted. She embraced the nebulous concepts of political idealism at a time when the pluralists were specifically rejecting Hegelian idealism and, instead, were attempting to fashion a more empirical understanding of group-individual relations. In spite of Follett's penchant for Hegel, her main contribution was to advance pragmatic pluralism by recommending policies designed to encourage individuals to organize into groups of all sorts — occupational

---

[98] Follett, *The New State*, 305.
[99] Follett, *The New State*, 262.

groups, neighbourhood groups, political groups, etc. The essence of democracy, according to Follett, is "creating a genuine collective will." "The technique of democracy," she argued, "is group organization."[100]

Conclusion

The arguments of Figgis, Cole, and Laski bring to light more clearly than do the arguments of Dewey and James the notions of power that come to pervade pluralist theories for the remainder of the century. It is likely that political pluralism was adopted by political scientists as one of their primary analytical tools because it provides a relatively economical way of conceptualizing complex power relations within liberal democracies. Indeed, a point of great similarity between British and postwar American pluralists was their insistence that power is distributed in a more complex way than is reflected in traditional conceptions of sovereignty and the state.

Two types of power were initially identified in this chapter. The first type is aggregative power. This dimension dominates Cole's analysis in that groups lend individuals power by facilitating the aggregation of resources (e.g., votes, influence, money). The power that is necessary to express or vindicate the individual's interests within the political realm is available to individuals through the group context. Aggregative power is also central to the way that Cole understood relations between groups. As a means of controlling the power of any one group for the purpose of retaining democratic values, pluralism made empirical sense. One could easily imagine aggregates of individuals and their resources striving to vindicate different interests or, as in later renditions, competing with each other for scarce resources, including a privileged position within the state. Single-group dominance must be prevented, under this scenario, to ensure that the various groups can properly function within their demarcated sphere and thus meet the various interests held by individual members. Liberal values such as tolerance, democracy, and equality become central to managing relations between groups in that liberal values also recognize that aggregates of individuals and resources should not be concentrated and put to the service of only one or two interests.

Developmental power is captured by Figgis's theory, parts of Laski's theory, and Follett's contribution. Laski's theory is especially in-

---

[100] Follett, *The New State*, 7.

teresting in this regard because, by weakening the role that groups play in personal development, Laski's pluralism is not simply distinct from other theories; it is inferior to them. Without justifying pluralism on the basis of personal development, Laski abandoned one of the key normative reasons for adopting pluralism. Consequently, he left his theory open to the criticism that, politically, it is unworkable because it promotes chaos in at least two ways. First, his ideal of freedom as the absence of constraint and his goal to undermine the conventional idea of sovereignty meant that there was no legitimate way of coordinating the actions of different groups. Therefore, the role of coordinator was unjustified. Secondly, the ideal of individual freedom that he embraced led him to insist that individuals should be the judge of the state's demands or the demands of other groups. The system must discourage the "unthinking acquiescence" that follows from automatic obedience. Therefore, the power of any group over the individual could not be justified. Freedom was defined by Laski as the opposite of being bound by association.

Pluralist theorists who emphasize that personal development occurs within the context of associating with others cannot embrace, as a central ideal of liberal democracy, a notion of individual autonomy that, beyond any other consideration, aims at preserving within the individual that aspect of herself to which no group has access. In other words, Laski's understanding of individual autonomy has no place within theories of pluralism sensitive to personal development. In an attempt to protect individuals from the potential tyranny of groups, Laski moved towards a concept of autonomy that negates the crucial relation between the individual and groups upon which pluralism is based.

According to the standards set by personal-development pluralists such as James and Dewey, and according to Follett's criticisms, this notion of autonomy ignores the central problem addressed by pluralism. Even though potentially tyrannical, societal groups are loci for personal development and also serve as contexts of meaning for the individual's life. One cannot deal with the potential tyranny of these groups by exclusive reliance on devices, such as rights, by which the individual can completely escape from them, without allowing the means to personal development to go by the wayside. According to the early American pluralists, this trade-off captures the weaknesses of classical liberalism. It is also a weakness from which Laski's theory suffers.

Laski's political theory consists of two incompatible commitments. As in Figgis's theory, pluralism for Laski is a means to guaranteeing group autonomy or to recognizing group personality. Independently of any commitment to the group, Laski argued for the individual's liberty to choose between group loyalties which included the choice to remain free of obligations to any group. So, first, his theory is committed to pluralism for the sake of group autonomy. Second, it is committed to individual rights for the sake of individual autonomy. There is no recognition from Laski that serious tensions exist between these commitments. Specifically, he fails to recognize that freedom from the potential constraints on individuals and groups has to be balanced with the social requirements for the development of individual and possibly group personalities.

The theories of both Figgis and Cole also fail to attain the appropriate balance between the requirements for individual autonomy from groups and the individual's needs regarding personal development which groups fulfill. Though Figgis recognized that groups play a role in personal development, his theory is like Laski's in that it invokes the elements of pluralist theory without understanding that these elements have to be balanced. According to Figgis, the individual is incapable of even formulating her goals without the guidance and influence of groups. Yet, Figgis's argument for why groups should be autonomous is distinct from his arguments for why they are important to individuals. Group autonomy is important because groups possess personalities which ought to be recognized. He does not advocate that group autonomy be respected for the sake of individual development. His priority seems to be to guarantee group autonomy in order to protect the well-being of groups — not the well-being of individuals. If his intention was to provide personal development and context to individuals by giving groups prominent status within the political and legal structure of society, he ignored the trade-off that exists between providing for individual development and protecting individuals from the potential tyranny of the group.

Cole's theory does not deal adequately with personal development. Cole highlighted the relation between the individual and the group strictly in terms of power. Without the group, the individual is powerless and therefore unable to reach her goals. The power relation between individuals and groups and the relation between groups and other groups is central to understanding the dynamic of politics. Democratic politics, Cole argued, could only be facilitated by allowing individuals to associate freely and then guaranteeing that no group dominates all other groups. Preventing single-group dominance had little to do with fostering a healthy personal development. Rather, Cole intended such protection as a means to recognizing the worth of all groups in society and as a means of undermining traditional theories of state sovereignty. Cole's argument denies dominance to any group in order to substantiate his opposition to the dominance of the state.

Cole's theory focused on aggregative power to the exclusion of developmental power. The individual comes to the group with desires and goals already intact. Because the individual is portrayed as fully developed, it is a simple matter for Cole to insist that the group should always be under the control of individuals. It makes no sense, he argued, to allow groups to control individuals unless one believes in the implausible concept of group personality. Yet, Cole's straightforward conception of the individual illustrates that he failed to appreciate the ambiguities of the individual-group relation. To insist that groups are created in order to serve individual needs is to beg the question of how to balance individual and group power if the group is responsible for the individual's development and is able to control the individual by controlling her goals and needs. Therefore, like Figgis and Laski, Cole did not recognize the balance that had to be attained between individual and group autonomy. The challenge for a reconstructed pluralism is to indicate how this balance can be struck.

IV
Individualists, Group Theorists, and Behavioralists

The central argument of this book thus far has been that political pluralism forms a tradition in which the themes of political power and personal development are intertwined. This chapter and the next turn to the distinctive pluralist theory of the postwar era.

Postwar pluralism is usually represented as a theory solely concerned about the distribution of power in Western democracies. As such, it seems to depart from the pluralist tradition that has been herein described. Particularly in contemporary accounts, postwar pluralism is thought to have nothing to say about personal development. The power which its advocates focused upon was aggregative power and, specifically, the resources that interest groups accumulate in order to influence public policy. Thus, in contemporary accounts of the doctrine, postwar pluralism is often called interest-group pluralism.

The argument developed here contends that this common depiction ignores the significance to postwar pluralism of the socialization processes carried out by groups. More specifically, the claim here is that the role of socialization in postwar political science is parallel to the role of personal development in earlier pluralist theories. This does not mean that socialization and personal development are taken here to mean the same thing. As a vehicle for personal development, pluralism depends upon an ethical commitment to the individual's well-being. Postwar theories of socialization exhibit no such commitment.[1]

---

[1] Hirst's argument suggests that Dahl's stance was evaluative and that pluralism contained standards that democracies had to meet in order to be considered minimally democratic. The evaluative nature of pluralism is far more apparent in Dahl's later works of the 1970s and 1980s. Dahl's earlier commitments, which are the focus of this analysis, were to value-neutrality. See Hirst's "Retrieving Pluralism," 156–57.

The argument developed here is that postwar pluralism was dominated by two themes — political power and socialization. Contemporary descriptions of postwar pluralism usually only recognize one of these themes, namely, political power. Therefore, they mischaracterize and misunderstand the nature of postwar pluralism. But they are not alone. Postwar pluralists themselves upheld an inaccurate image of their theory. This chapter focuses on the confusion regarding the commitment within postwar pluralism to individualism. This commitment, which was thought by many political scientists to accompany the behavioral approach to political phenomena, was, in fact, dangerously absent from many behaviorialist theories, of which postwar pluralism was one. The next chapter shows why political power in postwar pluralism is not as genuinely pluralistic as its advocates supposed. In each chapter, dispelling these confusions is a means of illuminating parallel confusions in contemporary diagnoses of liberalism's ills.

The conclusion that postwar empirical political science, which included pluralism, was not value-free is reached by many critics of the tradition. The project here and in the subsequent chapters goes beyond simply reestablishing this conclusion. Rather, this argument illustrates that the critical perspective through which to detect the flaws of postwar pluralism is, in fact, undermined by the sort of analytical methods prescribed by contemporary communitarians. The analytical methods focused on in this chapter pertain to the conflation by communitarians of different types of individualism. Communitarians conflate methodological, ethical, and atomistic individualism. Some of the interesting ramifications of this conflation are revealed here by exploring theories, such as pluralism, which rely on certain sorts of individualist commitments but not others. Postwar pluralism is particularly interesting in this regard because, in contrast to other pluralist theories already examined, its proponents explicitly embraced individualism, particularly methodological individualism. But, contrary to the claims of its proponents and critics, postwar pluralism, or more specifically, the behavioral portrait of the individual upon which it was based, was not individualistic in any but the most diluted sense of the term. This conclusion is not surprising given the intellectual traditions from which postwar political science developed. But, whether the absence of individualism can be considered a benefit or drawback of behavioralism is wholly dependent upon which type of individualism is lacking in it. By looking at the ways in which the absence of individualism caused deficiencies in postwar pluralism, it becomes clear why the supposition of communitarians that all varieties of individualism are connected is mistaken and dangerously misleading.

Any adequate theory of pluralism must distinguish between different types of individualism. More importantly, a reconstructed theory of pluralism must adhere to ethical individualism because, without it, a commitment to facilitating personal development cannot be central to the theory. As is more fully illustrated in the final chapter, the normative dimension of pluralism, signaled by a commitment to ethical individualism, ensures that a commitment to facilitating personal development is not reduced to the mere observation that socialization occurs in groups as it was in postwar pluralism. In other words, the crucial distinction between mere socialization and personal development is drawn within pluralist theory by ethical individualism.

The argument of this chapter is developed in three parts. First, I briefly explain the distinction between three types of individualism — methodological, atomistic, and ethical individualism — around which the argument is centered. The second part examines the intellectual traditions from which postwar political science developed. These include the influence of earlier pluralists, the group theory of Arthur Bentley, David Truman, and others, and finally, the impact of behavioralism. The second part is primarily devoted to determining the sort of individualist commitments found in postwar pluralism via behavioralism. The third part examines the implications for communitarianism of the foregoing argument by scrutinizing Taylor's analysis of individualism. Taylor is very critical of the general influence of individualism on political theory. His criticisms depend on conflating different types of individualism. His treatment and criticism of individualism raise doubts that his theory, and communitarianism in general, offers a better understanding of what individual development requires of politics.

One final note of explanation regarding the relation between postwar pluralism, behavioralism, and empiricism is required. The postwar theory of pluralist democracy was built on methodological foundations that were nearly an obsession in postwar political science. The idea central to postwar pluralism, that democracy is solely concerned with the distribution of power to groups rather than with participation, equality, or some other "democratic" value, rests on a bed of assumptions regarding the relation between political facts and values and regarding the nature of individual citizens within Western democracies. These assumptions comprised the empirical and behavioral standards developed and applied in postwar political science. One commitment born out of these standards was to construct nonevaluative theories of politics by assembling empirically verifiable facts. In democratic theory, these facts were supposed to be mainly about individual attitudes, values, beliefs, and behavior. From these facts, a distinctive portrait of the individual emerged. Democratic theorists, such as the pluralists, used the behavioral portrait as a starting point from which to build theories of democracy. The behavioral portrait of the individual assumed a similar role in these theories to the role assumed, in philosophical, liberal theories, by the individual in a state of nature or in the original position. In each case, assumptions regarding the nature of the individual resonate throughout the political theories in question.

Three Forms of Individualism

Three kinds of individualism are relevant to the theories discussed below.[2] The first and most controversial kind is *methodological individualism (MI)*. MI was taken by postwar empirical political scientists to be the methodological standard which any adequate explanation of political phenomena must meet. MI holds that all social phenomena are ultimately explicable or describable in terms of the dispositions, beliefs or behavior of individuals.[3] Groups are definable in terms of "either the behavior of the individuals composing the groups or the relations between these individuals or both."[4] Individualists of this sort specifically deny what methodological holists affirm: that the behavior *of* groups is sometimes not describable in terms of the individual behavior *in* groups. Methodological holists may give explanatory priority to the development or behavior of groups by explaining individual development or behavior in terms of the group.[5]

The controversy that surrounds MI is partly due to the fact that there are broader and narrower interpretations of what it entails. Its proponents in the social sciences invoke the doctrine primarily to affirm

---

[2] Steven Lukes distinguishes between six senses of individualism: political, religious, economic, epistemological, ethical, and methodological. Although I have no dispute with his distinctions, I have slightly redrawn the lines in order best to capture the sense of individualism in communitarianism and behavioralism. See Lukes, *Individualism*.

[3] See Watkins, "Methodological Individualism: A Reply," 58–62.

[4] Brodbeck, "Methodological Individualism: Definition and Reduction," 2.

[5] Elster, *Making Sense of Marx*, 6.

their conviction that social explanation should not rely on supraindividual entities or entities that cannot, at least in principle, be reduced to premises about individuals, their dispositions, roles, or relations. Critics of MI[6] have a narrower understanding of the doctrine. Even the most commonplace social phenomena, they argue, are explained only by employing concepts whose methodological content is not reducible without remainder to statements about individuals.[7] While groups do not exist separately from the individuals that comprise them, often a group's dynamic and influence cannot be reduced merely to the characteristics of individuals. Social scientists, argue the critics, try to avoid irreducible concepts by incorporating social phenomena into the character of the individuals they study. "Class structure" and the "party system" become traits of individuals (e.g., working-class deferential Conservatives) rather than irreducible social phenomena. This strategy, Lukes argues, serves only to avoid and ignore the methodological problem rather than eliminate it.[8]

Adherents to MI, such as Jon Elster, might counter the criticisms of Lukes and others by arguing that the critics have raised the stakes too high. The important methodological point is that phenomena *can* be reduced, *in principle*, to premises about individuals. Better explanations may not, in fact, contain such reduction. Political behavior, for example, may be more sensibly explained in terms of socialization than in terms of brain activity. Nonetheless, one should be able to reduce such explanation, if only in principle, and thus show that no supraindividual force determines individual behavior.

So, the broad interpretation of methodological individualism asks only that explanation not rely on supraindividualist entities such as a *zeitgeist* or perhaps a "group personality." The narrow interpretation insists that social facts cannot be reduced and that MI is therefore untenable. Given how important MI was to the postwar project, it is best not to predetermine what variant of methodological individualism was meant to inform the theory. Instead of resolving the dispute between the critics and proponents, this analysis will recognize both interpretations and seek out both in postwar pluralism.

The second type of individualism, which I shall call *atomistic individualism*, is central to Taylor's criticisms of liberalism. Atomism ad-

---

[6] For example, Lukes, *Individualism;* Mandelbaum, "Societal Facts;" Miller, *Fact and Method*.

[7] See especially, Mandelbaum, "Societal Facts."

[8] Lukes, *Individualism*, 121–22.

vances a view of human nature or the human condition in which the individual is autonomous and self-sufficient. According to Taylor's description, "atomism affirms the self-sufficiency of man alone or, if you prefer, of the individual"[9] in securing the conditions to lead a good life. It denies what theorists such as Aristotle argue, that "[m]an is a social animal, indeed a political animal, because he is not self-sufficient alone, and in an important sense is not self-sufficient outside a polis."[10] Individual self-sufficiency, according to Taylor, underlies the liberal rationale for protecting the individual's well-being by assigning primacy to individual rights. Rights are intended to protect the individual from state or societal interference. By making this protection a first principle of political organization, liberals assume that the individual can develop her protected capacities independently of state or societal involvement. Communitarians such as Taylor explicitly reject the atomist doctrine because they quite reasonably recognize that individuals need social nurturing and guidance before they are capable of enjoying their rights. Capacities must be developed in a social context before they can be protected. Therefore, Taylor argues, primacy should be accorded to certain social goods rather than to individual rights.

Ethical individualism, the third type, is a doctrine about how political phenomena should be evaluated, rather than how they should be explained or conceptualized. Ethical individualists hold that a political society should be primarily committed to individual well-being. Individual rights are mechanisms often used by liberals to secure this well-being. Another way to advance this commitment is to evaluate theories, policies, or societal principles in terms of whether they contribute to personal development. Without discussing or adopting a theory of rights, Dewey and Follett defended pluralism because it was a means to facilitate the individual's development.

Theories dedicated to ethical individualism are distinct from those which are not dedicated to it on the basis of whether they are committed, first and foremost, to ensure individual well-being or whether their priority is the well-being of groups or the community. This distinction is exhibited in theories or through policies that aim at securing some vision of group or community well-being at the expense of individual well-being.

---

[9] Taylor, *Philosophy and the Human Sciences,* 189.
[10] Taylor, *Philosophy and the Human Sciences,* 189.

The Intellectual Context: Groups and Group Processes

The Early Pluralists

Three features of the intellectual context are key to understanding the postwar variant of pluralism. The first feature is the influence that early pluralists, such as Laski, had on postwar pluralism, specifically on Dahl's theory. Although the works of Figgis, Cole, and Laski are given scant attention today, postwar American pluralists were directly influenced by these British pluralists. Robert Dahl, who is considered to be the leading proponent of postwar American pluralism, acknowledged the influence that British pluralists such as Harold Laski had on the formation of his own thought.[11] While a student at Yale from 1936–37, Dahl studied under Francis Coker, who, though a critic of Laski, was greatly influenced by Laski's arguments. Moreover, one of Dahl's earliest publications explored Cole's contribution to debates in British socialism between central planners and syndicalists.[12] Like Laski's and Cole's theory, Dahl's pluralism emphasizes the theme of political power. And like these British pluralists, he explores the extent to which one can claim that sovereign power is concentrated in the hands of one group or whether power is pluralistically distributed.

From Political Realism to Behavioralism

The second feature of the intellectual context is the impact of the group theories of politics developed primarily by Arthur Bentley and David Truman which laid the groundwork for much postwar political science. These theories contained strong assumptions about the individual's role in politics, many of which found their way into postwar theory. Bentley, like his friend and correspondent, John Dewey,[13] was committed to transposing the methods used in the physical sciences onto social and political analysis. He thought, that by making political analysis scientific, he could portray the individual in a more socially sensitive manner. By embracing the standards set in vogue by Einstein's theory of relativity, Bentley's work, like Dewey's, illustrates the wide-ranging nature of what was thought to be *scientific* reasoning in the social sciences. It also illustrates that scientific methods were

---

[11] See Dahl, *Democracy, Liberty and Equality*, fn 11, 281–82.

[12] Dahl, "Worker's Control of Industry and the British Labor Party."

[13] See Dewey and Bentley, *A Philosophical Correspondence, 1932–1951.*

thought to be consistent with, if not prerequisites for, socially sensitive theories.

In *The Process of Government,* Bentley criticized the "dead political science" of his day for focusing on "the most external characteristics of governing institutions."[14] Accurate analysis depends upon discovering the "raw material" of political phenomena and from it fashioning a tool with which to construct a more realistic understanding of how politics works. Neither political institutions nor laws and constitutions were the raw material of politics. Bentley also had no use for approaches that rest on "a postulated split of the individual from her social context."[15] He wanted to develop a method of analysis that offered a credible alternative to both the institutional approach to political research and to the "group mind" approach popular in so much political theory at the beginning of the century.

Bentley's method was supposed to have clear empirical underpinnings. He insisted that "[t]he way to find out how a thing works is to take it to pieces and examine the parts. . . ."[16] Identifying the raw material, he argued, is the "foundation upon which a coherent system of measurements can be built up."[17] In defining "group," for example, he carefully linked group activity to individual activity:

> [t]he term "group" . . . means a certain portion of men of a society, taken, however, not as a physical mass cut off from other masses of men, but as a mass activity, which does not preclude the men who participate in it from participating likewise in many other group activities.[18]

His scarce illustrations of the sort of groups he meant to include avoided what he condemned as "holistic intangibles."[19] His definition of government as "a differentiated, representative group, or set of groups

---

[14] Bentley, *The Process of Government,* 162. Leo Weinstein interprets Bentley's remarks quoted here to express an abandonment of political science as a discipline: "His use of political data for study is an expedient one, . . . [F]rom political science as a discipline, Bentley expected little," ("The Group Approach," p. 155). Bentley's ambitions, which he repeatedly expressed in his work, were to reform political science by fashioning a tool that could be used in political analysis as well as in other disciplines.

[15] Bentley, *Relativity in Man and Society,* 145.

[16] Bentley, *The Process of Government,* 254.

[17] Bentley, *The Process of Government,* 202.

[18] Bentley, *The Process of Government,* 211.

[19] Bentley, *The Process of Government,* 462.

(organ or set of organs) performing specified governing functions for the underlying groups of the population" was intended to steer clear of holism.[20]

Despite some affinity of his theory to MI, Bentley was attempting to construct a subtle position between the individualist and holistic perspectives. Paul Kress, who examines the idea of process in Bentley's theory, contends that, "Bentley's maximum program would no more tolerate the idea that phenomenal individuals could be examined and then aggregated as a group than it would the postulation of a group mind."[21] Sidney Ratner concurs that Bentley tried to avoid the pitfalls of methodological individualism and methodological holism:

> He rejects the idea that social groups or classes are more or less fixed entities as well as the thesis that persons exist as social atoms, independently of groups. To him each human being has diverse interests that he seeks to satisfy by taking joint action with others. He is a member of as many groups as he has interests.[22]

Bentley found the alternative to the isolated individual or the all-embracing group in Einstein's theory of relativity. On the basis of Einstein's notion that space and time exist on the same continuum, Bentley insisted that the individual and society occupy the same continuum. Individuals are socially constructed. They cannot be understood as separate from the social context in which they are observed because, not only does the individual define herself according to this social context, but the observer defines the individual according to socially established understandings. The individual is the product of ideas, feelings, and activities that exist in the social environment of which both she and her observers are a part. There is no way to isolate her from this environment.[23]

Social research often focuses on the individual because individuals articulate feelings and ideas through the use of language. Language itself is a social construct, and, together with feelings and ideas, language helps to define individuals in terms of social understandings. Any word that characterizes an individual embodies a set of socially

---

[20] Bentley, *The Process of Government*, 209.
[21] Kress, *Social Science and the Idea of Process*, 215.
[22] Ratner, "Introduction" in Bentley, *Relativity in Man and Society*, viii.
[23] Bentley, *The Process of Government*, 177.

recognized characteristics and socially constructed valuations. For instance, by identifying a person as a hero, one locates these social understandings in an individual personality or a set of individual capacities. The individual possesses these capacities, but the social context gives these qualities their meaning and significance.[24]

The raw material of political and social analysis is what Bentley called the "man-society process." "Man-society" was meant to be analogous to "time-space" on Einstein's continuum. The process part of the concept denoted the constant changes that man-society undergoes. Our social context is constantly being changed, if only slightly, by the efforts, activity or behavior of individuals. Therefore, any given observation of the man-society process captures only one phase of the process. Any given observation or study, is only able to focus on a cross section of the continuum. These cross sections are the groups in which individuals act in society.

> These joint activities, of which governmental activities are one form, are the cloth, so to speak, out of which men in individual patterns are cut. . . . The "President Roosevelt" of history, for example, is a very large amount of official activity, involving very many people.[25]

All decision making in politics, according to Bentley's theory, is the product of group interaction. The decisions of the Supreme Court of the United States — an institution chosen by Bentley specifically because it is supposed to be insulated from group pressures — are interpreted by him to be the result of interaction between groups which exerts influences on individuals who are members of the Court.

> We shall get a great deal nearer to an adequate statement of what is taking place if we analyze the great interest groupings of the country which were then active in the fields on which jurists had to center their attention, if we observe how these interest groupings made themselves manifest in the great cases that went before the court, if we note how these phases of the life of the nation were reflected in the personalities of the justices as well as in their reasonings, and if we thus get

---

[24] Bentley, *The Process of Government*, 5–6; Bentley, *Relativity in Man and Society*, 152–53.

[25] Bentley, *The Process of Government*, 176.

the cases and the theories and the precedent and the people
all stated in one common set of pressures. . . .[26]

The traditional institutional approach looked no further than the institutions themselves for the sources of institutional power. It missed the
group pressures which underlay all of the Court's decisions. If groups
were stifled by judges from advancing their interests, the judicial decisions

> would have been but temporary obstacles and would have
> been overwhelmed, not by any virtue in some other consti-
> tutional theory or reasoning, but by the power of the under-
> lying interests which pump all the logic into theory that the-
> ory ever obtains.[27]

Groups are closer to the reality of politics. The institutional approach, Bentley argues, obscured this reality to the detriment of democratic reform.[28]

The middle ground that Bentley sought between individualistic
and holistic approaches is captured by the social fact, a notion employed
throughout Bentley's analyses. A *social fact* is "any definable situation in
man-society, involving for its full definition, a statement in terms of activity, which is always cross-sectional."[29] Social facts are snapshots of
man-society. They are the relations between individuals and groups.
They reflect the social construction of the individual and thus admit the
"rich-life activity" that statistical analysis alone cannot capture.[30] Analyses that focus on the isolated individual do not reflect social facts because
they separate man from society. Isolated individuals do not represent all
that is relevant about groups.

> It is a "relation" between men, *but not in the sense that the in-
> dividual men are given to us first,* and the relation erected be-
> tween them. The "relation," i.e., the action, is the given phe-
> nomenon, the raw material; the action of men with or upon
> each other.[31] (Emphasis added.)

---

[26] Bentley, *The Process of Government*, 389.
[27] Bentley, *The Process of Government*, 390.
[28] Raymond Seidelman argues that, although Bentley wanted to separate scholarship from political advocacy, he was still a great advocate of political reform. See his *Disenchanted Realists*, 68.
[29] Bentley, *Relativity in Man and Society*, 94.
[30] Bentley, *The Process of Government*, 201.
[31] Bentley, *The Process of Government*, 176.

The group represents a different type of phenomenon.

> [Groups] are vastly more real than a man's reflection of them in his "ideas" which inadequately interpret or misinterpret to him his course; . . . Indeed the only reality of the ideas is their reflection of the groups, only that and nothing more. The ideas can be stated in terms of the groups; the groups never in terms of the ideas.[32]

For this reason, Bentley argued, individual activity is "of trifling importance" when one is interpreting some aspect of society. Group activity, on the other hand, "is essential, first, last and all the time."[33]

According to Bentley, all social and political events are part of the man-society process and are the product of group activity that takes place within this process. Because the objects of investigation cannot be isolated or separated from their environment, groups cannot be studied in isolation from each other. In this sense, all aspects of social existence are embedded in all other aspects. Analysis cannot escape this social embeddedness, since the *event* of observing the man-society process also occurs in a social context. Again relying on Einstein, Bentley argued that, just as "velocities drag their space and time with them" the observations of any one observer exist as a relation between that observer and the object being observed.[34] Therefore, the ethnic, economic or cultural biases of the observer must be considered before considering the meaning and significance of the observation made.[35] By accounting for the relativities of the statements and judgments of social research, "the study of man-society acquires a real relativity not unworthy to be brought within the lines of physical relativity. Then a science has arrived."[36]

Bentley's Legacy in Political Science

Though written in 1908, Bentley's most renowned work, *The Process of Government*, was not widely read within the political science community until the 1940s and early 1950s, at which time it came to be considered

---

[32] Bentley, *The Process of Government*, 206.

[33] Bentley, *The Process of Government*, 215.

[34] Bentley, *Relativity in Man and Society*, 23.

[35] Bentley, *Relativity in Man and Society*, 205–6. Also see Ratner, "Introduction" in Bentley, *Relativity in Man and Society*, vii, ix.

[36] Bentley, *Relativity in Man and Society*, 206.

"one of the great classics in political science."[37] Yet, even at the height of its popularity, political scientists failed to appreciate the subtleties of Bentley's theory. The more obscure epistemological problems which he attempted to solve by using the concepts of process and relativity were ignored. Following Bentley, political researchers

> could read Part One of *The Process of Government* as a welcome liberation from the formalism of constitutional law and institutional description, endorse its attack on prevailing modes of explanation, and then proceed to apply their instruments directly to the raw material of behavior with its locus in the individual.[38]

So, while Bentley was a contemporary of Dewey and was clearly influenced by similar considerations, his work was only appreciated and used in the postwar period. Moreover, it was only part of Bentley's legacy that made any impact. Political scientists applied what Kress calls Bentley's "minimum program" which consisted of two aspects: (1) a commitment to measure the raw material of politics, and (2) an affirmation that groups are the loci of political activity.[39]

The second part of the minimum program is clearly traceable in prewar political science. In the 1930s and 1940s, most political scientists in the United States and Canada adopted a group approach. Democratic theorists throughout this period defined democracy in terms of group freedom. For instance, T. V. Smith argued that, in a liberal democracy, the state's main function is to adjudicate conflicts between societal groups.[40] Conversely, under totalitarianism, the state is the only organization promoting the interests of individuals, and these interests must be either consistent with or subordinate to the interests of the state.

Also using the group approach, Pendelton Herring contrasted fascism and democratic forms of government. In Germany, the dominance of one party or one group over the whole country was thought to be the only way in which disparate groups could be integrated when Prussia united with the rest of Germany.[41] Conversely, the defining characteristic of democracy, Herring argued, is the existence of a multitude

---

[37] Ratner, "Introduction," in Bentley, *Relativity in Man and Society*, v.

[38] Kress, *Social Sciences and the Idea of Process*, 215.

[39] Kress, *Social Sciences and the Idea of Process*, chapter 6.

[40] Smith, *The Promise of American Politics*, 81–82.

[41] Herring, *The Politics of Democracy*, 57–59.

of groups with divergent interests that interact with each other in a flexible manner. The key feature of democratic politics is the "process of adjusting the interrelations of individuals, institutions, ideals and interests."[42] Adjustment takes place within groups of which political parties are the most important. Democratic parties aggregate and integrate the diverse interest groups within society and ensure that flexibility remains a virtue of group interaction.

Political scientists such as Smith, Herring, and others[43] shared with Bentley a commitment to rid political science of confusing abstractions. They rejected the formal institutional approach as superficial and also rejected the isolated individual as unrealistic or, in the case of Smith, impractical. At the heart of "real" politics and "realistic" notions of democracy, they argued, are groups, group activities, and group interests. But none of these theorists incorporated into their group approach the more detailed aspects of Bentley's project.

David Truman's work illustrates the limited ways in which many political scientists interpreted Bentley's theory. In *The Governmental Process*, Truman intended to revive and extend the group method pioneered by Bentley so that it would be a more useful tool for analyzing American politics. According to Truman, this meant grounding the approach more thoroughly in the behavior of the individual and thus ridding Bentley's theory of the intangible aspects of relations, activity and social facts.[44]

Truman's theory reflected the compromise that Bentley tried to forge between individualism and holism. Though he insisted that his method was grounded in the individual's behavior,[45] Truman agreed with Bentley that realistic analysis precludes the atomistic view that society is comprised of individuals "each assumed to have definite independent 'existence' and isolation, each in his own locus apart from each other."[46] Truman rejected nongroup approaches in which political and

---

[42] Herring, *The Politics of Democracy*, 27.

[43] For example, Beard, *The Economic Interpretation of the Constitution of the United States*, and Odegard, *Pressure Politics*.

[44] See Truman, "The Implications of Political Behavior in Research." Weinstein ("The Group Approach") criticizes Bentley for relying on too many intangibles. See Kress's analysis in *Social Science and the Idea of Process*, 215–19.

[45] Seidelman, *Disenchanted Realists*, 177; Truman, "The Implications of Political Behavior in Research," and "The Impact on Political Science of the Revolution in the Behavioral Sciences."

[46] Originally from Arthur F. Bentley, *Behavior Knowledge and Fact*, 29. Cited in Truman, *The Governmental Process*, 48.

economic man "exercised rational choice and acted independently for the maximization of individual advantage."[47] He later argued that "[w]e do not, in fact, find individuals otherwise than in groups. . . ."[48] Like Bentley and other group theorists, Truman juxtaposed the atomistic conception of individuals and the group approach. He understood that, by adopting the group approach, one was rejecting atomism. After a brief survey of the problems of individualism at the beginning of his study, Truman barely mentioned individuals in the rest of his analysis. Rather, he focused on arguing that the function of government is to establish and maintain order amongst groups.

In light of the current tendency in political theory to conflate distinct types of individualism,[49] Truman's argument may seem confusing. He clearly rejects atomism but also insists on methodological individualism: explanation of political phenomena must include only concepts that are reducible to premises about individuals. Although Truman insisted that individual behavior, not group activity or relations, is the raw material of his approach, his focus was the group. Focusing on the group, he argued, allows political scientists to include all politically relevant behavior about the individual. "The individual and the group are at most merely convenient ways of classifying behavior, two ways of approaching the same phenomena, not different things."[50] However, in terms of political power, the individual and the group are not the same phenomenon. According to Truman, even the individualists of the nineteenth century (he fails to identify which ones) understood the political powerlessness of individuals who act alone.[51]

Truman's focus on individuals and his rejection of the man-society process meant that his methodological commitments departed significantly from those of Bentley. Nonetheless, he advocated a socially sensitive theory of individuals, and he rejected the isolated, self-sufficient, and autonomous individual. As a premise for a political theory, atomism was an unrealistic one. He justified his focus on groups because individuals are naturally found in groups and because political power is a group concept in the sense that when individuals behave as a group they have the power to influence decision making. Therefore, the group

---

[47] Truman, *The Governmental Process*, viii.
[48] Truman, *The Governmental Process*, 48.
[49] This tendency is explored in part II of this chapter.
[50] Truman, *The Governmental Process*, 48.
[51] Truman, *The Governmental Process*, viii.

approach captures the individual's dependence on groups in terms of socialization and in terms of political power. And it accomplishes this
without mentioning the obscure man-society continuum, processes, activity, or relativity.

Truman's interpretation of group theory was thought to have improved Bentley's rendition because it eliminated some of the intangible
concepts that Bentley favored. These intangibles were replaced by the superior empirical methods of the postwar period to which Truman was
committed.[52] Behavioral methods were understood by Truman, as well
as most other political scientists of the postwar era, as superior because
they were supposed to be individualistic. There was no man-society
continuum. There were no social facts. Yet, there was also no atomistic
conception of the individual in society. There was purportedly only individual behavior, which, when aggregated, became politically significant, group activity.

Behavioralism and the Individual

It would be surprising to find emerging from this intellectual background theories that were staunchly individualistic in a sense that pre-
cluded the influence and importance of groups to politics unless these
theories were a reaction against the intellectual background described
above. But, postwar political science was quite the opposite of a reaction
against Bentley and Truman. Theories typical of the postwar period in
political science contain vestiges of Bentley's group approach and draw
on the tradition of theories, such as those of Dewey and Laski, whose central concern was balancing individualism and holism. Truman's group
theory is a good example of how postwar theory contained these traditional concerns, while, at the same time, adopting individualism as the
standard which solid, scientific methods should embrace. The postwar
tradition in these respects consists of the third feature of the intellectual context of postwar pluralism, namely, the behavioral tradition in political science.

Postwar political theories are often understood as being purely
individualistic in both their approach and their result. Like Truman,
behavioralists encouraged this misinterpretation by saturating their
work with scientific and individualistic rhetoric. In 1965, David Easton
described political behavioralism as "a *change in mood* in favor of scien-

---

[52] Young, *Systems of Political Science*, 91. Cited in Kress, *Social Science and the Idea of Process*, 215.

tific methodology, methods, and techniques. . . ."[53] (emphasis added).
Dahl also distinguished the mood of postwar behavioralism from the in-
novations of prewar political scientists. He defined behavioralism as

> an attempt to improve our understanding of politics by seek-
> ing to explain the empirical aspects of political life by means
> of methods, theories, and criteria of proof that are accept-
> able according to the canons, conventions and assumptions
> of modern empirical sciences.[54]

The behavioralists claimed their approach differed from prewar social
science in that they did not evaluate political phenomena according to
ethical standards. Doing so would entail violating their scientific creed.
"Ethical evaluation and empirical explanation," David Easton argued,
"involve two different kinds of propositions that, for the sake of clari-
ty, should be kept analytically distinct."[55] The goal was to construct a
"value-free science of politics" as Heinz Eulau called it.[56]

One reason why postwar behavioralists doing research on American politics provide an interesting foray into a discussion of how the
concept "individualism" is misused is because these behavioralists,
by their own account, claimed to be committed to individualism. Yet,
their theories actually contain very little evidence of individualism.
Like group theorists since the turn of the century, these political scientists rejected the formal institutional focus. They opted instead to
build explanation and description on the foundation of so-called brute
data. Behavioralists such as Bernard Berelson, Harold Lasswell, George
Catlin, and Eulau, and political scientists such as Dahl and David Easton who claimed at the time to adhere to the standards of research
that behavioralists embraced, enthusiastically adopted a methodology that putatively reduced social phenomena to premises about individuals. They described their theories as "a return to the individual";[57]
as focusing on "the acts of individuals, not of states";[58] as disclosing "the
pattern of individual acts behind the group act."[59] Their critics agreed
and argued that behavioral methods were unduly biased in favor of the

---

[53] Easton, *A Framework for Political Analysis*, 10.
[54] Dahl, "The Behavioral Approach in Political Science," 77.
[55] Easton, *A Framework of Political Analysis*, 7.
[56] Eulau, *The Behavioral Persuasion in Politics*, 134–36.
[57] Easton, *A Framework for Political Analysis*, 8.
[58] Catlin, *Science and Methods Politics*, 141–42.
[59] Lasswell, *Psychopathology and Politics*, 3.

individual.[60] To illustrate that their theories were actually lacking individualism — even of the methodological sort — I shall now turn to the three types of individualism discussed at the beginning of this chapter.

Behavioralism and Methodological Individualism

Methodological individualism has the most apparent affiliation with postwar behavioralism because the aim of behavioralists was to understand the political system in terms reducible to observations about individual dispositions, beliefs, and behavior. MI is generally supposed by philosophers of science to go hand-in-hand with an empirical approach because "empiricism holds that all terms must ultimately refer to what is observable, directly or indirectly, and that what we observe are people and their characteristics."[61] Behavioralists rejected explanations that relied on what appeared to be supraindividual structures and relations. The survey data they collected were the means by which the political process was broken down into its component parts; the answers of each individual to each question were the molecules from which an understanding of the political system and its laws could be constructed. Their purpose was, in the spirit of MI, to reduce the time span between cause and effect[62] and to generate laws of political activity based on these nuts and bolts of politics.

While the behavioral project has been criticized for accomplishing little except the endless accumulation of statistical data,[63] most behavioralists, and pluralists like Dahl who used this research, were primarily interested in aggregating the statistics and building theories of group interaction. For instance, Berelson explained his project as investigating "the voters' perception of politics, their reaction to the issues, their attention to the mass media, their influence on one another's political preferences," for the purpose of better understanding the processes of democratic elections.[64] The behavioral task, which was to understand democratic processes, was pursued by reducing these processes to the attitudes, dispositions, beliefs, and behavior of individuals within the process.

---

[60] See Taylor, *Philosophy and the Human Sciences,* 31. Also see K. W. Kim, "The Limits of Behavioral Explanation," 39–40.

[61] Brodbeck, "Methodological Individualism," 3.

[62] See Elster, *Making Sense of Marx,* 5–6.

[63] See David Ricci, *The Tragedy of Political Science.*

[64] Berelson, Lazarsfeld, and McPhee, *Voting,* vii.

In keeping with their methodological intentions, behavioralists generated conclusions about groups on the basis of research that focused on individual behavior. They categorized individuals according to variables such as class, race, religion, age, and gender. Establishing such categories made it possible for the research to be presented in the scientific form of lawlike generalizations such as: individuals who live in the same house tend to vote for the same party, or elites are more tolerant than nonelites, or the more involved an individual is in a group, the more likely her vote will correspond with the votes of other group members, etc. All of these generalizations reaffirm the central hypothesis of many voting studies, which is undoubtedly a plausible one, that voting behavior is influenced by the groups with which individuals are affiliated.

While plausible, the general explanatory hypothesis about voting behavior, along with the method of categorization used to generate it, actually compromised the sense in which the theories can be considered individualistic. The hypothesis about socialization was explored by concentrating on the individual exclusively as a member and a product of various groups. As a result, the studies disclosed conclusions that revealed more about the political behavior of *groups* than about the political behavior of individuals. Though the group behavior in question was linked to individual behavior, the behavioralists were only interested in the individual to the extent that the individual's behavior was captured by group behavior.

This first point may be obvious. The behavioral enterprise was not designed to predict the actual behavior of any *particular* individual. Some individuals, though falling under various classifications depending on their skin color, age, or religion, may or may not have actually shared the characteristic behavior of the groups to which they were affiliated. To use examples from Berelson's 1954 study: not all Blacks vote for the Democrats and not all young Catholics are Republicans. Only in terms of general group characteristics could the behavioralists offer plausible claims. When applied to human behavior, the scientific enterprise that aims at discovering norms is bound to treat individuals as less central to explanation in the sense that individual behavior which closely complies with the norms of groups counts more towards the social scientist's conclusions than behavior that does not comply with group norms. In this way, characteristics of groups are more accurately captured than are characteristics of any particular individual.

The group focus of these theories is more clearly inconsistent with both the broad and narrow interpretations of methodological individualism when one considers the common criticism of postwar behavioralism: that it produced a distorted and fragmented portrait of the individual voter. According to this criticism, the picture is distorted because the categories into which individuals are classified are better suited to the researcher's needs than they are descriptive of the individual's affiliation. For example, the category of "Protestant" includes such an array of individuals, all with different orientations to religion and/or to their religion (or is it the religion of their parents? or just one parent?), that it is unclear which individual characteristic of relevance is identified under this label. When data are aggregated, individual differences blend together, producing a single shade of Protestantism. Whether or not any individual actually matches this shade is unimportant given the purpose of the research. In the research, as in the society to which it applies, political significance is attached to the *group* characteristic and behavior, not to the *individual.*

The behavioralists' portrait was also one of a fragmented individual. In the voting studies, each fragment was not so much a role the individual played but a group with which the individual was affiliated. As in all pluralist theories, the fact of multiple affiliations, rather than the mere existence of affiliation, was central to postwar pluralism. In behavioralism, though, multiple affiliations posed a methodological challenge. The same individual may be white, young, female, and middle class. Comprehensively, her personality is a combination of all these fragments. However, the only way in which data are sensibly aggregated is to isolate each of these characteristics and separately discuss the voting tendencies of whites, of youths, of women, and of the middle class. Discussing each of these fragments showed again how the behavior of groups rather than that of individuals was the researcher's focus.

Attempts were made by postwar behavioralists to piece the fragments together because, without understanding the interaction between fragments, the individual's vote could not be predicted on the basis of social characteristics. A method of analysis had to be developed to deal with the multiple affiliations of each individual, since policy questions and elections activate many social characteristics and affiliations simultaneously. Two techniques were used. The first was to analyze composite groups. For example, research about young Protestant women was compared with research about youth, women, and Protestants. On the basis of comparing composites with primary groups, Berelson concluded, for example, that "Catholics vote more Democratic than Protestants regardless of class status or class identification or national origin."[65] At

---

[65] Berelson, et al., *Voting,* 75.

other times, he found contrary results; variables changed the political preferences so that, for example, "... younger members of the currently active minorities, Jews and Negroes, are more Democratic than their elders."[66]

The benefit of exploring the attitudes within composite groups is that, by isolating the composite from the primary group, the research might be able to decrease the deviation from the primary group norm. For example, the exceptions to the norm that Catholics vote Democrat may be accounted for by the composite of young Catholics, who tend to vote Republican. Moreover, the more composite the group was, the less fragmented and thus more plausible was the picture of the individual. In order to construct a less fragmented and more plausible picture of the individual, more and more groups of increasingly specific subtypes were continually added to the list. The more realistic the individual was made to appear through composite groups, and the more these composites could account for idiosyncratic behavior, the less simple and useful the behavioral project appeared. Studying composite groups decreased the usefulness of the behavioral information by greatly increasing the complexity of their explanations.[67] Their research methods were better suited to accounting for general tendencies of groups rather than predicting individual behavior.

The second technique was cross-pressure analysis. It aims at explaining what happens when different groups pull the individual's political preferences in different directions. If wealthy people tend to vote Republican and Blacks vote Democratic, how will wealthy Blacks vote? Analysis showed that, when an individual belongs to two groups, one of which supports candidate A and one of which supports candidate B, or if the individual is of two minds about a decision, she will withdraw from making that decision, make it at the last minute, lose interest in the election, or deny the importance of the election.[68]

There are four problems with cross-pressure analysis. First, the evidence that the phenomena existed was, according to critics and advocates, scant.[69] Secondly, the method conflicted with the rationale behind the composite group method. The behavior of individuals who

[66] Berelson, et al., *Voting*, 76.

[67] V. O. Key, *The Responsible Electorate: 1936–60*, 3–4.

[68] See Lazarsfeld, Berelson, and Gaudet, *The People's Choice*, 60–62; Berelson, et al., *Voting*, 284–85; Campbell, Converse, Miller, and Stokes, *The American Voter*, 42–48.

[69] For a critic see Amitai Etzioni, *The Active Society*, 451. For an advocate see Campbell, et al., *The American Voter*, 42.

were purported to be cross-pressured might be better interpreted as the behavior typical of members of a certain composite group.[70] The difference is between a) interpreting a behavior as caused by an individual being pulled in opposite directions, e.g., by race and income level and b) interpreting behavior as socialized and typical of individuals who share a particular "race-wealth" characteristic.

The third problem with cross-pressure analysis is the assumption that, within a situation of conflicting affiliations, the individual will avoid conflict rather than confront it; she will retain her contradictory loyalties rather than adjust them. Pluralists, such as Dewey and James, argued just the opposite conclusion: that conflicts of this sort are the vehicles for personal development because they force individuals to reassess their priorities and sometimes to reintegrate their personalities by changing the groups to which they are affiliated. Conversely, the behavioralists were notorious for assuming that the individual would respond to conflict by employing psychological-avoidance tactics. The cross-pressured individual is always portrayed as trying to reduce, avoid, or deny conflict. As Peter Sperlich argues, the view in political theory of individuals as primarily tension-reducing animals invites assumptions that favor stability over conflict, an assumption that was central to much postwar theory. In addition to being unsubstantiated, these assumptions can be dangerous when taken to an extreme. Sperlich extrapolates that "[t]o try to abolish or to suppress the conflict assertion side of politics means to try to forcibly impose a single consensus" and this imposition carries with it totalitarian implications.[71] (The theme of stability shall be explored further in the next chapter.)

The fourth problem is that cross-pressure observation is a clear example of the initial point made about behavioralism — that it allowed the individual to be swallowed by the group. In cross-pressure analysis, political preferences are determined wholly by social or group characteristics. The individual is a product of the groups to which she is affiliated rather than being, in any sense, an independent agent. Even when there is ample opportunity for her to act independently of group pressures — when groups are exerting contradictory influences on her — she does not autonomously decide between conflicting pressures. Rather, she withdraws from the task, unable to act at all.[72] The groups appear to

---

[70] Etzioni, *The Active Society*, 452.
[71] Sperlich, *Conflict and Harmony in Human Affairs*, 184.
[72] See Lazarsfeld, et al., *The People's Choice*.
[73] John Wahlke, "Pre-Behavioralism in Political Science," 13.

be the real actors in politics. In postwar pluralism, the competition among groups determines the direction of public policy because groups determine the political preferences and the political behavior of individuals. Therefore, understanding the political system means understanding the behavior of groups.

Individuals were the units of observation in postwar behavioralism, but they were not the units of interest and therefore often not the units about which conclusions were generated.[73] Though the group focus alone does not distance behavioral analysis from individualism, it points to at least three problems with identifying postwar behavioralism with MI.

First, behavioralism violated the narrow construal of MI by simultaneously maintaining that individual behavior is determined by groups *and* that group behavior is explicable in terms of individual behavior. In a sense, all theories of socialization will fail to meet the standards of MI narrowly construed. Of course, this might point to problems with this interpretation of MI rather than with theories of socialization. According to the narrow interpretation, observations about individual behavior cannot explain group behavior if individual behavior is itself explicable in terms of these groups. Either the individual determines the group's characteristics or the group determines the individual's characteristics. The problem with simultaneously maintaining both conclusions speaks to the central concern that critics of MI raise. The individualist method is inadequate to the task of explaining a political system if that method relies on premises (about individual behavior) that are themselves only explicable in terms of that system (i.e., the way in which groups are treated in the political system). In the case of behavioralism, facts about individuals are explained in terms of facts about groups, namely, the socialization process that takes place in groups. Simultaneously, the behavioralists argued that their methods generated conclusions about groups based on individual behavior. But which individuals were these? the same individuals who were being socialized by the group? Methodologically, this which-came-first problem might appear to be solved by incorporating the influence of past individuals who established the patterns of behavior by which present-day individuals are socialized. But then the behavior of past individuals has to be explained. Without belaboring the point further, the explanation cannot infinitely regress. Maurice Mandelbaum argues that, to engage in this sort of explanation is to commit the genetic fallacy, in this case, presuming that the origin of certain groups is identical with those same groups at present.[74] To avoid the genetic fallacy, one must run afoul of MI narrowly construed.

What is needed to save this explanation, short of embracing methodological holism, is the addendum that the behavior of groups, or more specifically, the effect of groups on individuals is not satisfactorily explained in terms of the behavior of individuals in groups (even though the existence of the group clearly depends on the existence of individuals). Adopting such a position is essential for any theory of socialization. Nonetheless, it is inconsistent with MI narrowly construed because it relies on concepts such as social facts, that are irreducible, without remainder, to individual dispositions, beliefs and/or behavior.

The second and third ways in which postwar behavioralism violates the strictures of MI apply to both the broad and narrow interpretations. In postwar behavioralism, individual characteristics were often not simply aggregated, they were blended. Blending meant that the group's characteristic coincided only very loosely with the characteristic of any individual who counted as part of the group. To cite the example previously used, the category of "Protestant" includes such an array of individuals, all with different orientations to religion and/or to their religion (or is it the religion of their parents? or just one parent?), that it is unclear what individual characteristic of relevance is identified under the label. When data are aggregated, individual differences are blended together, producing a single shade of Protestantism. Blending also occurred when generating conclusions about behavior. As the researcher aggregated individual responses to the questions, individual differences were lost in favor of conclusions that more accurately capture the behavioral tendencies of groups. Blending meant that the studies could not be reducible without remainder to premises about individuals. In this case, remainder is supplied by the researcher who chooses the relevant categories and who distills their content to a few central characteristics which are based on a prior knowledge of what counts as politically significant in the society in question. So, what is significant about the group "Protestant" for the voting studies excludes accounts of how each individual is associated with that sect in a unique way. Even if the conclusions about the group were based on what individual Protestants said about themselves in interviews or on questionnaires, what is of most significance in establishing the categories and defining what should count as a Protestant has little to do with the specifics of how an

---

[74] Mandelbaum, "Societal Facts," 179.

individual views herself. Rather, these groups indicate the categories that the researcher identified as politically significant in the society studied, and, more generally, they indicate how the individual is categorized by the society in which she lives. For this reason, the voting studies revealed much about the social context in which the researcher was situated before a single response was recorded. So, in sum, the three violations of MI by behavioralists center around not being able unproblematically to reduce group behavior to individual behavior because 1) individuals are, themselves, the product of group socialization and therefore cannot alone explain the character of the group; 2) individual characteristics were blended to formulate a group characteristic which, then, cannot be disaggregated back to individual characteristics; and 3) researchers were largely responsible for choosing which categories or characteristics were politically significant.

Behavioralism and Atomistic Individualism

A criticism of behavioral methods similar to the third reason why behavioralism violated MI was made by Taylor in his essay, "Interpretation and the Sciences of Man." Political scientists who claim to reduce political phenomena to brute data and explain social meaning by aggregating the individual, subjective assessments of political phenomena completely ignore the intersubjective dimension of meaning. This intersubjective meaning is incorporated into the categories and questions that comprise the studies. In comparative politics, these categories are applied by researchers from one culture onto another culture where their appropriateness is questionable:

> [American political science] proposes to understand the politics of all society in terms of such functions, for instance, as "interest articulation" and "interest aggregation" whose definition is strongly influenced by the bargaining culture of our civilization, but which is far from being guaranteed appropriateness elsewhere.[75]

Taylor's main point is that political scientists think that their categories are neutral when they are not. But, his analysis also reveals, though inadvertently, that the empirical methods, for all their flaws,

---

[75] Taylor, *Philosophy and the Human Sciences,* 42.

did not presume atomism. The mistake of comparative political scientists was not that individual respondents were stripped of culture or plucked from communities. Rather, the problem was that respondents from one culture were judged by the standards appropriate to a different culture. The individual does not escape the group. Rather, she is measured by the standards of a group or community with which she is *not* affiliated.

Taylor's discussion illustrates one reason why it is mistaken to label postwar behavioralism as displaying atomistic individualism. Atomism denotes an understanding of the self or the human condition in which individuals are conceptualized as self-sufficiently developing the capacities they need to enjoy a good life. Empirical political scientists did not conceptualize individuals by separating them from their attachments. The more common problem was that researchers often misunderstood the attachments that encumbered individuals and, as in comparative research, assumed that the behavior of individuals from non-Western cultures could be judged by standards more appropriate to Western cultures.

Outside of comparative research, behavioralists in the United States constructed a notion of the self that, if anything, was anti-atomistic. As early as 1930, an anti-atomistic portrayal of the individual was the central variable of a research technique and political theory that discredited individual participation in politics. At that time, Harold Lasswell was assessing political behavior by applying psychoanalytic theory to data gathered from prolonged interviews with individuals. On the basis of his research, he recommended that a preventive approach be taken to politics. Individuals ought to be insulated from political activities, even activities as seemingly benign as political debate. "Discussion," Lasswell argued, "frequently complicates social difficulties, for the discussion by far-flung interests arouses a psychology of conflict which produces obstructive, fictitious, and irrelevant values."[76] Lasswell further argued that the political system would not be crippled nor would individual well-being be threatened by a politics that relied less upon participation, since individuals do not have a good sense of what is in their interests anyway. "The examination of the total state of the person will frequently show that his theory of his own interests is far removed from the course of the procedure which will give him a happy and well-adjusted life."[77] In other words, political decisions are re-

---

[76] Lasswell, *Psychopathology and Politics*, 196–97.
[77] Lasswell, *Psychopathology and Politics*, 194.

moved from the individual's competence partly for her own sake. Since individual participation rarely makes a difference in the political arena, the political system also will not suffer: "[p]olitical demands are of limited relevance to the changes which will produce permanent reductions in the tension levels of society."[78] For Lasswell, politics is a matter of tension-reduction, and leaving this activity to the elite is a more efficient and safe way to achieve this end. The survival of democracy depends upon "improving the methods and the education of the social administrators and the social scientists," not by preparing the public for participation.[79]

In the postwar period, evidence was continually being compiled through voting studies which showed that individuals lack the capacity to make political decisions autonomously. Behavior was largely influenced by the groups to which the individual was affiliated. In their 1954 study, Berelson's team concluded that the typical voter is not a calculating decision maker at the polls. Rather, political choices are made like choices in music, literature, and fashion — either according to individual whims or, more often, according to the dispositions of the individual's friends or peers. Individuals, they argued, are incapable of collecting and understanding the information necessary to make an informed choice. Therefore, they vote the way that the people they trust vote.[80] In addition to Berelson's study, the lack of individual self-sufficiency was a clear implication of cross-pressure analysis. The individual withdraws from making a decision when group pressure fails to lead her in one direction rather than another.

Behavioralists did not write about a self in the abstract. They did not employ the same terms of intellectual discourse that liberal philosophers employ. But the socialized individual they portrayed played the same role in the theories of American democracy developed in the postwar period as the abstract individual plays in the philosophical accounts offered today. In both cases, the individual is the starting point from which theories of political organization proceed. The theories of democracy that were developed in the postwar period were specifically designed to respond to the behavioral portrait of the individual that was emerging. This portrait assumed that socialization rather than isolation was the backdrop to political interaction and behavior. Thus, postwar political science clearly rejected an atomistic conception of the individual.

---

[78] Lasswell, *Psychopathology and Politics*, 203.
[79] Lasswell, *Psychopathology and Politics*, 265.
[80] Berelson, et al., *Voting*, 309.

Behavioralism and Ethical Individualism

Postwar behavioralism had its greatest impact on political analysis and public policy through the conclusions it generated regarding the nature of individuals. The individual was not socially isolated or unencumbered. She was not self-sufficient. Rather, she was profoundly affected by her social environment and the multitude of attachments she had to others.

Much evidence was also compiled that showed the individual to be irrational and intolerant. Besides Lasswell's conclusions, numerous studies in the postwar period disclosed an American electorate willing to deny basic rights to groups such as communists or Blacks.[81] "The electorate," McCloskey concluded, "had failed to grasp certain of the underlying ideas and principles on which the American political system rests."[82] Voting studies showed that voters are rarely fully informed, that they are unable to bring information to bear on principle,[83] and that they are "almost completely unable to judge the rationality of government actions."[84] Dahl observed that the behavioral studies had drastically changed the way in which political scientists understood the voter, and, in the new portrait, "the face of the rational voter is all but invisible.[85] Although some of these conclusions were eventually challenged by political scientists, such as Key who questioned the standards of rationality imposed by the researchers, many postwar theorists drew on this portrait. They constructed theories of democracy that attempted either to minimize the damage the voter could do to the system or to explain why American democracy was resilient to the attitudes of the typical voter.

Ethical individualism holds that a theory, a policy, or a political system should be judged in terms of how well or poorly it secures individual well-being. One might argue that the behavioral project speaks past this category. Generally, postwar political scientists tried to avoid evaluating the political systems they described as a means to emulating scientific standards of research. For this reason, behavioralists were more unwilling to recommend ways in which democratic politics could

---

[81] See Stouffer, *Communism, Conformity and Civil Liberties;* Prothro and Grigg, "Fundamental Principles of Democracy;" McCloskey, "Consensus and Ideology in American Politics."

[82] McCloskey, "Consensus and Ideology in American Politics," 365.

[83] Berelson, et al., *Voting*, 309.

[84] Campbell, et al., *The American Voter*, 309.

[85] Dahl, *Democracy in the United States*, 285–86.

improve individual development even though they provided a wealth of information about the development (or lack thereof) of individual capacities and traits through political and social interaction. But within the democratic theories that applied behavioralist methods, ethical individualism had relevance because these theories advanced an interpretation of what democracy entails. And, according to many of these theories, democracy does not rely on ethical individualism.

Given the behavioral portrait of the typical voter, the need to protect the system from the intolerant and uneducated electorate unsurprisingly became a prominent theme in the postwar era. This theme pervades elite theories of democracy, some proponents of which argued that individuals ought to be discouraged from participating in democratic politics, even though, as was often pointed out, participation helped to develop a responsible citizenry. Mosca, Lippmann, Schumpeter, Pareto, and Michels acknowledged that political democracy requires that citizens be more politically adept than they are and that participation facilitates this adeptness.[86] But these theorists also argued that mass participation was dangerous and that it puts democracies at risk. Surrounded by the circumstances of the Second World War, Schumpeter warned that voters have a tendency to give into dark urges and to become receptive to any group, no matter how extreme, that has an axe to grind. The stakes were too high to make participation a worthwhile goal. "Many decisions of fateful importance are of a nature that makes it impossible for the public to experiment with them at its leisure and at moderate cost."[87]

Some critics of elite democracy focused their attacks on the complacent attitudes that Schumpeter and others theorists had towards the individual's potential development. Henry Kariel contended that the elite theorists and behavioralists considered only "man's dismal record" and not his ideal capacities.[88] Elite theorists developed a form of politics that specifically responded to the dismal record. C. B. Macpherson sarcastically noted, "[t]here is no nonsense about democracy as a vehicle for the improvement of mankind" within the empirical theories of democracy.[89] Instead, Schumpeter and other empirical democratic theorists focused their attention on the value and importance of political stability.

---

[86] This argument is made by Kaufman, "Human Nature and Participatory Democracy."

[87] Schumpeter, *Capitalism, Socialism and Democracy*, 263.

[88] Kariel, *The Promise of Politics*, 23.

[89] Macpherson, *The Life and Times of Liberal Democracy*, 78–79.

Dahl developed his theory partly in response to the hypothesis that a ruling elite exists in the United States.[90] The strength of his pluralist alternative to elite democratic theory rested on his appreciation of the complexity of democratic decision making. At the time, its strength was seen also to rest on the purported objectivity that his more sophisticated interpretation of the empirical methods lent his approach. The more sophisticated interpretation showed that the elite theorists either employed normative (nonempirical) reasoning or accepted unfalsifiable hypotheses.[91] But Dahl did not challenge the assumptions about the individual and her capacities upon which elite theories were built. He also argued that the stability of American democracy was made possible, in part, by the very low level of political activity in which the American electorate engaged.[92] In his 1961 assessment of the distribution of political power in New Haven, Dahl argued that political apathy is functional to this democratic system, given the pervasive ignorance about political matters of New Haven's electorate. Dahl cited the tolerance studies and the conclusions of Berelson's team, both of which endorsed political apathy because of the poor performance of voters.[93] He agreed with the consensus amongst behavioralists that most voters "operate at a low level of ideological sophistication," "with a small fund of political information": "often they lack the elementary information required even to be aware of inconsistencies between their views and what is actually happening in the political system."[94] This makes them feel incompetent to decide such issues even though they have the opportunity. But, evidence that few participated was not sufficient to establish that an elite ruled. Dahl challenged the elite theory on an empirical basis and avoided the normative question of whether an elite ought to rule. Moreover, he did not challenge the portrait of individuals found within many of these theories, nor the assumption that political apathy could be functional to democracy.

Most behavioralists who tried to reconcile their portrayal of the voter with the existence of democracy argued that political apathy allows American democracy to continue functioning. Classical theories that required the voter to be rational and eager to participate were unrealistic.

---

[90] Dahl, "Critique of the Ruling Elite Model."

[91] For example, if a given group was found not to be the true ruling elite, then, the theory went, there must be another group controlling the initial group.

[92] Dahl, *Who Governs?* 314–15.

[93] Prothro and Grigg, "Fundamental Principles of Democracy," 293; Berelson, et al., *Voting*, 314–15.

[94] Dahl, *Who Governs?* 319.

Berelson observed that "individual inadequacy provides a positive service for society."[95] Similarly, Prothro and Grigg observed that "[d]iscussions of consensus tend to overlook the functional nature of apathy for the democratic system."[96] These theorists accepted a status quo that did not improve the individual's incompetence rather than entertain any means of improving the individual's well-being. Explaining the status quo was acceptable within the parameters of empirical political science. Explaining ways to improve democracy and to improve individual well-being was not acceptable within these parameters.

The irrational, intolerant, and politically unsophisticated individual was accepted as the unchanging variable around which various democratic theories in the postwar period were described and designed. Most behavioral theorists explicitly rejected a participatory ethic even though they recognized that participation may improve the individual's political sophistication. But participation would also arouse a psychology of conflict and tension. It would bring to the foreground the individual's sense of her incompetence. Apathy avoided these problems.

One might argue that these theorists aimed at securing individual well-being via more direct efforts to guarantee the continuity of a stable, anticommunist, antifascist system. One might argue that these theories can be interpreted as having embraced a substantive view of individual well-being, though one that is very conservative and paternalistic. Perhaps Lasswell, Berelson, Dahl, and others thought the individual was better off with apathy than with an active and tension-inducing disposition towards politics. But, this argument, to be made convincingly, requires that the behavioralists argued for apathy or tension-reduction because these were key to individual well-being. Yet, no such argument was made. Rather, the assumption that tension or conflict ought to be avoided was part of an argument that focused on the system's stability, not the individual's well-being.[97] Postwar theorists, including elite theorists and pluralists, showed how apathy contributed to the system's stability *in spite of the fact that individual sophistication, potential and improvement were sacrificed.* If individual well-being could be thought of as central to these theories, it would be unclear whether any political theory could count as nonindividualistic in the ethical sense. In each of these theories, politics is seen as an arena of individual development. But

[95] Berelson, et al., *Voting,* 316.

[96] Prothro and Grigg, "Fundamental Principles of Democracy," 293.

[97] See also Harry Eckstein's, *A Theory of Stable Democracy.* Chapter 5 contains some discussion of Eckstein's theory.

the characteristics that ought to be developed according to the elite theorists and pluralists are conflict-avoidance and apathy. Postwar theorists revealed a willingness to sacrifice a political process more conducive to individual improvement for one that was less likely to disintegrate into communism or fascism.

While the behavioralists' intention was clearly to apply individualist methods, their scholarship did not generate individualistic or atomistic conclusions. Perhaps more so than any other political analysts, behavioralists would have found absurd the communitarian claim that the practices and policies of liberal democracies, such as the United States, are characterized by atomism. Notwithstanding their official affirmation of individualism, behavioralists generated group-centered, socially sensitive — if not socially determined — conclusions about the individual. Furthermore, these conclusions were produced by applying methods that aimed at disclosing the social-connectedness — not the atomism — of the participants in the political system. For all the many flaws of this type of political science, only an attenuated understanding of postwar behavioralism or, conversely, a very narrow use of the term *individualism* can lead one to conclude that either the methods used or the democratic politics described by postwar political scientists promoted or depended upon any variety of individualism. This conclusion not only raises problems for those who think that the postwar behavioral movement emulates individualism, but it reveals serious ambiguities, which are relevant to communitarianism, that arise when employing the term *individualism* in political analysis. I shall now turn to this issue.

Individualism in Communitarian Analysis

A popular position that has emerged from the current communitarian critique of liberalism mistakenly equates individualism with atomism and both with liberalism. Roughly speaking, adherents to this position hold that liberal theory and liberal society endorse an atomistic conception of the individual within society. Adherents to atomism conceptualize individuals as isolated from the social context in which they are found, as if they were unencumbered by any attachments or obligations to their families or their communities; in Hobbes's words, as if they were "sprung out of the earth, and suddenly, like mushrooms, come to full maturity, without all kind of engagement to each other."[98] Other aspects of liberalism are born out of and help reinforce atomism. Individual rights, for example, reaffirm the individual's isolation, as do liberal research methods, in that they focus on the individual as if she is isolated from society. Hobbes, Locke, Nozick, and Rawls are included amongst the theorists particularly guilty of these atomistic prejudices.[99] However, communitarians such as Taylor view atomism as a problem endemic to all forms of liberalism and to liberal societies.[100] We share "an atomistic-infected commonsense" whose magnitude must be recognized before it can be conquered.[101]

The communitarian claim that all liberal theory is based on an atomistic view of the individual ignores the pluralist theories explored so far, or, at least, must define liberalism so as to exclude pluralist theories. Communitarians tend to focus on the theories of philosophical liberals such as Hobbes or Rawls. But, the urgency of the communitarian case is based on the purported pervasiveness of destructive forms of individualism in liberal societies. Communitarians not only argue that individualism has infected the methods by which we construct our political theories but that it pervades our society and political practices.

As I have explained, the methods used by American political scientists of the postwar period who embraced the behavioral approach are individualistic only in a very narrow sense. Once one distinguishes between different types of individualism, the methodological problems of postwar behavioralism appear more clearly to be caused by a lack of a certain type of individualism — namely ethical individualism — rather than an excessive commitment to individualism. Communitarian analyses confuse the problems that may plague liberal-democratic methods or theories partly because they conflate various types of individualism. As has already been shown, the term individualism has a variety of meanings and failure to distinguish adequately different varieties of individualism can lead to significant confusion.

Contemporary communitarians foster this type of confusion. Taylor's recent work is particularly guilty of conflating individualisms. In

---

[98] Hobbes, *De Cive,* 109.

[99] See Taylor, *Philosophy and the Human Sciences,* and Sandel, *Liberalism and the Limits of Justice.*

[100] Although Taylor's analysis clearly links the atomistic doctrine to liberalism and to devices such as rights that are central to liberal doctrine, he exempts Rawls from the charge of atomism. See Taylor, "Alternative Futures," 193, fn 8. Nonetheless, Rawls continues to be implicated in reifying the modern identity which Taylor finds problematic. And, even if Taylor has special (though undisclosed) reasons to count Rawls as an atypical liberal, Rawlsian liberalism is central to Sandel's communitarian critique.

[101] Taylor "Cross-Purposes," 170.

his 1979 essay entitled "Atomism," his target seems to be narrow and clear. He criticizes the presumption, found in classical liberal philosophy, that individuals are self-sufficient. He ties, historically and conceptually, this atomistic presumption to the primacy-of-rights doctrine. The purpose of rights, Taylor argues, is to protect certain treasured capacities that individuals possess. Since individual capacities only flourish in certain types of communities, to be committed to the capacities entails being committed to these communities. Yet, posing these commitments in terms of one's obligation to sustain a certain type of society and culture directly challenges the primacy-of-rights doctrine. Moreover, accepting such obligations undermines the atomistic, self-sufficient portrayal of the individual found in liberal theory. The upshot of Taylor's argument is that a genuine commitment to individual well-being cannot be predicated on an atomistic conception of the individual or on the associated primacy-of-rights thesis.

In a later essay, Taylor restates the argument in terms of modern liberal culture. "The culture of rights pushed to a certain point, the habit of circumventing majority decision through court judgments, both presupposes and further entrenches taking a distance from community decision-making."[102] Liberal rights separate people from their communities because they presume self-sufficiency; they protect what has been supposedly developed elsewhere. Rights may be appropriate devices to promote the well-being of autonomous and self-sufficient individuals, but they are inappropriate devices for promoting the well-being of individuals who are in the process of developing these essential capacities within an expressly communal context. The slide between different varieties of individualism here is subtle but significant. Liberal individualism is assailed because it putatively represents a commitment to atomism. Yet, atomism is itself criticized by implicit reference to ethical individualism. Communitarian rhetoric, including that of Taylor, suggests the need for a wholesale movement away from individualism. And, indeed, the special privileging of community goods and traditions in communitarianism does signal an absence of ethical individualism. Yet, paradoxically, the very coherence of Taylor's critique of the primacy of rights entails a commitment to a variety of individualism.

In a 1989 essay, Taylor explicitly conflates the idea of atomism with methodological individualism, stating that atomists "are often referred to as methodological individualists."[103] He does not provide rea-

---

[102] Taylor, "Alternative Futures," 211.
[103] Taylor, "Cross-Purposes," 159.

sons why the notion of self-sufficiency to which the primacy of rights is attached must be connected to methodological claims about social explanation. And the reasons are far from obvious especially given the broader definition of methodological individualism. For instance, one can deny atomism while maintaining a sort of MI. That is, one can coherently argue that, since individuals are profoundly interdependent, their welfare is only secured within a communal context, while still maintaining that the communal context can be explained, in principle, without relying on supraindividualist entities. And even if critics of MI are correct to argue that most political or social concepts cannot be explained solely in terms of individual behavior, dispositions, and relations, this conclusion hardly says anything about whether or not individuals are self-sufficient in securing the good life or about whether individual rights rather than social goods ought to be accorded primacy.

The problem is exacerbated when strains of ethical individualism are mixed with the other types of individualism. Methodological individualists, Taylor argues, hold that "you can and ought to account for social goods in terms of concatenations of individual goods."[104] MI, he claims, discounts many social goods, including goods that involve friendship and intimacy, that are collectively enjoyed and collectively acquired. Because these goods are irreducible to individual goods, they are outside the individualist's purview. Here, Taylor's argument confuses the ethical and methodological categories. The methodological concern, at least in terms of what proponents of MI would pose, is whether friendship as a social practice can be explained in terms of the values, dispositions, and relations of individuals. The proponents of MI might disagree with their critics about whether friendship contains a social remainder. But no one would dismiss friendship as a value if it failed to be reducible to individualist explanatory premises. Ethically, the question posed is whether or not friendship, or any phenomenon whose value is being considered, is actually valued by individuals or contributes to individual well-being. Friendship passes this test with little effort. But some social phenomena do not so easily satisfy the standards set by ethical individualism. For instance, political stability, the central value in postwar democratic theory, is less successful in meeting the standards of ethical individualism because it can be secured at the expense of values more closely associated to individual well-being. This points to the central problem of postwar empirical democratic theory identified by critics such as Macpherson, Kariel, and many others. Stability is essential for the continuity of any so-

---

[104] Taylor, "Cross-Purposes," 159.

ciety, group, or system. But, the ethical individualist would insist that the extent to which it is valued must depend on how it affects the welfare of individuals, *not* merely how it affects the welfare of groups or systems. Because postwar political scientists did not assess the worth of stability in terms of individual well-being, and, moreover, seemed willing to sacrifice key aspects of individual well-being for the sake of stability, their theories fail to be ethically individualistic.

The key reason why behavioralism lacks ethical individualism is because it attempted to remove the ethical component from democratic theorizing. Similarly, the reason why it contained no theory of personal development is because its proponents were bent on merely describing development rather than prescribing means by which individuals could become more sophisticated, tolerant, rational, or autonomous than they were. Essentially what these theorists described were the processes and results of socialization. In both cases, the absence of ethical individualism is not caused, as it is in communitarianism, by conflating different types of individualism. Rather, it is caused by removing all ethical prescriptions from the theory. But this diagnosis might be too quick. Because, in spite of aspirations to the contrary, postwar political science did, in fact, advance value claims. Value was ascribed to the system, particularly its stability, and more generally, to the status quo. Socialization was a given, tension-reduction was good, and apathy was condoned. The sense in which these theories ascribed value to the system's stability shall be explored thoroughly in the next chapter. For now, I want to point out that, irrespective of the seemingly different routes they take, behavioralism and communitarianism arrive at strikingly similar results. In the seeming absence of any ethical commitments, behavioralism endorsed the system's stability as a primary value and drew the focus of democratic theory away from individual well-being — what is here called ethical individualism. It situated the individual within the context of her social affiliations and constructed her identity in terms of these affiliations.

Communitarianism, particularly Taylor's variant, conflates different types of individualism and is critical of the general package of individualism. It insists on viewing individuals as thoroughly social beings and on defining their identities in terms of the attachments that they possess. It contains ethical commitments but seeks to refocus the attention of democratic theory on the community or common good and away from the individual.

Distinguishing between different senses of individualism is the only way in which the rhetoric of behavioralist theories can be separated from their reality. The same, unsurprisingly, is true of communitarianism. Taylor seems to reiterate a commitment to the individual's well-being by illustrating how social goods and community are integral to that well-being. But, at the same time, his criticisms of liberal individualism depend upon sliding between one type of individualism and another. One result of this is that his analysis tends to saddle liberalism with commitments that it need not have. Unsurprisingly, critics of communitarianism have responded by arguing that there are various ways in which one might be a liberal without embracing atomism[105] or pointing out the various theorists usually thought to be liberals who do not fit the communitarian characterization of that tradition.[106]

Another result is that Taylor distances his alternative to liberalism from commitments that, it seems, he must endorse — namely, ethical individualism. The problem with liberalism which communitarians identify is that it uses the wrong tools in order to secure the individual's well-being. To be at all plausible, communitarianism must be interpreted as advancing an alternative notion of what it means to secure the individual's well-being. That is, the treasured human capacities which Taylor argues rights seek to protect, and which he seeks to develop, must be presumed by liberals and Taylor to serve the individual's well-being. They are treasured because individuals treasure them, and not, one presumes, because they are useful to a community or, like apathy in postwar behavioralism, consistent with maintaining the stability of a political system. The dispute, then, between liberals and communitarians must essentially entail a disagreement about how best to secure the individual's well-being. So, despite its rhetoric and arguments to the contrary, communitarianism must be ethically individualistic.

But, if one takes the rhetoric and anti-individualist arguments to heart, then the central aim of communitarianism is defeated. Without ethical individualism, personal development is reduced to mere socialization because, without a commitment to the individual's well-being, the social context becomes a noted fact of existence, as it was in behavioralism, rather than a potential vehicle for the improvement of individual well-being. By conflating different notions of individualism, communitarianism is dangerously misleading. Either it is ignoring its own individualistic commitments or it is proposing a vision of liberal society which is indefensible.

---

[105] For example, Kymlicka, *Liberalism, Community and Culture.*
[106] For example, Rosenblum, *Another Liberalism.*

Conclusion

The application of communitarian analyses to liberal society, as opposed to liberal philosophy, elicits further confusions. On the one hand, communitarians focus on the failure of liberal *theory* to grasp the genuine nature of individuals. On the other hand, communitarians purport to describe the malaise of liberal individualist *societies*, particularly the United States. Regardless of whether or not atomism pervades liberal philosophy, the urgent concern is that atomism informs current liberal politics, practices, and common sense; that individuals and not groups or communities are entitled to liberal rights; and that, armed with their rights, individuals retire to their isolated existences, leaving no one to care for the communities and social goods upon which everyone depends. This diagnosis of the ills of contemporary American society is based on philosophical interpretations of liberal principles, none of which claim to describe the reality of American politics. Should communitarians turn to interpretations of American political practices offered by political scientists, they would find fertile ground for certain types of criticism. But, in most of these descriptions, they would not find the "unencumbered" self or the atomized society. Moreover, one suspects that if communitarians took seriously the description of American politics offered in postwar behavioral theory, they would find little reason to condemn some of the individualist values to which philosophical liberals are committed. For in the absence of viewing these values as legitimate ideals, many postwar theorists accepted uncritically, first, the portrayal of the voter as irrational, intolerant, and far from autonomous, and second, a form of politics that perpetuated this reality. Berelson and many others concluded that public apathy is functional to democracy because they accepted this portrait. The resulting democratic theory was attacked for its uncritical acceptance of stability as the ideal of American democracy.[107] For the critics of empirical democratic theory, the problems of the American political system were partly attributable to the belief, on the part of scholars and decision makers, that American citizens are incapable of self-government because they are politically unsophisticated. In other words, the problem appears to be not a matter of relying upon the model of the rational and autonomous individual, but rather, of rejecting the model as either false or impossible and failing to view the political system as *prima facie* responsible for the well-being of individuals.

---

[107] See Duncan and Lukes, "The New Democracy."

Very little has been offered so far about the workings of postwar pluralist theory. That explanation is left for the next chapter. The assumptions examined here about the individual which underlie postwar pluralist theory were based on behavioral research and group theory rather than on the mechanics of pluralist politics. Pluralists incorporated a portrait that was similar to that which elite theorists incorporated in their theories. But pluralists took more seriously the plurality of groups in which individuals were socialized.

Both behavioral and group theory presupposed links between the social and political spheres. Bentley, Truman, Herring, Smith, and others treated groups as the primary political actors for reasons similar to those used by pluralists in the past: individuals acquired political power through groups and were socialized in groups. For both the group theorists and especially the behavioralists, individual development was a political issue in the sense that political attitudes, beliefs, and behavior were socialized. Apathy is a characteristic typical of certain groups, as is political activism. Cultivating certain characteristics or "treasured capacities" would entail fostering certain types of social situations. For example, political participation may have to be encouraged and expanded as one means to developing citizens who are politically sophisticated, competent, aware of their interests and possessing the ability to bring information to bear on principles. Conversely, if apathy is the characteristic prized because, for instance, it serves to strengthen stability, then the status quo would suffice. The link between individual development and politics was explicitly recognized in postwar theory. But, unlike in early pluralist theories, the course of individual development condoned by theorists was one which fostered the stability of the political system rather than individual well-being.

The analysis of individualism is more complex than is generally supposed because the term can denote many different things. The behavioralists understood their commitment to individualism in the very broad, methodological sense; explanations should be reducible to premises about individuals. Their theories were not meant to be individualistic in any other sense and, perhaps, were not individualistic even in the methodological sense. Contemporary communitarians conflate the different sorts of individualism, and, by doing so, they undermine the means by which to decipher problems like those found in behavioralism.

As a consequence, communitarians also confuse arguments relevant to liberal theory with those relevant to liberal societies. Thus far, I have argued that at least some of what might fall within the communitarian purview does not contain excessive individualism. The behavioral methods that dominated the social sciences and, particularly, political science, in the 1950s, 1960s, and 1970s did not contain this individualism. Moreover, individualism was absent from the interpretation that postwar political theorists offered of American politics. In the postwar interpretation, the political practices, institutions, and organization of the American political system were all directed at a unifying goal: the continuation or improvement of societal and political stability. The individual did not necessarily fare well in light of this end.

V

The Common Good
in Postwar Pluralism

The communitarian vision seems incredible in light of the long history, central to liberal mythology, of abuses that dissenters have suffered in the hands of otherwise conventional communities. Their diagnosis of the problem is built, according to Stephen Holmes, on the "implausible assumption that, in the century of Hitler and Stalin, liberalism remains the Great Enemy of mankind."[1] It seems incredible that communitarians actually think life would be better for individuals if communities adopted a communal notion of the good — one which sometimes has primacy over individual rights (to take Taylor's analysis seriously) — or if we returned to the heroic societies of ancient Greece, for which MacIntyre yearns[2] — or the pre-New Deal America found in Sandel's analysis.[3]

Although many liberals have criticized the communitarian vision of community for its conspicuous neglect of the insecurity of minorities and dissenters, more often than not the critics hesitate to define the communitarian alternative boldly because it seems so implausible that they actually intend to return us to Salem or Athens. For example, Rosenblum searches for the "most likely referent" to the communitarian alternative. She argues that the examples of "tribes, Puritan communities, Medieval Jewish ghettos" are meant to "illustrate moral and psychological propositions about 'belonging,' not political ones,"[4] even though these are the examples found in communitarian accounts. Other theorists attempt to fill in the blanks left by communitarians. Cary Nederman, for example, constructs from Medieval political theory the notion of communal functionalism and shows how this notion is faithful

---

[1] Holmes, "The Permanent Structure of Antiliberal Thought," 228.

[2] MacIntyre, *After Virtue*, especially chapters 9–15.

[3] Michael Sandel, "The Procedural Republic and the Unencumbered Self," 92–93.

[4] Rosenblum, "Pluralism and Self-Defense," 215.

to the standards set by contemporary communitarianism while it avoids the pitfalls of absolutism which are so often attributed to the communitarian vision.[5]

The route negotiated here aims to establish that postwar pluralism may stand as a referent to the communitarian vision. Postwar pluralism, I argue, meets the standards of community set by communitarians both through its methodological approach and its practical prescriptions. One need not go all the way to 17th-century Salem to find something that resembles the communitarian vision.

Postwar pluralism is, at first blush, an odd candidate to offer as an example of communitarian political theory. In fact, the first part of this chapter explains the ways in which postwar pluralism contains many characteristics deemed by communitarians to be typically liberal and is, for this reason, a good example of what contemporary communitarians find unsatisfactory about liberal theory. The fact-value distinction and emotivism, both of which communitarians claim underlie liberalism, are prominent aspects of postwar methodology and the accompanying pluralist theory. In these ways, postwar pluralism exhibits what communitarians fear most about liberal methods, namely, that they lead to fragmented and fractured communities governed by a neutral state.

But the level of analysis used to search for a notion of community partly determines the thickness of the notion discovered. Here the argument is that "liberal" commitments may lead to "communitarian" conclusions specifically in theories which adopt functionalist explanations of political or social practices. Most postwar empirical political science adopted functionalist explanations as a consequence of attempting to offer only value-neutral explanations. Thus, "liberal" commitments, such as value-neutrality, lead, I argue, to conclusions that parallel communitarian notions of community unity and values. Theories may contain many of the ingredients that communitarians suppose cause liberal theories to be hostile towards a common good (e.g., emotivism, fact-value distinction, a fragmented notion of community) but still embrace a notion of the common good that has close affinities to the conception of the common good which Nederman and MacIntyre identify. For this reason, I conclude that communitarians, such as MacIntyre, have misidentified the route by which theories are led to endorse a common good.

In the second part I argue that, taken superficially, postwar pluralism celebrates the fragmented community. Yet, just as there is often diversity and conflict between members of the same family, underneath

---

[5] Nederman, "Freedom, Community and Function."

the pluralism of American society, the pluralists hypostatized a substantive notion of communal value and good. But the notion of common good that they recognized and reaffirmed rightly invites serious criticism because, in postwar pluralism, communal good is purchased at the
price of individual well-being. The communitarian discussion of the
common good and particularly the methods by which, communitarians claim, politics ought to be analyzed and assessed leaves their theory open to the same criticism.

Part I: The Failure of Postwar Pluralism

Facts and Values in the Communitarian Critique

Contemporary communitarians argue that liberal theories and practices embrace the principle of neutrality. This principle states that justice
requires states or societies not to privilege some notions of the good life
over other notions. How this claim is to be interpreted is controversial.[6]
Nonetheless, neutrality is considered by communitarians to be a key
ingredient in theories which lack a notion of the common good. Communitarians argue that liberal neutrality is incompatible with recognizing the true nature and importance of community which, if nothing
else, entails privileging some notions of the good life over others.

The culture of value-neutrality originated, according to MacIntyre, in the intellectual project of the Enlightenment and continues to
inform moral philosophy, political science, sociology, and psychology.
Its legacy rests in the logical proposition that "from a set of factual
premises no moral conclusion validly follows."[7] The root of this idea is
found in principles advocated by some medieval philosophers and in the
work of Hume and Kant. However, not until the twentieth century is the
fact-value distinction considered to be a truth of logic. Early in this century, logical positivists made full use of the distinction when they set the
epistemological standards for vetting truth claims in the physical and social sciences. In moral philosophy, MacIntyre argues, positivism offered
its most barbarous manifestation through the doctrine of emotivism.
Originally, emotivism was a theory about the nature of moral language.

---

[6] See Dworkin, "Can A Liberal State Support Art?" in *A Matter of Principle*, and
Kymlicka, "Liberal Individualism."

[7] MacIntyre, *After Virtue*, 56.

Its pioneers, C. L. Stevenson and A. J. Ayer sought out the epistemological status of moral principles and moral argument by applying the distinction between facts and values to moral discourse.[8] Stevenson and Ayer argued that there is no scientific way to ascertain the objective truth of claims about what *ought* to be the case because truth claims only involve premises about what *is* the case. Without any basis in fact, moral propositions are not truth claims. At most, they are statements of personal preference and can claim no objectivity beyond this. "[I]n moral argument the apparent assertion of principles functions as a mask for expressions of personal preference."[9] According to emotivism, the claim, for example, that democracy is desirable masks a personal preference for democracy and nothing more.

MacIntyre argues that emotivism ultimately succeeded in a way that even the emotivists did not anticipate: "What emotivism however did fail to reckon with is the difference that it would make to morality if emotivism were not only true but also widely believed to be true."[10] Whether emotivism is true or not as a theory of meaning, individuals within Enlightenment-influenced (i.e., liberal) societies act as though moral values are nothing more than personal preferences. Today, according to MacIntyre, emotivism forms the core of liberal culture and is reflected in the liberal style of politics. His proof partly lies in the observation that individuals from the same culture and society are unable to agree on how to solve basic moral questions. In addition to disagreeing about which solutions are best, people disagree as to what should count as good reasons for holding their moral positions. MacIntyre illustrates this point by briefly surveying controversial issues (e.g., whether abortion can be justified) and two or three rival perspectives on each issue.[11] The rival perspectives, which are familiar enough to anyone who has even informally discussed with others issues such as abortion, are each logically coherent. But, when viewed as a package, the perspectives are conceptually incommensurable because each relies on a different set of premises; ". . . the rival premises are such that we possess no rational way of weighing the claims of one as against another."[12] Moral debate surrounding issues like abortion is interminable because individuals adopt incommensurable premises. Herein lies the cultural success of emo-

---

[8] Stevenson, *Ethics and Language;* Ayer, *Language, Truth and Logic.*

[9] MacIntyre, *After Virtue,* 19.

[10] MacIntyre, *After Virtue,* 19.

[11] MacIntyre, *After Virtue,* 6–7.

[12] MacIntyre, *After Virtue,* 8.

tivism. Moral premises are believed to have no objective basis. They are viewed as mere expressions of personal preference. Each individual has to adopt her own premises on the basis of her preferences. This renders moral debate futile because no one is required to share with others the standards for what is to count as a good reason to support or oppose a particular policy or position.

In one sense, empiricists in the social sciences cannot avoid dealing with values because the individuals whom they study hold moral and ethical beliefs that are expressed through voting, protesting, or other political or social behavior. So they respond to the fact-value distinction by converting values into data. They treat values, not as universal or societal truths (as facts should be), but rather, as personal preferences; the difference is between the statement "democracy is good" and the statement "democracy is the preferred system of political organization for ninety-nine out of one hundred people." This conversion is typical of empirical studies in political science. And often, empiricists believe that, once values are made into preferences, they can be treated as facts in the same way that the number of fingers or toes an individual has is a fact.

Yet, empirical political science is not simply about tallying preferences. Proponents also aggregated these preferences, compared them with the preferences of other groups and societies, explored their significance, and constructed concepts on the basis of their findings. Irrespective of whether or not they recognized it, political scientists incorporated values into their empirical analyses through all of these pursuits. But one of the most persistent problems of empirical political science, at least in the postwar years, was the reticence of its practitioners to realize that their analyses were not and could not be based wholly on objective facts. This methodological problem was stated and restated by the critics of empirical political science throughout the 1960s and 1970s. But some practitioners were also aware of it. In 1956, Gunnar Myrdal clearly explained the futility of seeking utter objectivity in the study of politics:

> There is no way of studying social reality other than from the viewpoint of human ideals. A "disinterested social science" has never existed and, for logical reasons, cannot exist. The value connotation of our main concepts represents our interest in a matter, gives direction to our thoughts and significance to our inferences. It poses the questions without which there are no answers.[13]

---

[13] Myrdal, *An International Economy, Problems and Prospects*, 1.

Myrdal concluded that the goal of a good social scientist is to be aware of the values which she incorporates and make these plain to the reader at the beginning of the study.

According to Taylor's 1971 essay, "Interpretation and the Sciences of Man," most social scientists did not heed Myrdal's advice. Instead they believed that, by relying on the brute facts of social experience, they could reach beyond the subjectivity of their own understandings of the social world. According to Taylor's interpretation, the empiricists believed facts can deliver one from subjective contexts because facts are free of interpretative slants. They are just facts — brute facts. And they can be strung together without interpretation intervening. Taylor illustrates how comparative political scientists actually believed that their research could escape the subjective world by taking as his example the approach adopted by Powell and Almond in *Comparative Politics: A Developmental Approach* (1966). In this study, the authors use brute facts to measure individual attitudes and orientations towards politics. Irrespective of the value-free methods at the measurement stage, the authors do not recognize that the categories of attitudes and practices being measured (e.g., interest aggregation and articulation) are themselves part of the subjective reality of a particular culture. In the science of comparative politics, Taylor explains, "[t]he not-surprising result is a theory of political development which places the Atlantic-type polity at the summit of human political achievement."[14] Many American political scientists thought they were discovering the nature of other political systems when all they were really discovering was how other systems fail to live up to the American understanding of politics.[15]

Social scientists become blind to communal boundaries when they embrace emotivism and empiricism. They believe that they transcend the cultural particularities of their own social and political scheme by turning political values into personal preferences — by separating facts and values. Yet, after tallying the preferences, they return facts to a context that reflects their own intersubjective reality or their interpretation of what the cultural reality studied entails. In either case, the researcher's values figure prominently into the conclusions. The problem within

---

[14] Taylor, *Philosophy and the Human Sciences,* 42.

[15] Taylor, *Philosophy and the Human Sciences,* 34. This is also the central problem of Almond and Verba's famous study, *The Civic Culture.* See critical analyses of this study by Pateman, "The Civic Culture: A Philosophic Critique"; Arend Lijphart, "The Structure of Inference"; and Alan Abramowitz "The United States: Political Culture under Stress" all in Almond and Verba eds., *The Civic Culture Revisited.*

empirical social sciences, according to both Myrdal and Taylor, is that empiricists think they are separating facts and values, but they are not and possibly cannot do so, at least, while doing political analysis.

In *After Virtue*, MacIntyre shows how liberal politics share with the social sciences an exuberance for the standards established by emotivism and empiricism. When moral values are understood to be nothing more than personal preferences originating in the individual's will, no communal basis exists upon which these values can be judged worthwhile or not. When a culture takes emotivism seriously, the only political scheme that can be justified is one that remains neutral between the ends that are chosen; one that protects the individual's liberty to choose her own ends. Liberalism embodies this type of scheme, and liberal rights offer this sort of protection to the individual. The liberal scheme, according to MacIntyre, perpetuates the fragmentation of moral discourse primarily by protecting the rights of each individual to be the legitimate author of moral value. Thus, moral debate about what justice requires, which projects are worthwhile, which acts are virtuous, and so on, are interminable within liberal society since rival premises are accorded equal respect. No moral standards can be authoritative except those, such as tolerance and neutrality, that perpetuate fragmentation.

At the same time as the liberal scheme guarantees tolerance to a wide variety of moral perspectives, it depends on moral debate remaining interminable and thus futile. The continuous plurality of coherent moral discourses is the only legitimate basis upon which liberalism can advocate value-neutrality. In turn, the value-neutrality it advocates perpetuates the interminable quality of moral debate. Thus, individual freedom to contribute to moral debate is purchased at the price of rendering these contributions futile. The argument, in short, is that liberal politics has internalized the desire to separate facts and values. Both liberal politics and empirical methods reflect a desire to dwell only on what can be objectively ascertained. Tallying preferences has become the mainstay of both for the purposes of objectivity.

But, does the analogy between methods and politics end here? Critics of empirical methods revealed the gap between what the empiricists desired to accomplish and what they, in fact, accomplished. What they could not accomplish was *actually* separating facts and values. Is a similar gap evident in liberal politics? That is, is a notion of the common good smuggled into liberal political practice in a way analogous to how values entered empirical theory? Certain aspects of communitarian analysis suggest that notions of the good are found in liberal political society. For example, Walzer argues that notions of the good in-here in social and political practices. His argument for a pluralistic notion of justice rests on the observation that different practices contain within them different sets of values or notions of the good.[16] Here, a close look at postwar methods and theory shows that a notion of the good or a set of values also informed these theories and the politics they prescribed.

Emotivism and Postwar Pluralism

The fact-value distinction, emotivism, the conversion of political values into mere preferences, and the resultant fragmentation of moral community are key aspects of the communitarian critique of liberalism. They are also central aspects of postwar political science. The project of finding a science of politics reaches back to the beginning of the century, to the work of Dewey, Bentley, and others. However, only after WWII did the distinction between a science and a nonscience in the study of politics become clearly dependent on divorcing moral evaluation from political science. Once political scientists were aware of logical positivism, perhaps as a result of reading Karl Popper's application of it,[17] they began to reformulate the project of their discipline. Leaders in the discipline incorporated the distinction between prescriptive and descriptive statements into their understanding of what constitutes political science. Their reformulations closely reflect positivist sentiments. For example, in *Political Science,* Vernon Van Dyke argued that the notion of science does "not relate to alleged knowledge of the normative — knowledge of what ought to be. Science concerns what has been, is, or will be, regardless of the 'oughts' of the situation."[18] Harold Lasswell and Abraham Kaplan argued that the basic concepts and hypotheses of political science should contain "no elaborations of political doctrine, or what the state and society *ought* to be."[19] David Truman concluded, "inquiry into how men *ought* to act is not a concern of research in political behavior."[20]

As the empirical approach rested on the fact-value distinction, the behavioral approach largely followed from emotivist premises. If moral values are nothing more than personal preferences, then the only legitimate

---

[16] Walzer, *Spheres of Justice.*
[17] See Ricci, *The Tragedy of Political Science,* 150.
[18] Dyke, *Political Science: A Philosophical Analysis,* 192.
[19] Lasswell and Kaplan, *Power and Society,* xi.
[20] Truman, "The Implications of Political Behavior Research," 37–38.

questions to ask regarding political values are those that refer to how many people hold which moral positions and, perhaps, how they came to hold these positions. For example, the only way to determine scientifically whether or not political participation is an important value in democracy is to study so-called democracies (for, other than the fact that people think a certain system is democratic, there is no way of determining what is a democracy) to discover whether people actually participate in politics or whether they think political participation is important.

This is exactly the method of analysis advocated by Dahl and Easton even though both of these theorists appeared to be aware of something like Myrdal's warning. Dahl argued, for example, that "[f]actual knowledge is not a 'substitute' for moral judgement, but it 'is' a prerequisite."[21] Easton noted that "in undertaking research we cannot shed our values in the way that we remove our coats."[22] Yet, he also maintained that facts and values are logically distinct and that values rest on emotional assessment; the factual aspect of a proposition "refers to a part of reality," while the moral aspect "expresses only the *emotional response* of an individual to a state of real or presumed facts"[23] (emphasis added). Easton called for "moral clarification" through a constructive approach that would "check the impact of moral views on theory."[24] While he was more cautious than those who claimed to adopt a value-neutral standpoint, he perpetuated the view that the mix of facts and values is an obstacle to rational inquiry by linking moral discourse to emotional responses. Notwithstanding his apparent cautiousness, his reasoning reflects the same emotivist arguments that motivated less cautious political scientists.

Dahl saw his project as limited to the task of establishing the factual prerequisites to moral evaluation. He considered himself to be a behavioralist, and he endorsed the empirical approach.[25] Dahl's work in the 1960s and 1970s received a warm reception in the behavioral community partly because he was able to overcome the hyperfactualism which threatened to characterize much of the empirical research by constructing a democratic theory out of the methods, assumptions, and data of behavioralism. This democratic theory was based on the idea of social, organizational, and institutional pluralism.

---

[21] Dahl, *Modern Political Analysis,* 106.
[22] Easton, *The Political System,* 225.
[23] Easton, *The Political System,* 89.
[24] Easton, *The Political System,* 228–32.
[25] See especially, Dahl, "The Behavioral Approach in Political Science."

The Fragmented Community in Postwar Pluralism

There are two preliminary notes to the following account of postwar pluralism. First, more than one theorist developed and used the ideas about democracy embodied in postwar pluralism, though only the work of Dahl is examined here. This is because Dahl's theory contains the clearest and most comprehensive treatment of postwar pluralism. Secondly, Dahl's arguments and methods have gone through significant transformations since the 1950s. Chief amongst these has been his present ambivalence about pluralism as the basis of democracy. Dahl now argues that pluralism must be guided by principles of distributive justice.[26] In light of these transformations, the following analysis focuses on Dahl's work in the 1950s, 1960s, and 1970s. However, some references will be made to Dahl's recent scholarship, in particular, his elaboration of pluralist theory in the last two chapters of *Democracy, Liberty and Equality*.

A communitarian might view postwar pluralism as a political celebration of the moral fragmentation that MacIntyre criticizes. From the start, Dahl's pluralist theory was founded on a fragmentation of community like that to which MacIntyre refers. At the social level, Dahl argued, a plurality of values is an indisputable fact about all large-scale democratic societies.

> The relatively homogeneous population of citizens united by common attachments to city, language, race, history, myth, and religion that was so conspicuous a part of the classical, city-state vision of democracy now becomes for all practical purposes impossible.[27]

As if to lend support to MacIntyre's observations, Dahl noted that, "[a]ll assertions as to the specific nature of a general, collective, public or national interest are, unless they are merely vacuous, themselves likely to become matters of public controversy."[28] A modern democratic nation-state cannot sustain the same practices as those found in the democratic polity of Ancient Greece.[29] In a similar manner, Sandel notes, the

---

[26] Dahl, *Democracy, Liberty and Equality*, chapter 10.

[27] Dahl, *Democracy, Liberty and Equality*, 228.

[28] Dahl, *Democracy, Liberty and Equality*, 256.

[29] Dahl explores the relation between nation size and democracy in a book he wrote with Tufte, *Size and Democracy*.

American nation is too large to sustain a substantive notion of community.[30] Unless a government intends to stifle social pluralism, which might mean imposing authoritarian measures, it must somehow peacefully manage the conflict that arises from it. Simple majoritarianism is inadequate for this purpose because it provides no safeguards against the exploitation of minorities. The behavioral surveys of voter attitudes provided good reasons to suspect that some minorities would not be tolerated by the majority. And the history of the United States, with its paradoxical origins as a slave-owning nation, and as a land to which persecuted minorities fled, emphasized the need for minority safeguards. Providing legal remedies, such as a system of laws or constitutional rights, was not a sufficiently powerful way of solving the problem, Dahl argued. "[I]n the absence of certain social prerequisites, no constitutional arrangements can produce a non-tyrannical republic."[31]

Dahl argued that the social will to guarantee safeguards for minorities could be cultivated by ensuring that a cohesive majority does not emerge. The majority has to be continuously fragmented so that it lacks the stability to victimize a minority. The task of ensuring fragmentation is made relatively simple by the immense diversity within pluralist society. Social pluralism ensures that, if some citizens agree on one issue, they will probably disagree on other issues. Reinforcing social pluralism through institutional mechanisms that give to groups, for example, favorable tax status or special access to government officials, guarantees that no stable consensus amongst citizens regarding key matters of public policy will emerge. In the United States, the conditions for fragmentation were optimal: "In the sense in which Madison was concerned with the problem then," Dahl noted, "majority rule is mostly a myth, . . . [and] [i]f majority rule is mostly a myth, then majority tyranny is mostly a myth too."[32]

The mechanics of Dahl's pluralism are set in motion when individuals affected by a given issue in the same way band together and make their voices heard as a group in the decision-making process. As in the theories of Cole and Laski, the group empowers the individual by giving to her the resources necessary to have her voice heard by the state or other groups. Each group competes, negotiates, and compromises with other groups for "influence resources," such as money or public support, which are used to influence government decisions. Be-

---

[30] Sandel, "The Procedural Republic and the Unencumbered Self," 93.
[31] Dahl, *A Preface to Democratic Theory*, 83.
[32] Dahl, *A Preface to Democratic Theory*, 133.

cause Dahl believed that no one influence resource dominates all the others in all or even in most key decisions and no group of more than a few individuals is entirely lacking in some influence resources," each group is forced to compromise with at least some others in order to acquire enough power to influence government decision making.[33] The direction that public policy follows depends on the nature of the coalition of minorities that dominates the policy-making scene at any given instant. The groups' reliance on each other creates an informal system of checks and balances in which no group is able to dominate the others. There is no chance for a minority to dominate a coalition because other minorities within the coalition will defect. Similarly, majorities are unable to pose a threat, since they are comprised of smaller groups, any of which may defect from the coalition if the policy direction changes. As Dahl put it,

> if there is anything to be said for the processes that actually distinguish democracy . . . from dictatorship, it is not discoverable in the clear-cut distinction between government by a majority and government by a minority. The distinction comes much closer to being one between government by a minority and government by *minorities*.[34]

In American democracy, Dahl argued, minorities rule where one aggregation of minorities achieves policies opposed by another aggregation.

Part of the novelty of Dahl's pluralism is that he provided empirical evidence to show that pluralism was, in fact, how communities in the United States are organized. The empirical techniques first revealed, he explained, many misconceptions about democracy. In his most popular work of the period, *Who Governs?*, Dahl argued that political power does not have to be distributed equally for a society to be a democracy. Because it is so difficult to mobilize resources, determining how they are allocated is an insufficient basis upon which to conclude that imbalances in power exist. Dahl also argued that mass participation is not a requirement of democracy, not because it leads to demand-overload, as some elite theorists believed, but because mass participation could simply not occur in a pluralistic society. Theoretically, the mass electorate could participate and would participate when an issue elicited intense approval or disapproval in them. However, such an issue hardly ever

---

[33] Dahl, *Who Governs?* 223–28.
[34] Dahl, *A Preface to Democratic Theory*, 133.

arises.[35] At most, issues incite the participation only of those groups that perceive the issue as central to their concerns and/or that are mobilized by skillful leaders.

According to Dahl's interpretation, the guarantee of freedom to participate rather than the actual participation of the whole electorate is central to all democracies. This freedom is guaranteed by a broad and general consensus — a democratic creed — that underlies the whole system. It is also guaranteed through the continual need to form coalitions and thus negotiate and compromise with other groups. The principle of neutrality by which the system operates requires that, within the parameters of maintaining the system, no set of interests is more justified than any other.

The checks and balances constitutionally written into the American decision-making process, through the distribution of powers to the Senate, the Congress, the Executive, the Courts, and the different levels of government, comprise another level of pluralism. Dahl explains that this institutional pluralism is the result of "interminable debates" amongst America's Founders over what sort of interests should be given the most protection in the newly formed republic.

> What they [the Founders] did was to create a framework of government which, once it had been accepted, might become either an aristocratic republic or a democratic republic. Which it was to be depended . . . on what was to happen later, over years and decades and perhaps centuries, among men outside the Convention and generations still unborn.[36]

The institutions of American government were made responsive to different interests and were ascribed different sorts of powers in order that they would compete with one another. This system of checks and balances ensured that power would not be concentrated in one group because the power of one institution could be set against the power of another one. At different times in history, different coalitions will succeed depending on the support they can secure. Thus, the direction and development of American democracy, he argued, is determined by the practical politics of coalition-building within the context of historical circumstance, not by a "logically conceived philosophical plan."[37]

---

[35] Dahl, *Who Governs?* 76–81.
[36] Dahl, *Pluralist Democracy in the United States*, 55.
[37] Dahl, *Pluralist Democracy in the United States*, 22.

To summarize the analysis so far: MacIntyre argues that moral fragmentation follows from a fragmentation of moral language and is caused, at its roots, by cultural emotivism. Dahl's analysis does not attempt to get at the emotive roots of social pluralism, although, like MacIntyre, he is extremely conscious of its pervasiveness in liberal democratic society. Rather, Dahl meant his project to be descriptive of the way in which American politics is pluralistic. Therefore, he was primarily interested in showing (1) that a pluralist distribution of power follows from social pluralism; (2) that the institutional and organizational machinery in the United States is designed to protect and perpetuate pluralism, and (3) when pluralism is great enough, it guarantees that neither a majority nor a minority will dominate society for very long. The stability of liberal-democratic society rests on the absence of agreement amongst members of the community as to community standards and priorities. And, in order to retain this stability, the state must remain neutral among these standards and priorities, even to the point of offering groups with different and contradictory priorities privileged access to state resources.

MacIntyre argues that a commitment to emotivism and the fact-value distinction underlie the fragmentation that characterizes liberal societies. Dahl and many other political scientists in the postwar period were committed to methods of just the sort that MacIntyre describes. However, they did not intend to advocate a theory of democracy that would follow from and be consistent with the assumptions contained in their methods. There is a distinction between a political scientist applying empirical methods when studying society (which is one of Taylor's concerns) and the prevalence, within the societies studied, of the fragmentation that underlies empiricism and emotivism. Both Taylor and MacIntyre suggest that a connection exists between the application of methods that separate facts and values and the emotive nature of society. MacIntyre argues that emotivism is the theoretical foundation of liberal politics. Supposedly then, the same historical foundations that led Dahl to endorse the empirical methods are imputed by MacIntyre to be responsible for creating the pluralist society that Dahl discovered when applying these methods. Dahl did not create pluralism in liberal society. Rather, he *found* pluralism while attempting to describe the way in which power is allocated in American politics. Remaining faithful to his empirical and behavioralist assumptions meant describing what democracy was like by considering "as a single class of phenomena all those national states and social organizations that are commonly called democratic by political scientists."[38] In this way, Dahl's work can be viewed as providing some confirmation of another observation of MacIntyre and Taylor: that there is a link between the methods used in the social sciences and the fragmentation that characterizes liberal culture. The link is that they both derive from a belief in emotivism.

The connection between theory and political practice is essential to the communitarian argument. It is not just that political scientists apply emotivist methods, it is that the societies which they study practise emotivist politics. This fact, alone, makes political science so relevant to the communitarian criticism.

Part II: The Common Good in Pluralism and Communitarianism

Despite their comprehensive criticisms of liberal political theory and practice, communitarians do not provide a comprehensive account of what they consider to be a better notion of community. It is partly for this reason that Nancy Rosenblum, Marilyn Friedman, Jeremy Waldron, Will Kymlicka, Amy Gutmann, and many others are unable to identify, without hesitation, the central claims of the communitarian alternative to liberalism. Nonetheless, a couple of general observations are usually made. Rosenblum, Friedman, and Kymlicka all point to the ways in which the communitarians focus on involuntary associations. "The communitarian approach," Friedman argues, "suggests an attitude of celebrating the attachments which one finds oneself unavoidably to have, the familial ties and so forth."[39] In Rosenblum's account, communitarians mean to replace the legalistic and formal structures that define relations between strangers with more informal ties; "In community, relations are not legalistic; obligations and personal inclinations coincide. In community, the regime appears *lovely* to its members."[40] This general assessment is reaffirmed by Waldron, Jules Coleman, and Gutmann, all of whom point out the primacy of affective ties in the reconstructed community. Communitarianism, Coleman argues, promotes a "vision of social ordering in which reliance on rights is replaced by the affective emotions."[41] Wal-

[38] Dahl, *A Preface to Democratic Theory*, 63.
[39] Friedman, "Feminism and Modern Friendship," 108.
[40] Rosenblum, *Another Liberalism*, 154.
[41] Coleman, "Comment: Rights, Markets and Community," 654.

dron points to family and friendships as the sort of relations that exhibit the appropriate communitarian flavor.[42]

According to communitarian sympathizers, even such attempts to characterize generally the communitarian alternative are inaccurate. Taylor deflects criticism directed at Sandel's notion of community by arguing that "Sandel has sometimes been read as though his point was to *advocate* a society that would have close relations analogous to a family.... This proposal has been, rightly, ridiculed."[43] Sandel also attempts to distance his notion of community from such interpretations. He argues that

> the yearning for community can no longer be satisfied by depicting the nation as a family or a neighborhood. The metaphor is by now too strained to carry conviction. The nation is too vast to sustain more than a minimal commonality, too distant to permit more than occasional moments of participation.[44]

Despite such disavowals, not only is an analogy between the family and society used throughout Sandel's work, Taylor also employs it by insisting, for instance, that the individual's obligation to maintain a healthy society is analogous to her obligations to her family.[45] Sandel likens the ties between members of a political community to ties between family members, specifically in terms of how these ties define one's loyalties and commitments.[46] Moreover, the constitutive conception of community for which Sandel argues is described by him as precisely the opposite of a voluntary association: "not a relationship they choose (as in a voluntary association) but an attachment they discover. . . ."[47]

Due to the clear disagreement between the communitarians and their critics regarding what their alternative to liberalism entails, here I try to use fairly uncontroversial aspects of their alternative when comparing communitarianism with postwar pluralism. In the first part, I compare how each type of theory analyzes the role that individual rights and the Supreme Court of the United States play in American politics.

---

[42] Waldron, "When Justice Replaces Affection."

[43] Taylor, "Cross-Purposes," 161.

[44] Sandel, "Democrats and Community," 22.

[45] Taylor, *Philosophy and the Human Sciences*, 203.

[46] Sandel, "The Procedural Republic," 90.

[47] Sandel, *Liberalism and the Limits of Justice*, 150.

The over-reliance on rights is key to the communitarian critique of American political practice, yet, the Court does not figure prominently in their analyses. In postwar pluralism, the Court occupies a minor role in explanations of politics. But, in each case, the material that is provided exposes a likemindedness in the approach taken and conclusions drawn.

In the second part, I survey communitarian theories in order to piece together a plausible and feasible understanding of how communitarians treat community values and the sense in which communitarian communities adopt teleological notions of the good. I then explore the similarities between functionalism and teleology and describe the role that functionalism played in postwar political science, including pluralism.

The Right versus the Good in the American Supreme Court

If no rational means exist to choose between competing conceptions of the good, what is wrong with organizing politics so that individuals retain the right to make their own choices regarding the priorities or interests they will pursue? And if they ought to be given this right, should the state not remain neutral between their competing conceptions? In terms of Dahl's theory, is democratic pluralism not the best way to accommodate social pluralism?

Communitarians provide two different types of arguments about why the liberal project is undesirable. Sandel offers the first type in his critique of liberal neutrality. He argues that a misguided reliance on individual rights is one consequence of liberal neutrality and the fragmented community. Along with MacIntyre and Taylor, Sandel argues that individual rights reinforce community fragmentation. Though Sandel concentrates on Rawls's theory of justice in order to illustrate his argument, his declared aim is to criticize the "political philosophy implicit in the practices and institutions in contemporary America."[48] Rawls's theory, according to him, is this political philosophy.

Rawls's theory, Sandel argues, attempts to put the right before the good. By this, he means two things: first, that, in Rawls's theory, "individual rights cannot be sacrificed for the sake of the general good," and second, "that the principles of justice that specify these rights cannot be premised on any particular vision of the good life."[49] In the course of es-

---

[48] Sandel, "The Procedural Republic and the Unencumbered Self," 81.
[49] Sandel, "The Procedural Republic and the Unencumbered Self," 82.

tablishing a theory of justice, Sandel argues, Rawls is forced to rely on the supposition, found in the difference principle, that the individuals within liberal democracies share in each other's fate. The difference principle requires that "[t]hose who have been favored by nature, whoever they are, may gain from their good fortune only on terms that improve the situation of those who have lost out. . . . In justice as fairness, men agree to share one another's fate."[50] Sandel argues that if moral luck is responsible for giving certain individuals precious assets and others handicaps, on what basis can Rawls argue that the individuals with the assets must aid those with the handicaps? Given that Rawls insists on the distinctiveness of individuals, he cannot claim that the community has any claim on individual assets. Just because the individual is not entitled to her attributes does not mean that the community is entitled to them. The difference principle, he argues, dictates that the community *is* entitled to them.[51] And though Sandel allows for the possibility that the obligation to share can be consistent with certain conceptions of the good, he argues that this possibility is inconsistent with Rawls's theory because Rawls purports not to favor any particular theory of the good.

Sandel's analysis of Rawls's theory has provoked thoughtful criticisms from numerous defenders of liberalism. However, here the issue is not whether Sandel has characterized Rawls's liberalism well or poorly. Rather, the issue is whether rights are given primacy over any conception of the good in the postwar pluralist interpretation of American political practices. In the empirical interpretation that Dahl and many others offered, rights play an insignificant role. But, empiricists like Dahl did not simply ignore the role of rights; they challenged the plausibility of any political theory that overlooked behavior in favor of political principles to which behavior may or may not conform. More importantly for the empiricists is whether liberal principles are consistent with the practices of liberal societies. If principles and practices are inconsistent, any incoherence that can be attached to the principles need not be an incoherence shared by American political practices. Dahl argued that political behavior and practice give rise to political principles, not *vice versa.* While the rhetoric of individualism, liberty and rights may be found in philosophical debates, decision making in the United States is the direct result of pluralist politics and not liberal principles.

Nowhere does Dahl illustrate his position better than in his analysis of the judicial system. Dahl shows that the courts, which are sup-

---

[50] Rawls, *A Theory of Justice*, 101–2.
[51] Sandel, "The Procedural Republic and the Unencumbered Self," 90.

posed to be insulated from the pressures of pluralist politics so that they may perform their function as forums of principles, are, in fact, deeply embedded in the pluralist framework. Empirical evidence suggested that the Court was rarely able to block a "determined and persistent law-making majority on a major policy."[52] By examining instances in which the Supreme Court held federal legislation unconstitutional in the first half of the century, Dahl found that the cases usually fell into three categories: (1) the law was a minor piece of legislation which had no great consequence for minority rights; (2) if it was a major policy, it was the work of a previous administration whose policies the present administration opposed, or (3) coalitions of the President and a majority of each House of Congress were able to reverse the Court's policy by tinkering with the policy or by amending the Constitution.[53] The conclusion that followed from this evidence was that,

> [e]xcept for short-lived transitional periods when the old alliance is disintegrating and the new one is struggling to take control of political institutions, the Supreme Court is inevitably a part of the dominant national alliance. . . . Acting solely by itself with no support from the President and Congress, the Court is almost powerless to affect the course of national policy.[54]

Judicial autonomy, Dahl noted, is a myth that is dispelled by examining the empirical evidence.

The way in which Dahl arrived at this conclusion has much to do with the structure of his empirical interpretation of politics. His commitments to empiricism did not allow him to view the evidence on the Court's performance that contradicted the rhetoric of neutrality and rights as proof that the Court was not fulfilling its mandate. In the empirical approach, primacy has to be given to the practices rather than to the rhetoric of American democracy. The mandate of the Court had to be discovered through the role it fulfilled. The approach eliminated any basis upon which to argue that the job of the Court is to direct the course of national policy according to abstract principles of justice because the empirical evidence suggested that this is not what the Court actually did.

---

[52] Dahl, *Pluralist Democracy in the United States*, 163.
[53] Dahl, *Pluralist Democracy in the United States*, 157–63.
[54] Dahl, *Pluralist Democracy in the United States*, 167–68.

According to Dahl, another powerful reason to suppose that the Court was not primarily a minority-protecting institution was that, "[i]f the Court did in fact uphold minorities against national majorities, as both its supporters and critics often seem to believe, it would be an extremely anomalous institution from a democratic point of view."[55] Moral approbation only indirectly figures into Dahl's observation. Dahl's main point is that the Court's legitimacy would be jeopardized if it consistently disagreed with the policies and values that the majority of American citizens endorsed. For this reason, the role that the Court is able to fulfill is limited to conferring "legitimacy on the fundamental policies of a successful coalition."[56] The Supreme Court cannot stand apart from the pluralist system. Rather, it is entrenched in the political and social flux created by the bargaining, negotiating, and compromise of political activity.

This position, or one that is strikingly similar to it, is adopted by Alasdair MacIntyre and animates one of the few assessments in his work of contemporary American political practice, namely his analysis of the American Supreme Court. It is worth noting first that he contrasts his position to that of liberal philosopher Ronald Dworkin, who sees the Court's function as "invoking a set of consistent *principles*, most and perhaps all of them of moral import, in the light of which particular laws and particular decisions are to be evaluated."[57] With these principles in hand, Dworkin evaluates various Court decisions to determine whether they are good or bad ones — i.e., whether they are consistent with the principles or not. MacIntyre disagrees with this approach and opts for one that is based on, not principle, but practice: not on an ideal vision of a supreme court, but on a functional view of the Supreme Court situated within its communal context — namely the United States. He notes that in the *Bakke* case the decision written by Mr. Justice Powell contained two seemingly incompatible views: "The Supreme Court in *Bakke* both forbade precise ethnic quotas for admission to colleges and universities, but allowed discrimination in favor of previously deprived minority groups."[58] The views are incompatible if one uses a Dworkinian approach to explain and assess them. But, using practice and function, MacIntyre suggests that the decision makes a great deal of sense. The Supreme Court, he argues, "play[s] the role of a peacemak-

---

[55] Dahl, *Pluralist Democracy in the United States*, 267.
[56] Dahl, *Pluralist Democracy in the United States*, 168.
[57] MacIntyre, *After Virtue*, 253
[58] MacIntyre, *After Virtue*, 253.

ing or truce-keeping body by negotiating its way through an impasse of conflict, not by invoking our shared moral first principles."[59] It is unable to invoke shared moral principles, according to MacIntyre, because "our society as a whole has none."[60] But even if the United States had such principles, it is unclear in MacIntyre's account that the Court would not continue to be a peacemaker and truce-keeper. "One function of the Supreme Court," in MacIntyre's view, "*must be* to keep the peace between rival social groups . . ."[61] (emphasis added).

MacIntyre applies methods of analysis that ascribe authority to the standards he argues must be adopted in order that communal practices and traditions can be resurrected and/or protected. Instead of going outside the community and importing principles, MacIntyre tries to assess a practice or institution according to the purpose it serves within the context of an actual historical community. Justice Powell's decision is incorrectly assessed in terms of abstract principles and more aptly assessed in terms of the ethnic conflicts that characterize American politics and the function of the Supreme Court in proposing compromises. According to MacIntyre, it seems as though there is no common good that one can refer to in assessing the judgment. But even if there were a common good, should the judge not still address the political practices and the institutional functions when deciding between claims of conflicting groups? In MacIntyre's account, one must continue to take the practices and functions seriously because it is through these that the good is expressed.[62]

Dahl also deliberately distanced his approach to the Supreme Court and to American democratic politics as a whole from approaches that relied on claims about individualism, liberty, rights, and other liberal principles. Whether or not rights are *theoretically* able to contribute to or undermine the goals of liberal democracy was besides the point in Dahl's analysis of politics. Rights, like other principles, are relatively powerless in the face of contradictory practices and preferences held by governing coalitions of minorities. To put his conclusions in a style more familiar to contemporary argument: within pluralistic democracy, practices, not rights, have primacy and, in the absence of certain back-

---

[59] MacIntyre, *After Virtue*, 253.
[60] MacIntyre, *After Virtue*, 253.
[61] MacIntyre, *After Virtue*, 253.
[62] On a slightly different note, this aspect of MacIntyre's discussion is a fine example of what Holmes calls the "shifting target" of communitarians: "Antiliberals tend to oscillate woozily between criticism of liberal theory and criticism of liberal society." Holmes, "The Permanent Structure of Antiliberal Thought," 234.

ground conditions — i.e., certain patterns of behavior — democracy cannot exist and rights are powerless. Furthermore, these background conditions do not depend on the content of a constitution or the activism of the courts. Rather, they are the result of the compromises made between the various groups within pluralistic societies. Dahl would then agree with MacIntyre's conclusion that "[t]he nature of any society . . . is not to be deciphered from its laws alone, but from those understood as an index of its conflicts."[63]

The compatibility on this point of MacIntyre's and Dahl's positions is curious, since, according to MacIntyre's analysis, Dahl's conclusions, with their empirical and emotive foundations, should be quite different from his own. Dahl's theory clearly endorses key assumptions that communitarians claim are typical of liberalism. But, it did not rely on the notion of rights to describe American politics and, moreover, held that rights are not fundamental to American political practices. Rather than rights influencing political practice, often the two are inconsistent. The primacy of rights is inconsistent with the political dynamic of pluralist politics. The influence of rights did not permeate the attitudes of the electorate, since toleration and equal respect are not values held dear by most voters.[64] Rights-based liberalism was inconsistent with the pattern of Supreme Court decisions given that, in several instances, the Supreme Court did not uphold the rights of minorities. Evidence did not suggest that these patterns of behavior are the manifestation of liberal-rights ideology because, when the two are inconsistent, one could better explain the political system by referring to behavior.

The Common Good

Despite this apparent convergence on the role of rights and the Supreme Court, communitarians would distinguish their vision from that of postwar pluralism on the basis of the value-neutrality which was central to the pluralists' account. If the pluralists did not use rights to entrench neutrality, then they used an analogous mechanism.

---

[63] MacIntyre, *After Virtue*, 254.

[64] Dahl incorporated this assumption into his work on the basis of the behavioral survey of voter attitudes and aptitudes. In addition to endorsing the behavioral methods throughout his work, Dahl often commented on the irrationality and lack of sophistication that characterized the typical voter. For two examples see *Democracy in the United States*, 285–86, and *Who Governs?* 319.

In this respect, the communitarians at first appear to be correct. The liberal quest for a politics that is neutral between different conceptions of the good is a definitive aspect of pluralist politics. Different ideals of the good are protected in the political arena and made to compete, negotiate, and compromise with each other to determine which conception(s) will temporarily direct public policy. The pluralist method of political decision making implicitly recognizes that, on the one hand, there is no objective means to determine which is the most worthwhile conception, and, on the other hand, there must be some means of deciding which vision of the good will direct public policy. Even though Dahl does not ground the maintenance of the system in the *right* to free assembly and the *right* to express different political opinions, in effect, such liberties are respected because people believe that no one association should dominate the others or that no one set of political opinions should be heard to the exclusion of others. A commitment to value-neutrality might be thought to underpin these beliefs. The communitarians might argue that, even without explicitly relying on rights, the pluralists managed to place the right before the good.

Nonetheless, two other arguments worth considering show the surprising affinity between postwar pluralism and the communitarian conception of the common good. The first is found in Dahl's argument that underlying pluralist society is a democratic creed that binds the disparate groups of society. The sense of commonality represented by the democratic creed includes highly abstract notions such as "a belief in democracy as the best form of government, in the desirability of rights and procedures insuring a goodly measure of majority rule and minority freedom, and in a wide but not necessarily comprehensive electorate."[65] The creed includes a commitment to principles that are thoroughly liberal in nature. It also defines membership in the political community in the strictest sense. Rejecting the creed is *not* a matter of individual right, according to Dahl. "To reject the democratic creed is in effect to refuse to be an American. As a nation we have taken great pains to insure that few citizens will ever want to do anything so rash, so preposterous — in fact, so wholly unAmerican."[66] Like the common good that Sandel describes, the democratic creed underlying pluralist politics is a criterion of membership in the community. To reject the communal creed is to renounce one's membership.

---

[65] Dahl, *Who Governs?* 316.
[66] Dahl, *Who Governs?* 317.

Dahl's democratic creed defines membership in the American political community in a manner that is surprisingly illiberal because it
denies to the individual the choice of belonging to the political community on her own terms. But, the communal acceptance of a democratic
creed will not, in the end, constitute a common good of the sort sought
by communitarians. Arguably, the democratic creed fails to constitute
a common good because it reaffirms the principles by which value-neutrality is accommodated. After all, the democratic creed simply signals
a commitment to neutral decision-making procedures and tolerance towards minorities. Some liberal philosophers have argued that the common commitment to these procedures and values testifies to the sense
of community that liberal society upholds. "Liberalism cannot be based
on skepticism," argues Ronald Dworkin. "Its constitutive morality provides that human beings must be treated as equals by their government,
not because there is no right and wrong in political morality, but because that is what is right."[67] According to Dworkin, the neutrality that
allows the individual to choose between different life-plans *is* the vision of the good promoted through liberal politics.

Communitarians find this response unsatisfactory, and they
would not accept that the democratic creed provides a notion of the
common good. If neutrality can count as a common good, Taylor argues, it is a different type of good from that which communitarians
seek. Taylor explains that communitarians use the term *good* in the
narrow sense to indicate life plans or ways of living that are valued. In
the liberal formula that Dworkin provides, the good is being construed
in the broadest sense, to indicate "something that is valued." Taylor argues that

> [p]rocedural liberalism cannot have a common good in the
> narrow sense, because society must be neutral on the ques-
> tion of the good life. But in the broader sense, where a rule of
> right can also count as "good," there can be an extremely
> important shared good.[68]

So, it is not quite right that liberalism lacks a notion of the good, according to Taylor. Rather, liberalism lacks a notion that is narrow enough
for communitarian purposes. Dahl's democratic creed may not be an
adequate conception because it is not narrow enough.

---

[67] Dworkin, *A Matter of Principle*, 203.
[68] Taylor, "Cross-Purposes," 172.

Taylor's distinction between the broad and narrow senses of the good is useful for distancing the communitarian conception from the liberal one. But, interestingly enough, it exposes one reason why ambiguity surrounds the communitarian conception of common good. Taylor's distinction poses, *prima facie,* a problem for the communitarian critique of Rawls's difference principle constructed by Sandel and reaffirmed by Taylor. Like Sandel, Taylor insists that the sharing invoked by Rawls's difference principle entails a "sense of mutual commitment" that could be sustained "only by encumbered selves who shared a strong sense of community."[69] Yet, Taylor is no clearer than is Sandel in explaining why sharing one's endowments requires extraordinary social bonds. The social bonds required for the tax-back schemes of welfare liberalism (for that, in practice, is what Rawls's notion might demand) need be no greater than the bonds required to establish minimal institutions of government. Both consist of rules by which individuals must live if they want to live in society together. Both limit the possible life-plans one could pursue. Yet, both are, nonetheless, compatible with an instrumental view of society and are consistent with a multitude of diverse life-plans.

The communitarians criticize the difference principle because it implies the existence of a common good. However, the good it implies is surely not narrow enough to violate the neutrality that communitarians insist is characteristic of liberalism. The good that Sandel finds in Rawls's doctrine must be the good broadly conceived. Yet, if it is the good broadly conceived, there seems to be no reason to criticize Rawls. As Taylor points out, where a rule of right can also count as good, liberalism contains a notion of the good. Communitarians are not concerned about this sense of the good. Again, if it was their concern, they could not sensibly describe liberalism as a doctrine that puts the right before the good because the right and the good would be identical.

On this point, Sandel and Taylor appear to disagree. As these arguments stand, Sandel's critique of Rawls is subject to one of the central criticisms that Taylor has of Dworkin's notion of community. Although, there is no requirement that the theories of Sandel and Taylor be consistent, the inconsistency between them leaves one wondering what the communitarian alternative to liberalism is, even at a very general level. Sandel is correct in exposing a notion of the good in Rawls. However,

[69] Taylor, "Cross-Purposes," 172.
[70] MacIntyre, *After Virtue,* 57–58.

this broad notion of the good is not something that Rawls or his students would deny affirming — although, along with Taylor, they might deny that it is a notion of the good in the communitarian sense. In terms of postwar pluralism, the democratic creed is acceptable in Sandel's argument and unacceptable according to Taylor.

Narrowing the Conception of Communal Good

It has been shown that communitarians can, to some degree, resist one way of trying to establish an affinity between postwar pluralism and communitarian theory. However, the second argument, to which I now turn, poses a greater challenge for communitarians. It takes its cue from MacIntyre's argument that values and goods are latent within practices, institutions, and communities. This argument provides a key to determining what, for communitarians like MacIntyre, counts as a common good. For MacIntyre, one has to restructure political analysis in order to reveal the values endemic to a particular community. The liberal project, he argues, illustrates that, unless there exists a common context of meaning, facts and values are disparate. Before the liberal project was conceived, the context for facts about the world was supplied through teleological world-views such as those contained in Aristotelianism and Scholasticism. Teleology circumvents the fact-value distinction by employing a distinctive functional analysis. As MacIntyre explains, "[f]rom such factual premises as 'This watch is grossly inaccurate and irregular in time-keeping' and 'This watch is too heavy to carry about comfortably,' the evaluative conclusion validly follows that 'This is a bad watch.'"[70] The argument is valid because "watch" is a functional concept. It is defined according to the function that, characteristically, it is expected to serve. In the classical tradition, MacIntyre points out, the notion of a "good man" was also defined in functionalist terms:

> according to that tradition to be a man is to fill a set of roles each of which has its own point and purpose: member of a family, citizen, soldier, philosopher, servant of God. It is only when man is thought of as an individual prior to and apart from all roles that "man" ceases to be a functional concept.[71]

For MacIntyre, functionalism is tied to a teleological understanding of political morality. Teleological theories contain within them an evalua-

---

[71] MacIntyre, *After Virtue*, 59.

tive notion of what counts as good in terms of whatever subject is being analyzed. As in functionalism, a teleological approach asks, for example, what counts as a good person? or what counts as a good watch? The notion of good in both instances is primary. Conversely, deontological theories try to avoid defining the good. They hold that, above all conceptions of the good, and prior to them, there must be the right for individuals to choose their own good. In deontological theories, which, according to communitarians, include all liberal theories, questions of right are placed prior to questions of good.

Cary Nederman notes the relation between communitarian and functionalist visions of politics in his analysis of the communal functionalism, which he finds in the political theories of John of Salisbury and Marsiglio of Padua. Communal functionalism reflects a communitarian understanding "that a community is defined in terms of a substantive good or set of goods that generate a fundamental civic identity within which all members are embedded and to which they ought to be socialized."[72] It meets these standards without falling into the trap, attributed to communitarians by liberals, of circumscribing all individual diversity. Diversity itself is a functional good for the community in this theory. Drawing from John's organicism and Marsiglio's theory of perfection through differentiation, Nederman identifies the two central characteristics of communal functionalism. First, it takes "as its point of departure the tasks and activities which make possible a given society at its particular level of development." "Citizenship," Nederman explains, in terms a behavioralist would also use, "is rooted in what individuals *do*, rather than what they *are*."[73] Second, communal functionalism views community in terms of diversity which is directed towards a particular end. "Without surrendering a doctrine of substantive common good, communal functionalism permits the communitarian to construct a framework within which to understand the diversity of interpretations of that good and to appreciate the necessity of the diversity itself."[74] This approach situates the individual firmly within a communal context but maintains "a meaningful role for personal volition" by turning diversity into a functional good.[75]

While diversity is crucial to the attractiveness of communal functionalism, it is functionalism rather than diversity that ties this theory to

---

[72] Nederman, 977.
[73] Nederman, 983.
[74] Nederman, 983.
[75] Nederman, 985.

communitarianism. Under communal functionalism, personal liberty is protected because this is interpreted, by John and Marsiglio, as the best route to communal well-being not to individual well-being.[76] On this basis, communal functionalism poses a sharp contrast to liberalism by Nederman's own account.

Liberalism, according to communitarianism, leads to individual anomie. It encourages individuals to define their own ends and thus places the individual prior to and apart from any conception of the good. By ascribing rights to the individual, it protects her from conceptions of the good that she has not chosen but that may be imposed on her by society. Because of their deontological foundations, liberal societies do not and cannot possess a sufficiently robust shared notion of the good. Yet, without a shared notion, the values by which the individual assesses whether or not she is a good person are not necessarily shared by others. Her neighbors, friends, and coworkers lack the means to recognize, let alone assess, her virtues. Thus, liberalism undermines the functional means of uniting facts about her behavior with moral assessments as to whether her behavior is good or bad. Only when people share a notion of the good (even if, as in Nederman's account, they interpret that good differently) can such assessments take place.

In the absence of authoritative standards, liberalism erects value-neutrality and forums of free choice. The individual becomes the sole judge of her actions. Yet, she has no criterion upon which to base her assessments other than her feelings, emotions, and preferences. Without community, she cannot rationally assess the moral worth of her actions. According to MacIntyre, rational assessment depends on commonly accepted standards of what is good in any given instance. Taylor also insists that rationality is context-dependent. Rational standards are erected by communities. Communitarianism shows how liberalism has relocated the task of erecting these standards from the community to the individual. By doing so, liberalism has robbed these standards of their significance, undermined the purposes for which these standards were used, and, thus, destroyed the primary basis of community. A *telos* provides a context in which the parts of society can be assessed. In order to meet the requirements of communitarianism, a notion of the common good must also supply such a context.

---

[76] Nederman, 984.

Postwar Pluralism and Communal Goods

The postwar theorists had no intention of constructing a teleological view of American politics. In fact, they had no intention of endorsing any particular value in the course of describing the system. Doing so would have violated their commitment as empiricists to value-neutrality. Yet, the sort of political system that is portrayed by postwar pluralists is not a paradigm of value-neutral politics, except in the superficial way that pluralist politics allows. In addition to the democratic creed, postwar theories endorsed the value of stability as key to the proper functioning of any coherent democratic system.

  From the inception of the postwar interpretation, critics have attacked the theory for favoring stability over any other political and democratic value. The charge that these theories were not value-neutral is usually coupled with the charge that what most obviously compromises neutrality in empirical democratic theory is the positive endorsement of stability. The importance of stability, according to Graeme Duncan and Steven Lukes, meant that the new, empirical way of theorizing *about* democracy became a new theory *of* democracy.[77] The features of politics that are central to this new theory are those essential for stability and equilibrium, not those required for democracy. William Connolly reaffirmed this assessment. The principal aim of postwar pluralist theory, he argued, is to ascertain the relationship between the existing system of conflict resolution and the maintenance of stability.[78] Pluralist politics did not interest Dahl because it provided the highest ideals of democracy. Rather, pluralism was prized because it stabilizes what might otherwise be an unstable and conflict-ridden environment.

As previously discussed in chapter 4, postwar theorists unsurprisingly had a special interest in the political system's stability, given the historical circumstances of postwar United States and given the behavioral portrait of the individual citizen as irrational, intolerant, and lacking political sophistication. One might expect to find stability in theories that meant to *describe* postwar democracies. But, the pluralists did not merely discover a preoccupation with stability in the societies they studied. Stability was central to the methods used by the postwar theorists and, therefore, was incorporated into their explanations through the very approach they took to political explanation.

---

[77] Duncan and Lukes, "The New Democracy."
[78] Connolly, "The Challenge to Pluralist Theory," 20.

The methodological route by which stability entered their explanations starts with the premises of behavioralism. Behavioralism, as Sperlich explains, came to political science via psychology. Psychological research often involved studies of pathological personalities. Research aimed at easing these pathologies by discovering tension-reducing techniques. The goal was to find ways of stabilizing abnormal personalities. Stabilization and tension-reduction are generally themes which pervade biology and physics, the sciences from which psychology has traditionally drawn many of its assumptions. In each of these sciences, homeostasis, harmony, equilibrium, and stability are the states towards which things tend or ought to tend.

The assumptions that guided psychological research were incorporated into political analysis along with the methods of studying human behavior. In the political science of the 1940s, mainstream models of political behavior favoring homeostasis, stability, and conflict reduction were not often criticized. In fact, Sperlich contends, the cross-pressure analysis, so popular in the 1950s, 1960s and part of the 1970s, was drawn from these models and directly depended on assumptions favoring stability. Proponents of cross-pressure analysis, including Lipset, Truman, Dahl, Almond, Verba, Kornhauser and Eckstein, explicitly endorsed stability as one of the most important values of political societies. Not only did their methodologies assume the benefits of stability, but, at the same time, these theorists endorsed stability in spite of their commitments to remain value-neutral.

By the 1960s and 1970s, leading political scientists adopted a less hostile attitude towards conflict. However, the development of new, conflict-friendly perspectives did not depose stability as the key value of political interaction. Often political systems were thought of as self-sufficient entities in the sense that the health of the system could be assessed by the extent to which equilibrium or homeostasis was obtained. The most important use of this analogy was made by Easton in developing the idea of systems analysis. Easton likened political society to a system in the sense that it has an environment in which it exists and which partly determines its character. Systems analysis assesses the ways in which the system responds to stress occurring in its environment or internally through coping techniques that may alter its structure and processes. It also explores the feedback mechanisms that allow the system to persist under stress.

Easton's theory is a good example of how political scientists in the postwar era attempted to deal with value-neutrality. Easton realized

---

[79] Sperlich, *Conflict and Harmony in Human Affairs*, 171–74.

that facts about politics were useless unless placed in a framework.[80] Like MacIntyre's and Taylor's insistence that facts need a context in order to make sense, Easton insisted on giving political facts a political context. The context he chose is as value-neutral as any context could be because it does not rely on values that are extraneous to the system studied. The context is the system itself, which tries to function and cope with various sources of stress it encounters.

However, the notion of a system is not value-neutral at all given Easton's supposition, which was shared by many other theorists, that the system is self-maintaining. The political system was thought to be like a living organism except in one crucial respect — that it does not age, decay, or die. Its chief goal is sustenance. Its coping and feedback mechanisms ensure its continued survival. The harmonious interaction of all parts of the system is the prime condition for the system's sustenance, i.e., its well-being. A system is stable or in a state of equilibrium when the demands on its mechanisms do not exceed the mechanisms' capacities to cope with these demands.

Dahl and many other postwar theorists endorsed the perspective that systems analysis offered.[81] However, even without Easton's help, the structure of their arguments would have been similar to Easton's argument in ways that are relevant to this analysis. Easton made explicit through systems analysis what was implicit in most of these theories, namely, that the different aspects of a political system work as part of a whole whose unifying purpose or function is perpetual existence. Systems analysis is a kind of functionalist analysis, and functionalist analysis was and is prevalently used in empirical political science.

Functionalism and Teleology

The link between communitarian approaches to communal values and postwar pluralist approaches is clarified once one understands the links between functionalism and teleology. According to Sperlich, functionalism is the dominant method of explanation and assessment in the social sciences. If one is not a functionalist, according to some theorists, one is a reductionist or raw empiricist.[82] According to Eugene Meehan's

---

[80] Easton, *The Political System,* 78.

[81] See especially, Dahl, "A Behavioral Analysis of Political Science," 85.

[82] Kingsley Davis, "The Myth of Functionalist Analysis as a Special Method in Sociology and Anthropology," 759–61.

analysis in 1967, "[f]unctionalism, or 'systems analysis,' is the predominant conceptual framework in contemporary political science."[83]

Key amongst the communitarian specifications for a common good is that a political theory or political society have a teleological structure. Explanations in the social sciences, particularly in the postwar period, have a functionalist structure, and functionalism and teleology offer very similar approaches to political analysis. Functionalism is a method of explanation in which the characteristics of the parts are explained in terms of the function they play in the whole. In systems analysis, the whole is understood to be the political system. Thus, the structure of a political institution is explained according to the function the institution fulfills in the system. The practices of the institution are explained according to the role they fulfill in sustaining the institution for the purpose that the institution fulfills in the system. The institution is assessed in terms of how it contributes to sustaining the system.

The structure of functionalist approaches is the same as that of teleological ones. Both explain and assess the parts of a whole in the context of the characteristics, ends, or aims of the whole. In MacIntyre's words, "the subject is analyzed according to its function" and "the parts have to been seen in terms of their roles in order to determine whether they are good or not."[84] Sperlich affirms that functionalist explanations often take teleological form, and he points to the work of Robert Merton and Ernest Nagel, both of whom recognized the similarities between these two forms of explanation.[85]

Functionalism and teleology are not identical. While functional explanations are basic to scientific approaches, teleological explanations are not.[86] Teleological explanations presume that the whole must embody a purpose whereas functionalist explanations do not. For example, in order for explanation to be teleological, it is insufficient for the parts of a watch to be explained in terms of how they keep the watch ticking. They must be viewed as contributing to the watch's purpose as an accurate time-keeping device. Teleology presumes that the parts of a system are intentionally designed to participate in unfolding the purpose or end of the whole. This intention is lacking in functionalist explanations, and it is also lacking in systems analysis where maintaining the system does not necessarily entail endorsing it.

---

[83] Meehan, *Contemporary Political Thought*, 68.

[84] MacIntyre, *After Virtue*, 58–59.

[85] See Sperlich, *Conflict and Harmony in Human Affairs*, 213.

[86] See Emmet, *Function, Purpose and Powers*.

Yet, functionalist explanations can become teleological ones when the system's maintenance becomes the reason for endorsing the system.[87] For example, a purely functionalist account would simply take note of the role the Court plays in maintaining the stability of a political system. A teleological account would endorse the notion of stability as good and would endorse the Court's actions as good when they sustain or improve political stability. As Sperlich notes, ". . . functionalists seem to be uncomfortable with instability and imbalance . . . they tend to move from the analytic to the therapeutic with great ease, and sometimes without realizing that this shift has taken place."[88] What Sperlich calls "therapeutic" are prescriptive statements that theorists make in light of what is perceived to be the system's goal — namely sustenance, harmony, or stability. "Indeed, functionalist theory often has a strong prescriptive component: harmony is not only natural but also *right*."[89] Myrdal concurred: "a description of social institutions in terms of their functions must lead to a conservative teleology."[90]

The line between describing a system as stable and endorsing it for this reason was crossed by many postwar theorists. With the help of systems analysis, theorists were able to argue sensibly that changes to the system that overburden the coping techniques or dismantle the feedback mechanisms are *bad*, while those that enhance a system's ability to attain a healthy balance are *good*. Their analyses may have disregarded all values extrinsic to the system and thus been objective within the parameters that a functionalist assessment of a particular political system allows. But even though postwar pluralists did not look beyond the political system they described for the values by which they assessed this system, they nonetheless assessed the system. They endorsed as good those aspects that contributed to the system's stability. Like Easton, Dahl recognized that conflict itself is functional to democratic politics in the United States. Therefore, amongst the conditions that maintain the system's stability are the cross-cutting conflicts of pluralist politics. The democratic creed served also to promote stability, as did the legitimating function that the Supreme Court performed. In fact, all aspects of the system were ultimately explained and assessed according to a view that made stability the central value of democracy.

---

[87] Emmet, *Function, Purpose and Powers*, 47.
[88] Sperlich, *Conflict and Harmony in Human Affairs*, fn 58, 213.
[89] Sperlich, *Conflict and Harmony in Human Affairs*, 213.
[90] Myrdal, *An International Economy*, 151.

Dahl and most other behavioralists were also quick to expose the values, traditionally claimed as democratic ones, that are not essential for the system's sustenance. In a manner that testifies to the unreflective subjectivism within their own theory, the postwar theorists often dismissed the standards that informed the democratic cultures that Rousseau or Mill defended. They insisted that the standards to which American democracy should be held ought to be more realistic ones than those of the past. Because they were not satisfied with looking towards the rhetoric of American political values, for example, as found in the Constitution and, instead, opted to examine the actual practices of the system, they found that these practices did not fulfill the traditional expectations of liberal-democratic theory. Thus, it followed that equality was not necessary for democratic government to exist. Similarly, a high voter participation was not a characteristic of the political practices of so-called democracies. The conclusions they drew were that, beyond a certain modicum — in fact, the same modicum actually attained in American politics — civic virtue, equality, and participation have no essential function in democracy. As Dahl argued, "it is inaccurate to say that one of the necessary conditions for "democracy" is extensive citizen participation."[91] Voter apathy, on the other hand, could be viewed as performing a "positive service," in Berelson's words, because it ensured that intolerant and unsophisticated voters would be less likely to place demands on leaders and thus less apt to waste the system's resources. Apathy ensured that the coping and feedback mechanisms would not be overly taxed by demands. Like conflict and pluralism, apathy was not simply noted as a fact about American democratic politics. It was regarded as a functional aspect of the system. Insofar as functionalism invited the theorists to assess functional components as good components, apathy could be considered a good aspect of American democracy.

So, within much postwar theory, stability was treated as if it was the purpose for which all institutions of the system were designed. It was the value by which all other values and behavior within the system were assessed. It was the context in which political practices could be rationally assessed. In this sense, stability was a communal value which helped to define the communal good.

It can also be regarded as a communal value which seemed to have clear priority over individual well-being. This point was also explored in the previous chapter but additional illustrations are easy to

---

[91] Dahl, "Hierarchy, Democracy, and Bargaining in Politics and Economics," 87.

offer. In assessing the "democratic personality," for instance, Lasswell argued that the purpose of nurturing a democratic personality is to help stabilize democratic values "which are being challenged as never before."[92] The structure of his study made personal development a means to democratic stability rather than considering democracy to be a means to personal development. Similar priorities are found in Eckstein's book entitled *A Theory of Stable Democracy*. Eckstein argues that, for the purpose of promoting societal stability, authority patterns that exist in the social and familial spheres ought to be parallel to those in the political spheres. "[A] government will tend to be stable," he argued, "if its authority pattern is congruent with the other authority patterns of the society of which it is a part."[93] Since pure democracy, Eckstein argued, is impossible and undesirable in social and familial arenas, the only way in which government will have "a high capacity to control social relations toward desired ends" is if it possesses some authoritarian elements as well.[94] If Eckstein was concerned about the individual's well-being, he would have compared the well-being of individuals in a more authoritarian, but stable, system to their well-being in a less stable, but partially liberal, system before endorsing the former. But, his primary interest was stability. Stability was secured by getting the correct form of mixed government to match the mix in social and familial institutions.

In Dahl's analyses, stability also seems to have primacy over individual interests in American democracy. For example, Dahl implied that the Court is justified in not upholding minority rights over majority preferences because its legitimacy would be threatened in the process. Within his functionalist framework, it makes little sense that an institution's role would involve it in affairs that threaten its legitimacy and thus threaten the system's stability. On this basis, he concluded that the Court's role is not meant to meet individual interests by protecting minority rights. Instead, its role ought to be assessed functionally, in terms of how well it contributes to stability by conferring legitimacy on the policies of the national law-making majority.

Dahl's interpretation of the role that political participation plays in a democracy again favors the political system's stability over more individualistic values. Healthy, pluralist democracy, according to Dahl, need not be a system whose chief aim is to vindicate individual interests. Hypothetically, individuals may have many complaints because the plu-

---

[92] Lasswell, *Power and Personality*, 122.
[93] Eckstein, *A Theory of Stable Democracy*, 6.
[94] Eckstein, *A Theory of Stable Democracy*, 32.

ralist system is not fulfilling their interests. What is essential to the health of the system is that people do not usually act on their complaints. In Dahl's terminology, all that is necessary for democracy to exist is that the rules in place are strongly endorsed by a powerful minority and weakly opposed by the majority. This situation could obtain, as Dahl noted, even if the interests of some are ignored in the political process.[95] In this way, his interpretation falls well short of one in which individual rights have primacy over ideas of communal or societal good.

Nor is stability somehow identical to the concept of individual interests in postwar pluralism. As argued in chapter 4, stability was not viewed in postwar theory to be a prerequisite to fulfilling individual interests. This does not mean that stability is a trivial concern for a political community or that it is unconnected to individual interests. But, Dahl and other behavioralists and pluralists did not view stability as a *means* to individual improvement. Rather, stability was treated as an end in itself. And, in some circumstances, it was an end for which individual interests had to be sacrificed.

Dahl argued that pluralism is beneficial because it contributes to peaceful conflict-management not individual well-being. In Eckstein's argument, congruent authority patterns are important because they engender stability, not because they are vehicles to human improvement. And, in many of these theories, apathy is condoned because apathy means that fewer voters who are intolerant, irrational, and politically unsophisticated will participate in politics.

With these observations in place, we can now consider how the communitarian account seems to allow the stability prized by postwar pluralists to be accepted as a common good. According to Taylor, an adequate and sufficiently narrow conception of the good must meet three conditions. First, it must be a good espoused by society itself. It is analogous to the individual's life-plan.[96] Community cannot be viewed as an instrument "designed to seek merely convergent goods." It must have a vision of its own and, through this vision, it must be able to command "strong spontaneous allegiances from its members. . . ."[97] Second, it must be a shared good both in the sense that it is attained collectively and it is enjoyed collectively.[98] And third, it must have primacy over individual rights and cannot be identical with these rights.

---

[95] Dahl, *Who Governs?* 314–15.
[96] Taylor, "Cross-Purposes," 172.
[97] Taylor, "Cross-Purposes," 172–73.
[98] Taylor, "Cross-Purposes," 169.

It is primarily Taylor's third criterion that the value of stability in postwar pluralism meets. As for the other two criteria, the frustration is not only that stability does not seem an appropriate good but that no political value seems appropriate. It is unclear what sort of value *could* be shared by a community in the sense that Taylor intends. The examples Taylor uses to illustrate his point, namely an intimate conversation and a musical concert, are unhelpful in that, as instances of valued activities, they are not directly relevant to a political community. An intimate conversation with a close friend cannot be duplicated at the political level. And attempting to duplicate it would destroy what is especially valued about the shared experience — namely, its intimacy. The passive enjoyment that one gets out of a musical concert, including the chance to discuss the event with a friend afterwards, and to select a concert next time according to *our* mutual tastes, are all aspects of the experience "Mozart-with-you" as opposed to "Mozart-alone." Yet, they are not aspects that have any analogy at the political level. These examples are sure to embody a sense of sharing that is irreducible to individual, "atomized" experience. And it is clear that this sense of sharing is what Taylor seeks at the political level. However, the examples fail to disclose what this sense of sharing would look like at the political level and to what sort of political value it could be attached.

Partly because of the political inappropriateness of Taylor's test, MacIntyre's methodological approach to communal value and the useful reconstruction that Nederman provides have been the focus here. In both cases, functionalism or teleology provides the key to revealing communal standards and assessing communal practices. MacIntyre uses this approach to assess Justice Powell's decision in *Bakke*. Like a postwar political scientist, he makes sense of the decision by searching out the function it performed. Functionalism becomes translated into teleology once the decision is applauded for performing this function; teleology emerges from functionalism, to borrow MacIntyre's words, once the "peacekeeping" and "truce-making" functions of the Court are seen as good purposes the Court fulfills. MacIntyre does not cross this line in his analysis (although the value-laden nature of the word *peacekeeping* might suggest otherwise). And quite possibly he would not consider stability to be an adequate communal value. But this does not mean that stability and all that it entails was not or is not one of the primary communal values of the American state and other states.[99] Postwar democratic theory showed that

<hr/>

[99] Stability is endorsed as constitutive of the common good in contemporary liberal philosophy. For example, William Galston identifies "social peace" which includes "so-

stability had primacy over individual rights. It was a value according to which the political practices and other components of the system could be explained, assessed, and, ultimately, endorsed. This may not make stability adequate in the sense of being a value that a community should desire to attain above all others. However, the communitarians stipulate no means of distinguishing a good *telos* from a bad one. MacIntyre's prescription for retrieving communal values entails a method whereby communities scrutinize their existing practices and retrieve the good which these practices serve from the communal functions they perform. This method allows different communal values to be embodied in each local form of community. His argument is that *a* conception of the good is necessary, not *any* *particular* conception. Any conception of the good that could unite facts and values by providing the context he deems essential would seem to be adequate. Stability provides this context.

Conclusion

By using empirical political science as a referent for the communitarian notion of community, this analysis has drawn attention to the communitarian approach to communal values, practices, and goods. Evaluating the nature of methods is essential to the communitarian diagnosis of the ills of liberal societies. The liberal methods which include primarily emotivism and the fact-value distinction lead to societal fragmentation and the priority of rights. Rights and fragmentation then become constitutive of the political practices found in liberal societies. But, as MacIntyre found when assessing *Bakke*, when these practices are scrutinized, it is oftentimes not rights one finds. When the empirical investigators of the postwar era focused on the practices of the United states, they did not find that either rights or fragmentation explained the course of American politics. While rights comprised the rhetoric of the Court's role, in reality this institution was meant to fulfill the dual function of endorsing the policy preferences to which current pluralist politics led and protecting its own legitimacy in the process. Protecting rights took on secondary importance to these purposes.

As for the fragmentation that pluralism denoted, at another level there seemed to be more than sufficient evidence of communal values

---

cial arrangements and political mechanisms directed toward the compromise of differences and the amelioration of conflict," as the first of ten elements which together comprise a liberal conception of the common good. See Galston, "Defending Liberalism," 628.

and goods. And empirical political science did not lack the resources to construct a notion of the good because of its propensity to separate facts and values and its endorsement of emotivism. In fact, the opposite is true. Empirical methods led the postwar theorists to focus on political practices. In explaining these practices they adopted functionalism and systems analysis. They established a context of meaning through functionalism in which the system's stability and sustaining this stability became the primary values or goals of the system. Many of these theorists crossed the line between description and prescription — between functionalism and teleology — by concluding that institutions, values, circumstances, and behavior that threaten the system's stability are, therefore, undesirable.

The problem with postwar pluralism, and postwar empirical political theory in general, is not that it fails to generate a common good that is commensurate with the communitarian conception of the good. The difficulty is that the tests proposed by communitarians in order to identify the common good are satisfied by the notion of political stability prized by postwar pluralists. I have argued here that, with regards to the values endorsed by American postwar politics, the problem is not that postwar United States did not endorse a set of communal values, but rather, that it did endorse a set of values, and the values it endorsed were oppressive. In particular, stability as a communal value and goal meant that political freedoms to free speech, free association, and the right to choose one's own good were denied to many Americans in the 1950s and 1960s.

Significantly, it is in terms of methodological approach that communitarians and empirical political scientists have the most in common. The central problem with empirical political science was contained in its methods. The problem was that the methods offered no critical perspective from which to analyze the undesirable and potentially unethical trends in political practice. By focusing on the practices, the behavior which underlay these practices, and the socialization processes that motivated this behavior, political scientists robbed themselves of the means by which to criticize these practices. Much of their work was dismissed for being theoretically flawed and for being unduly conservative. The same complaints can be launched against communitarianism.

Postscript

By the late 1970s, Dahl's disposition altered towards pluralism and particularly towards the prospects of the political pluralism which he developed being an adequate basis for upholding democratic values. The problem, Dahl admitted in 1978, was that a system which relied solely on the interplay between associations to decide how resources ought to be distributed will systematically alienate the disadvantaged and disorganized groups in society.

> It is hardly open to doubt that organizational pluralism and the institutional guarantees of polyarchy are not sufficient conditions for a high degree of equality in the distribution of political resources, or, more broadly, status, income, wealth, and other key values.[100]

Moreover, he argued, organizational pluralism may perpetuate group self-interest. Along with Grant McConnell[101] and Theodore Lowi,[102] he noted that the common good gets short shrift as groups vie for self-serving goals. In general, Dahl observed, organizational pluralism may lead to a general "disillusionment and discontent with the constitutional structure of the polyarchy and more, to polyarchy in general or even to the desirability and feasibility of democracy itself."[103]

The new approach to democracy that Dahl then developed was not one that rejected pluralism as much as it injected normative content into pluralist theory. In *Democracy and Its Critics*, Dahl completely abandons the nonvaluational stance he assumed in the 1950s and frames his analysis with the question, "By what criteria are we to appraise the worth of democracy whether as an ideal or as an actuality?"[104] Part of the answer to this question, Dahl argues, is contained in the idea of intrinsic equality. Polyarchy or political pluralism is the preferred form of democracy because it presents the best way for the interests of all citizens to be given the appropriate consideration.[105] In a manner that echoes Dewey's initial formulation, Dahl states, ". . . the public good is not necessarily a monolithic goal that can or should be realized by a single, sovereign government. . . . 'the public' will consist of many different publics, each of which may have a somewhat different good or set of interests."[106]

---

[100] Dahl, "Pluralism Revisited," 199.
[101] McConnell, *Private Power and American Democracy.*
[102] Lowi, *The End of Liberalism.*
[103] Dahl, "Pluralism Revisited", 199.
[104] Dahl, *Democracy and Its Critics,* 84.
[105] See especially Dahl, *Democracy and Its Critics,* chapters 20, 21.
[106] Dahl, *Democracy and Its Critics,* 295.

So, one explanation for why Dahl abandoned the empirical approach to democracy is because it failed to be the means to vindicate the values, such as equality, that he thought to be important. As he stated in 1978, the problem with polyarchy as a theory of democracy is that it could eventuate in a "stable equilibrium of inequalities."[107] Here, I have argued that a normative commitment to ethical individualism is required to avoid this eventuality. Political pluralism, as well as communitarianism, is bound to tend towards a stable equilibrium of the status quo unless values, which may not be currently adhered to in many communal practices, but which are nonetheless ethically compelling to the community, are entertained as possible standards for that community. As elaborated in the next chapter, ethical individualism, as pursued through pluralist politics, offers such a compelling standard.

---

[107] Dahl, "Pluralism Revisited," 200.

VI
Personal Development
and the
Requirements of Community

A reconstructed theory of political pluralism is primarily committed to offering individuals the means to a healthy personal development. By way of drawing together the themes pursued
in earlier chapters, I shall explore further the resources by which pluralism facilitates a clearer understanding of what healthy personal development entails. I have already argued that personal development
cannot be equated with mere socialization. Yet, like socialization, personal development requires a social context. As I shall argue, to draw accurately the distinction between socialization and personal development is a central challenge for contemporary liberal politics. A
reconstructed pluralism can go some distance in meeting this challenge.

Socialization is the process by which individuals come to exhibit characteristics, behavior, attitudes, and beliefs either through involuntary or nonvoluntary association in groups.[1] In light of its involuntary or nonvoluntary character, socialization is often understood
as presenting obstacles to the development of individual autonomy. So,
when we say that an individual voted for one party rather than another because of her socialization, the implication is that, whether or
not the standards to which she adheres as a result of her socialization
are independently rational, she does not adhere to them because they
are independently rational. Rather, they mark her personality and influence her behavior because they are the standards of the groups in
which she is born and/or raised. On the basis of this understanding of
the term, socialization and not personal development is central to postwar political theory and plays a definitive role in shaping postwar
pluralism.[2]

---

[1] The distinction between involuntary and nonvoluntary association is explored
below.

171

While communitarians claim to be committed to personal development, their theories treat self-development as though it were no different from socialization. Thus, communitarian accounts of self-development are built around the recognition and celebration of obligations
and affiliations that individuals possess without consenting to them.
Moreover, the failure of liberals to recognize that many associative ties
are not based on voluntary consent is largely what motivates the communitarian critique.

The recognition that identity consists of unchosen components
seems to be what attracts many contemporary theorists to the communitarian position, or some portion of their position. For instance,
Young finds attractive the arguments of Sandel and Barber against the
atomistic view of the self. She claims that Sandel replaces the liberal
self with one whose identity is a product of what it shares with others, "of values and goals that are not external and willed, as liberalism
would have it, but constitutive of the self."[3] While Young finds the
communitarian view of the constitutive self appealing, she rejects the
vision of community that communitarians claim accompanies this self.
The undifferentiated community, she argues, is no different from the individualist vision in that "each entails a denial of difference and a desire to bring multiplicity and heterogeneity into unity though in op-
posing ways."[4]

Like the early pluralists, Young tries to locate her alternative between the seemingly "exhaustive dichotomy" of individualism and
communitarianism. Her alternative relies on privileging social groups
in representative institutions through protective policies. Protecting social groups provides the means by which difference is respected. It
avoids the exclusionary pitfalls of undifferentiated community while
not reducing society to an aggregation of atoms. In this ideal, which
Young explores through the analogy of big city life, "groups do not
stand in relations of inclusion and exclusion, but overlap and inter-
mingle without becoming homogeneous."[5]

Young wants to protect group difference in order to remedy one
of the key causes of group oppression. "Liberal social ontology," she

---

[2] Although, it is worth noting that postwar pluralists found that the socialization
trends were most clearly evident amongst peer groups rather than, intergenerationally,
amongst family members.
    [3] Young, *Justice and the Politics of Difference*, 228.
    [4] Young, *Justice and the Politics of Difference*, 229.
    [5] Young, *Justice and the Politics of Difference*, 239.

argues, "has no place for a concept of social groups."[6] In earlier chapters, I indicate that pluralism can provide such a place. An adequate account of political pluralism must contain the resources to protect simultaneously group difference and individual difference within groups.[7] An adequate theory of personal development must go beyond recognizing that social groups constitute individual identity and address precisely *how* identity is being constituted and whether, within the group, socialization, or, even worse, indoctrination, is replacing personal development. Moreover, it must do so without simply imposing the standards and practices of one group upon another. The communitarian proposal is problematic because it fails to distinguish social contexts conducive to personal development from those that merely trap individuals through socialization. This failure has threatened the soundness of the communitarian position and motivated a search for alternatives, such as pluralism, which avoid communitarian excesses. Nonetheless, the principal strength of communitarianism, namely its emphasis on the social dimensions of personal development and their implications for democratic politics, also comprises the focus of any plausible alternative.

Without abandoning this insight, a better approach to theories of democratic politics must take into account the different degrees of embeddedness which characterize individual-group affiliations. Some discussion of the different degrees of embeddedness figures into critiques of communitarianism, though not always directly. For instance, many challenges to communitarianism employ insights derived from feminism or cultural studies. Both gender and culture offer good examples of the dangerous undercurrents and potential destructiveness of the attachments that constitute our identity. Belonging to a group that is disadvantaged in the larger society is bound to have a profound and, in some instances, a negative impact on the individual's identity. This is because our identity is not solely our own creation but is also a function of how others understand and treat us. As Taylor explains it, ". . . our identity is partly shaped by recognition or its absence, often by the *mis*recognition of others, . . ."[8] For this reason, the mere fact that one is socially situated provides no reason to endorse *all* social situations and any standards they happen to set.

---

[6] Young, *Justics and the Politics of Difference*, 228.

[7] See Eisenberg, "The Politics of Individual and Group Difference in Canadian Jurisprudence."

[8] Taylor, *Multiculturalism and The Politics of Recognition*, 25.

The distinction between socialization and personal development constitutes a central problematic of feminism and cultural critique. As the debate in feminism over the "ethic of care" reveals, the discovery of a distinctive moral voice typical of women need not be viewed as a source of empowerment. It might instead be seen as a product of oppression[9] or as a justification for further oppression.[10] Feminist theory alerts us to the dangers of celebrating socially constructed identities. It also struggles with the project of distinguishing socialization from self-development.

Needless to say, this analysis cannot broach all dimensions of these problems. The aims here are more modest. I shall first return briefly to communitarianism and show that the distinction between socialization and personal development is inadequately drawn there. Second, I shall develop a way of getting at this distinction which uses the resources of pluralism. The pluralist alternative which I propose relies on distinguishing between different ways in which one can belong to a group or community. These different ways are expressed through the categories of voluntary, involuntary, and nonvoluntary association. Finally, I conclude by identifying nine lessons for reconstructing political pluralism which are extracted from the analyses of historical and contemporary accounts of the doctrine.

Communitarianism and Personal Development

Communitarians criticize liberalism for failing to facilitate personal development. Taylor argues that the primacy-of-rights doctrine to which liberalism is committed wrongly assumes that individuals can develop their capacities in the absence of a social context. That is, either liberalism holds a view of self-sufficient development, or it assumes that individuals develop their capacities prior to entering society. Taylor's evidence that liberal philosophies embrace this sort of commitment is found in the theories of Hobbes, Locke, Nozick, and Rawls, all of which embrace or utilize the idea of a state of nature or something similar to it. Taylor argues that real liberal societies must be concerned with *developing* human capacities rather than assuming their existence. Capacities worthy of society's respect are developed within a social context, and they derive much of their meaning and significance in that social context. Rights are designed to *protect*, not to develop, these capacities.

---

[9] See MacKinnon, *Toward a Feminist Theory of the State*, 51.
[10] Okin, *Justice, Gender and the Family*, 15.

Rights assume that these capacities have already been developed. Therefore, the self-sufficiency that they are designed to protect makes rights the wrong instruments to *develop* capacities.

The limitations of rights as protective devices would pose no problems if rights were not given the primacy that they are in liberal societies. The primacy of rights, rather than the rights themselves, is the reason why Taylor claims that liberalism assumes self-sufficient development. The *protection* of capacities is given primacy over the *development* of capacities. This puts the cart before the horse; "for to assert the rights in question is to affirm the capacities, and granted the social thesis is true concerning these capacities, this commits us to an obligation to belong."[11] Rights actually undermine the possibility of individual development because they effectively separate the individual from the community and thus cut her off from the instrument of her development. The obligation of individuals to a social and political context of a particular sort should be given primacy over rights by those committed to personal development. Taylor argues that, if liberals believe that a social context is necessary for development, as communitarians do, they ought not to make the obligation to rights primary but, rather, they should insist that our fundamental obligation is to belong to or sustain a society of a certain type.[12] Instead, liberals make this type of obligation conditional on individual consent. As Taylor argues, "our obligation to belong to or sustain a society, or obey its authorities, is seen as derivative, as laid on us conditionally, through our consent, or through its being to our advantage."[13] It is the secondary status of this obligation to which Taylor's objections are directed.

Sandel and MacIntyre entertain the same sort of social thesis about individual development. For MacIntyre, the individual *qua* individual, outside or insulated from community, cannot lead a good life. The notion of a good is always tied to one's life circumstances and the role one fulfills in those circumstances. What is the good life for a farmer may not be the same as what it is for a stockbroker. MacIntyre explains that one's good is a product of the social roles one inhabits and with which one approaches the circumstances of life.

> I am someone's son or daughter, someone else's cousin or
> uncle; I am a citizen of this or that city, a member of this or

---

[11] Taylor, *Philosophy and the Human Science*, 98.

[12] Taylor, *Philosophy and the Human Sciences*, 188.

[13] Taylor, *Philosophy and the Human Sciences*, 188.

that guild or profession; I belong to this clan, that tribe, this nation. Hence what is good for me has to be the good for one who inhabits these roles. . . . These constitute the given of my life, my moral starting point.[14]

These roles define one's good because they constitute one's identity. They cannot be "stripped away in order to discover 'the real me.' They are part of my substance, defining partially at least and sometimes wholly my obligations and my duties."[15] Liberalism putatively negates these roles, or, at least, it attempts to abstract the individual from them. It erects an official policy of value-neutrality and rejects a teleological conception of the good. Its abstract notion of the individual reaffirms value-neutrality largely because it makes no sense to bind individuals *qua* individuals to any particular notion of the good. But again, it makes no sense because a teleological notion of the good, which is the only comprehensible notion according to MacIntyre, is always tied to the practices of individuals within roles and contexts. In the end, MacIntyre argues, if one rejects the teleological/Aristotelian conception, as have most post-Enlightenment thinkers, one "cut[s] oneself off from the shared activity in which one has initially to learn obediently as an apprentice learns . . ." and "debar[s] oneself from finding any good outside of oneself."[16]

Sandel relies on similar criticisms of the abstract self in his analysis of Rawls. He is mainly critical of Rawls, on the one hand, for attempting to abstract the individual in the original position from the interests that she actually possesses and the roles that she actually fulfills and, on the other hand, for thinking that such an abstraction is possible. Sandel argues that the attachments we possess are constitutive of, not incidental to, the sort of people we are. Rawls's attempt to abstract individuals from these attachments behind the "veil of ignorance," in order for them to reflect rationally on principles of justice, is a hopeless project. No self remains, Sandel argues, once the self has been stripped of all its constitutive attachments. Community in the strong sense — the "constitutive conception" of community — "describes not just what they *have* as fellow citizens but also what they *are*, not a relationship they choose (as in a voluntary association) but an attachment they discover. . . ."[17]

---

[14] MacIntyre, *After Virtue*, 220.
[15] MacIntyre, *After Virtue*, 33.
[16] MacIntyre, *After Virtue*, 258.
[17] Sandel, *Liberalism and the Limits of Justice*, 150.

The constitutive conception of community allows for hardly any distance to exist between the individual and her attachments. The relation is not voluntary. Instead, it is cognitive; "the self came by its ends not by choice but by reflection. . . ."

> Unlike the capacity for choice, which enables the self to reach beyond itself, the capacity for reflection enables the self to turn its lights inward upon itself, to inquire into its constituent nature, to survey its various attachments and acknowledge their respective claims. . . .[18]

Sandel argues that the liberal ethic which "puts the self beyond the reach of its experience, beyond deliberation and reflection" denies to the self the "expansive self-understandings" that result from self-reflection.[19] Instead of understanding the ways in which our identity is constituted by our attachments and commitments, "the liberal self is left to lurch between detachment on the one hand, and entanglement on the other."[20] Detachment results from believing in liberal practices such as rights. Entanglement results from misunderstanding the constitutive nature of both the attachments which people inevitably possess and the respective claims on the self which accompany these attachments.

Voluntary, Nonvoluntary, and Involuntary Associations

The types of self-development that are central to communitarian analysis, and, according to their critique, are discounted by liberalism, are involuntary and nonvoluntary. Communitarians claim that liberals ignore those aspects of the self that cannot be shed as easily as are affiliations with political parties and social clubs. The autonomous individual in liberalism is problematically conceptualized as making autonomous choices free from external constraints.[21] Communitarians are mostly interested in associations and obligations that are constitutive of the individual in the sense that no self exists apart from these constitutive elements. These attachments are ones that the self can come to understand and reflect on but cannot choose to keep or to discard. They

---

[18] Sandel, *Liberalism and the Limits of Justice,* 153.
[19] Sandel, "The Procedural Republic and the Unencumbered Self," 91.
[20] Sandel, "The Procedural Republic and the Unencumbered Self," 91.
[21] Gould, *Rethinking Democracy,* 35.

are part of one's identity and bring with them commitments and loyalties that are not based on consent or choice.

While one's gender, race, religion, or nationality may not be shed as easily as are one's affiliations with political parties or social clubs, all of these groups elicit in different individuals a variety of senses of belonging. Constitutive attachments bring with them different degrees of embeddedness. For example, being a woman is far more constitutive of my identity than is being a Canadian. Ceasing to be a woman may be more problematic than ceasing to be a Canadian. Yet, this does not mean that I could not *want* to detach myself from either affiliation. Rather, it means that, more often than not, individuals find it easier to change the nature of the collectivity in question than to change their affiliation to it. That is, women try to change what it means to be a woman in contemporary society rather than trying to become men.

An adequate theory of personal development requires that a distinction be drawn between at least three different types of associative ties: (1) voluntary, (2) nonvoluntary, and (3) involuntary. *Voluntary associations* preserve the individual's autonomy to change her values and dispositions when other values and dispositions seem more reasonable or appealing. So, individuals can move from one political party to another depending on which party offers the most reasonable political vision or strategy. In two senses, a voluntary context facilitates personal development. First, voluntary associations are contexts in which one's values and dispositions are formed and in which these values can have meaning and significance. Second, individuals learn how to exercise choice by making choices.[22] Values are voluntarily adopted rather than imposed or deposited. The obligations, commitments, and loyalties one assumes as a result of affiliation are, like the affiliation itself, voluntarily assumed. The individual remains an autonomous actor. Primarily because of this autonomy, personal development is relatively unproblematic within voluntary associations in the sense that destructive values will not be *imposed* on the individual as they might be, for example, on a child raised by racist parents. Nonetheless, as Gould points out, "some choices may in fact be pernicious for self-development or inhibit it. . . ."[23] So, the volun-

---

[22] Gould also finds the exercise of choice to be crucial to personal development. See *Rethinking Democracy*, 46–47, as well as chapter 11 for an interesting discussion of the democratic personality. In addition, Dahl recently has drawn on Mill in discussing the beneficial role that democracy plays in cultivating various individual characteristics. See *Democracy and Its Critics*, 91–92.

[23] Gould, *Rethinking Democracy*, 46.

tariness of association does not ensure that good choices will be made and that development will be healthy. Rather, it provides the least complicated context in which mistakes can be corrected once they are discovered.

Nonvoluntary affiliations are affiliations one has from birth or are formed in circumstances in which an individual cannot exercise volition. Typically, nonvoluntary affiliations cannot be easily shed. Being a woman or Black or disabled is a nonvoluntary affiliation. Being a Canadian or a Catholic may also be nonvoluntary in the sense that one's identity continues to be bound to the affiliation even once it is left behind. Thus, converting from Catholicism to Judaism often does not entail discarding all elements of Catholicism or adopting all elements of Judaism. Rather, it usually means becoming a "Jewish convert" or an "ex-Catholic," even in one's own eyes. The nonvoluntary element of such affiliations refers specifically to those aspects of the affiliation that exist independently of the individual's choice to participate in cultivating the association. Even though they shape identity, nonvoluntary affiliations are, at least in the first instance, beyond the scope of individual volition.

Many of the groups studied by postwar pluralists were nonvoluntary in this sense. Often researchers would categorize individuals based on whether they possessed a characteristic over which they had little or no control such as gender or race. These associations were known as "cohorts." Individuals may be affiliated to a cohort by virtue of a characteristic they possess, but they do not, in any meaningful sense, participate in this association. Participation is usually the sign of a more voluntary commitment to the values and perspectives of an association.

It is revealing of the false value-neutrality of postwar political science, as well as the nature of nonvoluntary associations, that these studies were necessarily based on more than simply the common possession of a given characteristic. The researchers were interested only in those cohorts that had politically significant behavior. Therefore, one of the researchers' responsibilities was to determine which cohorts are politically significant and which are not. Political significance was determined according to whether, statistically, individuals possessing a certain characteristic act in a way that is politically distinct from individuals not possessing the characteristic. So, one would expect groups, such as women or Blacks, to be statistically significant while others, such as redheads or football fans, to be insignificant, at least in the context of American politics.

But if all cohorts are based on nonvoluntary affiliation, and, as such, need not involve active commitments by their members to the values of the group, why do some cohorts and not others exhibit politically significant behavior? Part of the answer might be that some individuals in the cohort are active advocates of values or perspectives typical of the cohort. For instance, perhaps feminist attitudes are more prevalent amongst women than men because more women than men belong to feminist organizations.

Another part of the answer leads in the opposite direction and discloses the sense in which affiliations can be *involuntary*. Individuals affiliated to various cohorts are socialized in a certain way because they possess a certain characteristic. Cohorts display distinct political behavior because the characteristic that determines membership in a group, such as gender or race, also influences the way in which individuals possessing the characteristic are treated in society and by the state. In other words, socialization processes which affect those belonging to a politically significant cohort do not only involve voluntary interaction *within* the group (e.g., women interacting with other women). Often socialization entails interaction between members of the cohort and individuals in the wider community who treat those possessing the characteristic in question differently from those who do not possess it. *Involuntary* association is an association that the individual actively rejects but, at the same time, cannot avoid because the association is linked to a characteristic that she possesses nonvoluntarily, such as being a woman or Black, and this characteristic influences how she is treated by others.

The characteristics that determine membership in nonvoluntary cohorts cannot be shed or rendered insignificant simply by an act of the individual's will. Race, culture, or gender constitute one's self regardless of one's choice in the matter. One consequence of the nonvoluntary nature of such attachments is that these characteristics are constitutive of the person. But, the nonvoluntary aspect of such affiliations is rarely problematic. There is no problem coming to terms with one's gender or culture *per se*. Rather, the problems lie in embracing those aspects of gender and culture that are directly linked to disadvantage. In other words, it is only the involuntary aspects of politically significant nonvoluntary associations that raise difficulties for individual identity. Socialization processes have a great deal to do with how those who do not belong to the cohort treat those who do belong. This factor determines why certain cohorts are politically or socially significant while others are not.

The involuntary aspect of socialization means that many *contingent* factors are attached to the possession of certain characteristics within different societies. In some societies, being female may be associated with being maternal or emotional. Clearly, these contingent factors play a formidable role in socialization. Yet, they need not be accepted as *constitutive* in the same way as are the nonvoluntary characteristics that underlie them. There is an important difference between not wanting to be a woman and not wanting to be treated as society typically treats women, even though both the characteristic and the treatment influence one's personality and identity. To be sure, the distinction between the characteristic and the treatment — between the nonvoluntary and involuntary affiliations that we possess — may be difficult to draw. However, this difficulty counts as no more of a reason to treat all that is potentially contingent as constitutive of one's identity (as communitarians do) than does treating all that is constitutive as contingent of one's identity (as communitarians argue liberals do).

When communitarians discuss constitutive components of the self and obligations to belong, they have, in various instances, failed to appreciate the distinction among nonvoluntary, involuntary, and voluntary affiliations. Furthermore, they make no distinction between contingent and constitutive aspects of identity. Taylor fails to make these distinctions in his discussion of the obligation that exists between the individual and the social context in which her capacities are developed. He argues that the priority given to rights rather than obligations in liberal theory is illegitimate. "Illegitimate," in this context, can be interpreted as a factual claim: whether liberals like it or not, the bonds between individuals and societies are nonvoluntary and, therefore, our obligation to our social context is beyond our control. Our obligations derive from our nature as social animals. In discussing what is meant by an obligation to belong, Taylor notes that the type of obligation he is searching for is not analogous to obligations which individuals forge *outside* their families. One can only assume then, that these obligations are similar in some senses to those assumed within a family. Extrafamilial obligations, he argues, "are freely taken on in contracting marriage, friendships, and the like."[24] He then adds that "[t]he only involuntary associations are those between generations: our obligations to our parents and those to our children. . . ."[25] But even these obligations are not the same as one's obligation to belong to a society. However, the disanalogy, he explains, is not because of their involuntary (or nonvoluntary) aspect, but because these obligations "do not necessarily involve continuing associations" and "are not a condition of our continued

[24] Taylor, *Philosophy and the Human Sciences*, 203.
[25] Taylor, *Philosophy and the Human Sciences*, 203.

development."[26] The nonvoluntary tie between the individual and society indicates that the individual is dependent on society for her development. She belongs to society whether she likes it or not because she will not develop certain capacities outside society.

This nonvoluntary fact can be recognized without insisting that her "obligation to obey authority or an authority of a certain type" is also nonvoluntary.[27] As Holmes argues, "the fact that human potentials develop only in social settings . . . has no implications at all for what people are morally obliged to do."[28] Take, for example the family analogy. Taylor's claim that the social thesis carries obligations with it means that, since children are dependent on their families for their development, they are obligated to their families in the sense that they ought to participate in their family's decisions and, at times, willingly sacrifice their own interests for the sake of their family's welfare. This observation follows from the communitarian insistence that individual interests should not or do not automatically trump common interests when conflicts arise. In a political context, these obligations are not simply a matter of gratitude, as they are in the familial context. Rather, they are grounded in an understanding, which children may not possess, that one depends on a community in order to flourish.

The problem with the analogy is that, while some children should feel obligated to their families irrespective of whether they want to assume this obligation or not, other children, who are mistreated or neglected by their families, should not be obligated — *whether they assume any obligations or not.* Whether one is or ought to be obligated to one's family is conditional upon whether one's family treats one well.[29] It is not simply conditional upon whether one depends on a familial context for development. Neglected children may still depend on a family context. But their dependence cannot be the criterion for deciding whether they are obligated to their particular family. Familial obligation depends on the nature of one's family.

Similarly, the social thesis cannot make any claims regarding obligations to submit one's interests to the authority structures and institutions that exist within the social context of development. As Leslie Green argues, "even if our moral nature depends on institutions that nurture our essential capacities, that does not show that we cannot support such

[26] Taylor, *Philosophy and the Human Sciences*, 203.
[27] Taylor, *Philosophy and the Human Sciences*, 188.
[28] Holmes, "The Permanent Structure of Anti-Liberal Thought," 233.
[29] See also Holmes, "The Permanent Structure of Anti-Liberal Thought," fn 25, 286.

institutions without accepting their claim to create duties for us, and thus without acknowledging the authority of the state."[30] Supporting the social context is importantly distinct from sacrificing one's interests to this context. For Green, the need for political consent rests on this distinction.

At a societal level, the individual's obligation to a particular society must surely depend on the nature of that society. Black South Africans can hardly be criticized for not assuming their obligations to uphold the traditions and practices of the apartheid society in which they were born and to which their identities may be bound in some ways. Again, obligations are not simply a matter of needing a society — but, rather, depend on needing a specific type of society — a point which Taylor emphasizes[31] despite the contrary implications of parts of his argument. In other words, obligations to a society or social context cannot follow from the claims of the social context. Rather, obligations are based on the extent to which one sees a particular society or parts of it as constitutive of the person that *one wants to be* — as opposed to the person *society wants one to be* or the person that one presently is. The individual's affiliations need not be considered by her to be constitutive of her identity. Often, affiliations are subjects of reflection, struggle, and rejection by those on whom they are imposed.

In sum, the communitarian project with regards to self-development seems deeply problematic. By failing to grasp the significance of the distinction between voluntary, nonvoluntary, and involuntary association, communitarian self-development leads to the uncritical acceptance and celebration of given social roles. Self-development is thus reduced to mere socialization.

Personal Development in Pluralism

The behavioralists and postwar pluralists also failed to distinguish between voluntary, nonvoluntary, and involuntary groups. For instance, although "Black Americans" and "Republican Party members" are distinct types of groups with regards to the voluntariness of their members' ties to the group, this distinction is not explored in postwar theory. The extent to which characteristics are constitutive or contingent was irrelevant to the postwar project, as was the distinction between

---

[30] Green, "Consent and Community," 111.
[31] Taylor, *Philosophy and the Human Sciences*, 197–98.

socialization and personal development as processes whereby behaviors, values, and beliefs are adopted. Mostly, behavioralist research established correlations between values, beliefs, or behavior, and particular cohorts. Their project was to add political values to the list of contingent values already associated with various cohorts.

One can find some behavioral studies that seem to be sensitive to the distinction between different degrees of embeddedness. For example, in *The American Voter,* Campbell et al. conclude that an individual who identifies strongly with a group is more likely to exhibit voting behavior that is typical of the group. Yet, no attempt is made in this study to distinguish voluntary from other forms of association nor is there any discussion about which process of attitude-formation is more conducive to individual well-being. Behavioralists were only concerned with the final behavior and not with the process by which behavior is adopted. If one is only interested in whether more Black voters support the Republicans or the Democrats, it makes little difference whether or not the individual voter has an active and reflective role in constructing the norms and values that are manifest in the group's behavior. Only when one is interested in the process by which the decision is made will the individual's agency become pertinent and the distinction between voluntary, nonvoluntary, and involuntary associations take on political and moral significance.

Although communitarians claim to be interested in this process, they fail to appreciate these distinctions as well. They start with the correct observation that not all aspects of the self are voluntarily embraced by the individual. The contribution of political sociology at this point is helpful in emphasizing the communitarian point; all is not a matter of autonomous choice in these socialization processes. However, communitarianism offers no means of distinguishing characteristics that are constitutive of an individual self from those many identity-constituting characteristics that can and should be rejected by the individual. To borrow MacIntyre's metaphor, the individual should not be forced to be an "apprentice" in roles that will only continue to rob her of her potential.

Involuntary affiliations clearly ought not to be accepted by individuals as constitutive of their identity. Yet, who but the individual is able to decide whether a given value, attitude, disposition, or behavior constitutes their self or is imposed by society? By giving this decision to the individual, we adopt a liberal notion of the self in which all aspects of the individual's identity will potentially be treated as contingent by her. The self is imagined to be unencumbered, even though this is impossible. The alternative to the unencumbered individual is even less appealing. By allotting this decision to society, we pretend along with communitarians that no distinction exists between nonvoluntary and involuntary affiliations: that I am what society tells me I am even if that portrait seems unappealing and false to me.

Advocates of individual rights are correct to view rights as devices which can empower the individual to decide which of her affiliations are nonvoluntary and which are involuntary. As Gould notes, the moral principle from which rights are derived is that human beings ought to have access to the necessary conditions of self-development.[32] Rights which guarantee freedom of conscience, religion, and association make more accessible the choices that contribute to personal development.

This is not to say that rights are sufficient to empower the individual nor that, with rights, the individual will judge wisely all the time. A plurality of contexts is also required to empower the individual and to cultivate in her good judgment through the development of critical perspectives. But even a multiplicity of attachments will not guarantee that individuals make good choices. One consequence of making the individual the sole negotiator of her identity — the sole judge of whether something is a contingent or constitutive aspect of her identity — is that mistakes in judgment are bound to occur. No guarantee exists that the individual will make the right choices; I might find out, at many points in my life, that I have been wrong about the sort person I am or even about the sort of person I want to be. As a result, the attachments I cultivate and discard are bound to change. The choice between different political schemes in this respect is not between schemes that allow mistakes to be made or those which do not but, rather, between those that allow the individual or the community to make such mistakes. I am not the only one who could be mistaken about what my identity should consist in. Mistakes of this sort are made all the time by communities when they treat as constitutive characteristics that are contingent. It is preferable for two reasons that individuals and not communities be empowered through mechanisms such as rights to enter or escape associative ties even if, at times, mistaken choices are made. First, as Kymlicka argues, "a valuable life has to be a life led from the inside."[33] Second, communities often have vested interests in distorting the identities of some portion of their membership. As those who fight oppression and disadvantage observe,

---

[32] Gould, *Rethinking Democracy,* 64.
[33] Kymlicka, "Liberalism and Communitarianism," 183.

often no incentive exists for society or the majority in society to empower disadvantaged groups if doing so means taking or threatening
to take power away from those who dominate.

Political pluralism provides no guarantee against mistakes in
judgment. But it minimizes their likely occurrence and their tena-
ciousness. Political pluralism provides some of the crucial means by
which the individual can correct mistakes by encouraging her to cultivate alternative perspectives and providing the political means by
which such perspectives can develop in society. Friedman recognizes
the importance of developing such alternative perspectives and calls attention to the role that some voluntary communities play in displacing
our ties to the traditional communities in which we are born.[34] The
community of choice is particularly significant for individuals whose
origins are riddled with ambiguities, ambivalences, and oppressions.
Friedman emphasizes that the virtue of communities of choice is that
they can displace old and possibly oppressive attachments. An additional virtue emphasized in political pluralism is that some communities can mediate the confusions or challenge the oppressions found in
other communities. As Hirschman observed in his classic study of economic and political organizations, politics is more often a game about
voice — about transforming that from which one cannot exit.[35] Often we
do not sever old attachments, even when they are oppressive. Rather,
we try to transform the communities into which we are born. Friedman is correct in recognizing that some communities offer the resources
by which the individual can critically scrutinize her attachments to
other communities.[36] Understanding how to transform some of the
groups to which we belong, or realizing that some of them should be
transformed, is one of the great benefits that our other attachments or
communities offer.

Conclusion

I have argued that a reconstructed notion of political pluralism can address the shortcomings of rights-based liberalism and communitarianism. It recognizes the crucial role of group power in facilitating individual development without naively endorsing the unlimited and

---

[34] Friedman, "Feminism and Modern Friendship," 111.
[35] Hirschman, *Exit, Voice and Loyalty*, 16–19.
[36] Friedman, "Feminism and Modern Friendship," 112.

concentrated power of community. Personal development depends on individuals cultivating multiple attachments so that they can use the perspectives developed in one context to scrutinize the values and standards of other contexts. The works of James, Dewey, Figgis, Cole, Laski, Follett, Dahl, and others help to develop historical hindsight regarding the potential that pluralism holds. Although I shall not offer here a comprehensive reconstructed account of political pluralism, nine lessons which are central in shaping a reconstructed theory can be extracted from the analyses of past pluralists.

First, political power is deeply implicated in personal development, and a strong connection exists between the distribution of power to groups in society and the ability of group members to enjoy healthy personal development. This observation is hardly novel. It is recognized in jurisprudence, in psychology and sociology, and in our common sense. But its implications are often ignored in political science. The debilitating effects of racial oppression and segregation on African American children in the United States formed the cornerstone of Thurgood Marshall's 1954 argument in *Brown v. the Board of Education*.[37] More recently, Brown and Gilligan's study of the drastic loss of self-esteem experienced by female adolescents is plausibly interpreted as the result of girls being introduced to and socialized into the values and standards of the relatively disadvantaged and powerless group they are about to join — namely adult women.[38] The importance to children of role models undergirds the same point, namely, that the political powerlessness of identity-constituting groups has a profound effect on individual self-development.

Because individual well-being depends on group power and its distribution, no theory of group power and politics can be entirely divorced from the normative issues surrounding personal development. This contains the second and third lessons for a reconstructed pluralism. Second, political pluralism aims at securing individual well-being and, as such, is individualistic. The communitarian critique has given rise to an exaggerated suspicion of individualism and a mistaken conflation of distinct types of individualism. One lesson to be extracted from postwar pluralism is that theories which fail to connect individual well-being and group power risk endorsing oppressive schemes of communal politics. Individual well-being is central to any plausible democrat-

---

[37] See Kluger, *Simple Justice*, chapter 14.
[38] See Brown and Gilligan, *Meeting at the Crossroads: Women's Psychology and Girls' Development*.

ic theory or account of community politics — including, as I have argued, communitarianism. The debate between liberals and their critics is centered around which is the best strategy to secure this well-being and not whether it should be secured at all. However, some accounts of democracy examined above ignore the individual in favor of group personality or societal stability and, for this reason, are unacceptable.

Third, and again related to postwar pluralism, political pluralism must be reconstructed as a normative theory. The strength of the tradition lies in linking social interaction, the distribution of power amongst groups, and individual development. By avoiding the ethical dimensions of group politics (i.e., its consequences for individual development), theorists have been led either to endorse the status quo, as did the postwar pluralists, or, following the later Laski, to construct a theory which ignores what is largely politically significant about groups, namely, that they shape individual development.

The fourth lesson for a reconstructed pluralism is that any plausible approach in democratic politics to personal development must involve a balance between our engagement and disengagement with groups. Individual attachments to communal contexts provide the means to self-development both in offering an environment of interaction and sharing within the community, and in cultivating a critical perspective from which to scrutinize attachments to other communities. This critical perspective is key to James's and Dewey's pluralism. Part of their reasoning for insisting on a plurality of contexts is so that various parts of the personality can be developed simultaneously. They considered the all-embracing community to be dangerous because it perverts individual development by offering only one avenue of development.

The state's role under political pluralism has not been discussed here as extensively as it has been in other contexts.[39] In the theories examined above, the pluralistic state is conceptualized in a variety of ways, including as an umpire amongst all groups and as a group in competition with other groups. On the basis of the material analyzed, most pluralists have viewed the state as a group with distinct interests. The reconstructed notion of political pluralism favored here aims at avoiding state intervention in shaping the substantive values that define communities. Instead, it attempts, as much as possible, to rely on the individual's multiple affiliations to provide a critical perspective

---

[39] For a recent discussion of the state and the pluralist approach see Almond, "Return to the State," and accompanying critiques by Nordlinger, Lowi, and Fabbrini.

by which the individual can judge the worth of these values. So, the fifth lesson is that political pluralism can provide the means to healthy individual development without requiring societal or state scrutiny of the substantive values of any community. I have argued that the individual is the best judge of whether various communities advance or distort self-development. Individuals are bound to make mistakes in judgment, but they are more likely than are communities to correct such mistakes by discarding attachments and transforming associations. The individual ought to be, in this sense, the sole negotiator of her identity.

By insisting that, within a pluralist framework, the individual is treated as the sole negotiator of her identity, she is in no way cast as unencumbered or as not requiring communal contexts for healthy development. If political theory and practice is to be sensitive to the distinction between personal development and socialization, and, in general, to the different degrees of individual embeddedness in groups, individual agency to decide whether an association is voluntary, involuntary, or nonvoluntary must be preserved. One might portray affiliations as if they are voluntary in order to emphasize that, ultimately, the individual must be treated as the author of her own personal development even though, in many senses, she is not. This position contrasts sharply with that of the postwar pluralists who treated all associations as if they are nonvoluntary ones. Because behavioralists were not concerned with personal development as a means to enhancing individual well-being, it made no difference to them whether an individual voluntarily or involuntarily identified with the characteristic with which her cohort was affiliated. To the contrary, the autonomy and power to change one's relation to a group or to change the nature of the group would only complicate the socialization norms that behavioralism sought to establish. Rather than focusing their concerns on healthy individual development, these theorists sought to establish correlations between group memberships and political behavior.

So the sixth lesson for a reconstructed pluralism is that political power must be assessed on a group-societal basis as well as on an individual-group basis. For individuals, rights may provide one source of power by which certain choices can be made, specifically choices to leave associations which are oppressive. Under pluralism, membership in a plurality of associations is also a crucial source of empowerment. Groups require such protection as well. Just as groups are morally responsible for the well-being of individual members, the political structures and institutions of society ought to be assessed in terms of whether they contribute to the well-being of societal groups. Figgis, Cole, and Laski highlight this dimension of pluralism in arguing that groups develop distinctive personalities in the context of society and through their interaction with other groups. Young also emphasizes this dimension in illuminating how the individualistic focus of the concept of discrimination obscures and even denies the structural and institutional framework of oppression.[40] The justness of these structures ought to be assessed on the basis of the impact they have on groups or on individuals as members of groups. If some groups, such as cultural minorities, are found to be relatively powerless, they may require special rights that other groups may not require.[41]

The remaining lessons are all linked to the transformative element required of all collectivities, whether they are directly political or not, in order that they do not become oppressive to their members. The seventh lesson is that, according to the pluralist perspective, any means which offer to groups special protection from the cultural marketplace must ensure the continuation of pluralism. Groups that use their autonomy to stifle pluralism within their ranks can justify their actions only if they demonstrate that their actions facilitate healthy individual development and that healthy development is threatened by allowing pluralism within the group. According to the pluralist position on the relation between politics and individual development, groups which are antipluralistic will be hard pressed to show that their opposition to pluralism advances their members' development. Nonetheless, the fragility of some cultural communities leaves open the possibility that such an argument can successfully be made. In most cases though, groups which are antipluralistic cannot be considered democratic organizations and, further, they invite the suspicion that they oppress and distort the healthy development of their members.

Doubtlessly, readers have recognized that the distinction between groups, communities, and associations has not been drawn in this book and, moreover, has been ignored when it is drawn by others. This distinction usually rests on the degree to which the individual's identity and development is shaped by different types of collectivities and thus the degrees of embeddedness one expects to characterize each collectivity. For instance, "association" usually connotes ties that are more voluntary than those which characterize "communities." On the basis of embeddedness, there are two reasons why the distinctions between different

---

[40] Young, *Justice and the Politics of Difference*, 196.
[41] Kymlicka, *Liberalism, Community and Culture,* especially chapters 7, 8, 9.

types of collectivities have not been drawn here. Each consists of an additional lesson.

The eighth lesson is that communities, cultures, and associations consist of individuals who vary with respect to the closeness of their ties to the group. Amongst individuals belonging to the same culture, one can find some for whom involvement in the traditions of their community is central to their identity and others for whom escaping or transforming their culture helps to define the person they are. The same evidence can be found in religious groups, political parties, and amongst men and women. The diversity of attachments to a particular group is ignored if we insist on identifying a particular group as, e.g., a "community" rather than an "association." This distinction determines the standard degree of embeddedness one should expect to find amongst all members of that collectivity. Since individuals will vary with respect to their ties to groups, some, if not most, individuals will fail to meet the standard. The standard will either over- or underestimate the closeness of their ties to the group in question and, in any case, will ignore the different ways of belonging that individuals construct for themselves. Futile debates about membership, and about who counts as a Jew, a woman, an Aboriginal, a liberal, etc., etc., arise from drawing such misleading distinctions.

This distinction also spawns injustice, as the ninth and final lesson illuminates. Many of the values of collectivities to which we each belong are imposed by societal forces external to the group upon which they are imposed. In terms of membership, this often means that the standards of belonging to a collectivity might consist of values that are not only contingent to individual identity but are imposed by external forces. At one time or another, we all find ourselves hostage to the standards of others which aim to determine whether we are "real women" or "true men" and which lead to our being treated better or worse than other members of our group as a result of failing to meet such expectations. The struggle to transform our communities and attachments is central to identity politics. A reconstructed theory of political pluralism is better suited than is communitarianism to provide the conceptual resources through which identity politics can be explored.

Autonomy and voluntariness need not translate into freedom from all social attachments and obligations. Rather, the goal is to free individuals from any specific attachment that is destructive to her wellbeing. Political pluralism provides the resources for this sort of autonomy. By enjoying membership in many groups, individuals have the resources to determine the nature of their relation to any specific group or to change the nature of the group to which their affiliation is un-avoidably involuntary. Communitarianism does not offer these re-sources. Communitarians point out that liberalism does not sufficient-ly recognize that individuals are embedded in social contexts. Yet, some of these contexts, as illustrated above, are detrimental to the individu-al's well-being. For this reason, communitarians have reiterated the challenge to which the reconstruction of political pluralism is the best response.

Bibliography

Abramowitz, Alan. "The United States: Political Culture Under Stress." In G. Almond and S. Verba (eds.), *The Civic Culture Revisited*. Boston: Little Brown and Co., 1989.

Adorno, T. W., E. Frenkel-Brunswick, D. J. Levinson, and R. N. Sanford. *The Authoritarian Personality*. New York: Harper and Brothers, 1950.

Almond, Gabriel. "The Return to the State." *American Political Science Review* 82:3 (1988).

———. "The Intellectual History of the Civic Culture." *The Civic Culture Revisited*. Edited by G. Almond and S. Verba. Boston: Little Brown and Co., 1980.

Almond, Gabriel, and S. Verba, eds. *The Civic Culture: Political Attitudes and Democracy in Five Nations*. Princeton, N.J.: Princeton University Press, 1963.

Arendt, Hannah. *The Origins of Totalitarianism*. 2nd ed. New York: Meridian Books, 1958.

Ayer, A. J. *Language, Truth and Logic* (1936). New York: Penguin Books, 1971.

Bachrach, Peter. *The Theory of Democratic Elitism: A Critique*. Boston: Little Brown and Co., 1977.

Bachrach, Peter, and Morton S. Baratz. "Two Faces of Power," *American Political Science Review* 56:4 (1962).

Barber, Benjamin. *Strong Democracy: Participatory Politics in a New Age*. Berkeley: University of California Press, 1984.

Barker, E. "The Discredited State." *The Political Quarterly* 5 (1915).

Beard, Charles. *The Economic Interpretation of the Constitution of the United States*. New York: Macmillan and Co., 1913.

Bellah, Robert, Richard Madsen, William Sullivan, Ann Swidler, and Steven M. Tipton. *The Good Society*. New York: Alfred A. Knopf, 1991.

Bentley, Arthur F. *Behavior Knowledge Fact*. Bloomington, Ind.: The Principia Press, Inc., 1935.

———. *Relativity in Man and Society*. Revised with introduction by Sidney Ratner. New York: Octagon Books, Inc., 1968.

———. *The Process of Government: A Study of Social Pressures*. Chicago: University of Chicago Press, 1908.

Berelson, Bernard R., Paul F. Lazarsfeld, and William McPhee. *Voting: A Study of Opinion Formation in a Presidential Campaign.* Chicago: University of Chicago Press, 1954.

Berlin, Isaiah. *The Hedgehog and the Fox.* New York: Simon and Schuster, 1953.

Bernstein, Richard. "One Step Forward, Two Steps Backwards; Richard Rorty on Liberal Democracy and Philosophy." *Political Theory* 15:4 (November 1987).

Bosanquet, Bernard. *The Value and Destiny of the Individual.* London: Macmillan and Co., 1913.

Brodbeck, May. "Methodological Individualism: Definition and Reduction." *Philosophy of Science* 25 (1958).

Brown, Lyn Mikel, and Carol Gilligan. *Meeting at the Crossroads: Women's Psychology and Girls' Development.* Cambridge, Mass.: Harvard University Press, 1992.

Campbell, Angus, Philip E. Converse, Warren E. Miller, and Donald E. Stokes. *The American Voter: An Abridgment.* New York: John Wiley and Sons Inc., 1964.

Catlin, George E. *Science and Methods of Politics.* New York: Alfred A. Knopf, 1927.

Chapman, John W. "Voluntary Associations and the Political Theory of Pluralism." *Voluntary Associations,* vol. 11 of *Nomos.* Edited by J. W. Chapman and J. R. Pennock. New York: Atherton Press, 1969.

Cohen, Joshua. "Moral Pluralism and Political Consensus." In *The Idea of Democracy.* Edited by David Copp, Jean Hampton, and John E. Roemer. Cambridge: Cambridge University Press, 1993.

Cohen, Morris. *Reason and Nature.* New York: Harcourt, Brace, 1931.

Coker, Francis. "The Technique of the Pluralistic State." *American Political Science Review* 15:2 (1921).

Cole, G. D. H. *Social Theory.* New York: Frederick A. Stokes Co., 1920.

Coleman, Jules. "Comment: Rights, Markets and Community." *Harvard Journal of Law and Public Policy* 11:3 (1988).

Connolly, William. "The Challenge to Pluralist Theory." *The Bias of Pluralism.* Edited by William Connolly. New York: Atherton Press, 1969.

Dahl, Robert A. *Democracy and Its Critics.* New Haven: Yale University Press, 1989.

———. *Democracy, Liberty and Equality.* Oslo: Norwegian University Press, 1986.

———. "Pluralism Revisited." *Comparative Politics* 10:2 (1978).

———. *Democracy in the United States: Promise and Performance.* 2nd ed. Chicago: Rand McNally, 1972.

————. "The Behavioral Approach in Political Science: Epitaph for a Monument to a Successful Protest." *Behavioralism in Political Science.* Edited by Heinz Eulau. New York: Atherton Press, 1969.

————. *Pluralist Democracy in the United States: Conflict and Consent.* New Haven: Yale University Press, 1967.

————. *Modern Political Analysis.* Englewood Cliffs, N.J.: Prentice-Hall Inc., 1963.

————. *Who Governs? Democracy and Power in An American City.* New Haven: Yale University Press, 1961.

————. "Critique of the Ruling Elite Model." *American Political Science Review* 12 (1958).

————. "Hierarchy, Democracy, and Bargaining in Politics and Economics." In *Political Behavior, A Reader in Theory and Research.* Edited by Heinz Eulau, Samuel J. Eldersveld, and Morris Janowitz. Glencoe, Ill.: The Free Press, 1956.

————. *Preface to Democratic Theory.* Chicago: University of Chicago Press, 1956.

————. "Workers' Control of Industry and the British Labor Party." *American Political Science Review* 41:5 (October 1947).

Dahl, Robert A., and Charles E. Lindblom. *Politics, Economics, and Welfare.* New York: Harper and Row Publishers, 1953.

Dahl, Robert A., and Edward R. Tufte. *Size and Democracy.* Stanford: Stanford University Press, 1973.

Davis, Kingsley. "The Myth of Functionalist Analysis as a Special Method in Sociology and Anthropology." *American Sociological Review* 24 (1959).

Deane, Herbert A. *The Political Ideas of Harold Laski.* New York: Columbia University Press, 1955.

Dewey, John. *John Dewey: The Essential Writings.* Edited with introduction by David Sidorsky. New York: Harper and Row Publishers, 1977.

————. *Freedom and Culture.* New York: Capricorn, 1963.

————. *The Problems of Men.* New York: Philosophical Library, 1946.

————. *The Philosophy of John Dewey.* Edited by P. A. Schillp. Chicago: Northwestern University Press, 1939.

————. *Liberalism and Social Action.* New York: G. P. Putnan's Sons, 1938.

————. "The Future of Liberalism" (1935). *Dewey and His Critics.* Edited by Sidney Morgenbesser. New York: Journal of Philosophy Inc., 1977.

————. *The Quest for Certainty.* London: Allen and Unwin, 1930.

————. *Individualism Old and New.* New York: Minton, Bach and Co., 1930.

———. *The Public and Its Problems*. New York: Henry Holt and Co., 1927.

———. *Reconstruction in Philosophy*. New York: Henry Holt and Co., 1920.

———. *John Dewey: Lectures in China, 1919–1920*. Edited by Robert W. Clapton and Twuin-chen Ou. Honolulu: University of Hawaii Press, 1973.

———. *Essays in Experimental Logic*. Chicago: University of Chicago Press, 1916.

———. *Studies in Logic*. Chicago: University of Chicago Press, 1903.

———. "Psychology and Social Practice" (1900). *The Middle Works, 1899–1924*. Vol. 1. Edited by Jo Ann Boydston. Carbondale, Ill.: Southern Illinois University Press, 1976.

———. "Austin's Theory of Sovereignty." *Political Science Quarterly* vol. 9, (1894).

———. "Ethics of Democracy." In *The Early Works of John Dewey, 1882–1898*. Edited by Jo Ann Boydston. Carbondale, Ill.: Southern Illinois University Press, 1973.

Dewey, John, and Arthur Bentley. *A Philosophical Correspondence 1932–1951*. Edited by S. Ratner and J. Altman. New Brunswick, N.J.: Rutgers Press, 1964.

Duncan, Graeme and Steven Lukes. "The New Democracy." *Political Studies* 11 (June 1963).

Dworkin, Ronald. *A Matter of Principle*. Cambridge, Mass.: Harvard University Press, 1985.

———. *Taking Rights Seriously*. Cambridge, Mass.: Harvard University Press, 1977.

Dyke, Vernon Van. *Political Science: A Philosophical Analysis*. Stanford: Stanford University Press, 1960.

Easton, David. *A Framework for Political Analysis*. Englewood Cliffs, N.J.: Prentice-Hall Inc., 1965.

———. *A Systems Analysis of Political Life*. New York: John Wiley and Sons Inc., 1965.

———. "Categories for the Systems Analysis of Political Life." *Varieties of Political Theory*. Edited by David Easton. Englewood Cliffs, N.J.: Prentice-Hall Inc., 1956.

———. *The Political System: An Inquiry into the State of Political Science*. 2nd ed. New York: Alfred A. Knopf, 1953.

Eckstein, Harry. *A Theory of Stable Democracy*. Princeton, N.J.: Center of International Studies, 1961.

Eisenberg, Avigail. "The Politics of Individual and Group Difference in Canadian Jurisprudence." *Canadian Journal of Political Science* 27:1 (March 1994).

Eisfeld, Rainer. "Pluralism as Critical Theory." *Praxis International* 6:3 (October 1986).

Elliot, W. Y. "The Pragmatic Politics of Mr. H. J. Laski," *American Political Science Review* 18:2 (1924).

Ellis, E. D. "The Pluralistic State," *American Political Science Review* 14:3 (1920).

Elster, Jon. *Making Sense of Marx*. Cambridge: Cambridge University Press, 1985.

Ely, John Hart. *Democracy and Distrust*. Cambridge, Mass.: Harvard University Press, 1980.

Emmet, Dorothy. *Function, Purpose and Powers*. London: Macmillan and Co., 1958.

Etzioni, Amitai. *The Active Society: A Theory of Societal and Political Processes*. New York: The Free Press, 1968.

Eulau, Heinz. *The Behavioral Persuasion in Politics*. New York: Random House, 1963.

Eulau, Heinz, et al., eds. *Political Behavior, A Reader In Theory and Research*. Glencoe, Ill.: The Free Press, 1956.

Figgis, J. Neville. *Churches in the Modern State*. London: Longmans, Green and Co., 1913.

Follett, Mary P. "Community is a Process." *The Philosophical Review* 28:6 (1919).

———. *The New State*. New York: Longmans, Green and Co., 1918.

Frankel, Charles. "John Dewey's Social Philosophy." *New Studies in the Philosophy of John Dewey*. Edited by Steven M. Cahn. Hanover, N.H.: University Press of New England, 1977.

Freeden, Michael. *The New Liberalism: An Ideology of Social Reform*. Oxford: Clarendon Press, 1978.

Friedman, Marilyn. "Feminism and Modern Friendship." In *Communitarianism and Individualism*. Edited by Shlomo Avineri and Avner de-Shalit. Oxford: Oxford University Press, 1992.

Friedrich, Carl J., and Zbigniew K. Brzezinski. *Totalitarian Dictatorship and Autocracy*. Cambridge, Mass.: Harvard University Press, 1965.

Galston, William. *Liberal Purposes: Goods, Virtues and Diversity in the Liberal State*. Cambridge: Cambridge University Press, 1991.

———. "Defending Liberalism," *American Political Science Review* 76 (1982).

Garson, David G. *Group Theories of Politics*. Sage Library of Social Research, vol. 61. Beverly Hills: Sage Publications, 1978.

Gaus, Gerald. *The Modern Liberal Theory of Man*. London: Croom Helm, 1983.

Gierke, Otto. *Associations and Law: The Classical and Early Christian Stages.* Edited and translated by George Heiman. Toronto: University of Toronto Press, 1977.

——. *Natural Law and the Theory of Sovereignty 1500–1800,* vol. 1. Translated with introduction by E. Barker. Cambridge: Cambridge University Press, 1950.

Gould, Carol. *Rethinking Democracy: Freedom and Social Cooperation in Politics, Economy and Society.* Cambridge: Cambridge University Press, 1988.

Green, Leslie. "Consent and Community." *On Political Obligation.* Edited by Paul Harris. London: Routledge, 1990.

Gunnell, John G. *The Descent of Political Theory: The Geneology of an American Vocation.* Chicago: Chicago University Press, 1993.

Gutmann, Amy. "Communitarian Critics of Liberalism." *Philosophy and Public Affairs* 14:3 (1985).

Held, David. *Models of Democracy.* Stanford, Calif.: Stanford University Press, 1987.

Herring, Pendleton. *The Politics of Democracy: American Parties in Action.* New York: W. W. Norton and Co., 1960.

Hirschman, Albert O. *Exit, Voice and Loyalty: Responses and Decline in Firms, Organizations and States.* Cambridge, Mass.: Harvard University Press, 1970.

Hirst, Paul Q. "Associational Democracy." In *Prospects for Democracy: North, South, East, West.* Edited by David Held. Cambridge: Polity Press, 1993.

——. "Introduction" to *The Pluralist Theory of the State: Selected Writings of G. D. H. Cole, J. N. Figgis, and H. J. Laski.* Edited by Paul Q. Hirst. London: Routledge, 1989.

——. "Retrieving Pluralism." In *Social Theory and Social Criticism.* Edited by W. Outhwaite and M. Mulkay. Oxford: Basil Blackwell, 1987.

Hobbes, Thomas. *De Cive* (1642). In *The English Works of Thomas Hobbes of Malmesbury,* vol. II. Edited by Sir William Molesworth. London: John Bohn, 1966.

Holmes-Laski Letters. *The Correspondence of Mr. Justice Holmes and Harold J. Laski, 1916–1935,* vol. 1. Cambridge, Mass.: Harvard University Press, 1953.

Holmes, Stephen. "The Permanent Structure of Antiliberal Thought." In *Liberalism and the Moral Life.* Edited by Nancy Rosenblum. Cambridge, Mass.: Harvard University Press, 1989.

Horn, Robert. *Groups and the Constitution.* Stanford, Calif.: Stanford University Press, 1956.

Hsiao, K. C. *Political Pluralism: A Study in Contemporary Theory.* Ithaca, N.Y.: Cornell, 1927.

James, William. *Radical Empiricism and a Pluralistic Universe.* New York: Longmans, Green and Co., 1943.

———. *A Pluralistic Universe. The Works of William James.* Edited with introduction by Richard Bernstein. Cambridge, Mass.: Harvard University Press, 1977.

———. *Principles of Psychology,* vol. 1, *The Works of William James.* With introduction by Gerald Myers. Cambridge, Mass.: Harvard University Press, 1981.

Kariel, Henry S. *The Eclipse of Citizenship: Power and Participation in Contemporary Politics.* New York: Holt Rinehart and Winston, 1968.

———. *The Promise of Politics.* Englewood Cliffs, N.J.: Prentice-Hall Inc., 1966.

Kaufman, Arnold S. "Human Nature and Participatory Democracy." *The Bias of Pluralism.* Edited by William Connolly. New York: Atherton Press, 1969.

Kaufman-Osborn, T. V. "John Dewey and the Liberal Science of Community." *Journal of Politics* 46 (November 1984).

———. "John Dewey and the Politics of Method." Ph.D. dissertation, Princeton University, 1982.

Key, V. O. *The Responsible Electorate, 1936–1960.* Cambridge, Mass.: Belknap, 1966.

Kim, K. W. "The Limits of Behavioral Explanation in Politics." *Apolitical Politics.* Edited by Charles A. McCoy and John Playford. New York: Crowell, 1968.

Kluger, Richard. *Simple Justice.* New York: Vintage, 1975.

Kornhauser, William. *The Politics of Mass Society.* Glencoe, Ill.: The Free Press, 1959.

Kress, Paul. *Social Science and the Idea of Process.* Urbana: University of Illinois Press, 1970.

Kymlicka, Will. "Liberal Individualism and Liberal Neutrality." In *Communitarianism and Individualism.* Edited by Shlomo Avineri and Avner de-Shalit. Oxford: Oxford University Press, 1992.

———. *Liberalism, Community, and Culture.* Oxford: Oxford University Press, 1989.

———. "Liberalism and Communitarianism," *Canadian Journal of Philosophy* 18:2 (June 1988).

Laski, Harold J. *The Grammar of Politics.* 2nd ed. London: Allen and Unwin, 1930.

———. *Liberty in the Modern State.* London: Faber and Faber, 1930.

———. *The Foundations of Sovereignty and Other Essays*. New York: Harcourt, Brace and Co., 1921.

———. *Authority and the Modern State*. New Haven: Yale University Press, 1919.

———. "The Pluralistic State." *The Philosophical Review* 28 (November 1919).

———. *Studies in the Problems of Sovereignty*. New Haven: Yale University Press, 1917.

Lasswell, Harold. "Psychology Looks at Morals and Politics." *Introductory Readings on Political Behavior*. Edited by S. Sidney Uliner. Chicago: Rand McNally, 1961.

———. *Psychopathology and Politics*. New York: Viking Press, 1960.

———. *Power and Personality*. New York: W. W. Norton and Co., 1948.

Lasswell, Harold, and Abraham Kaplan. *Power and Society*. New Haven: Yale University Press, 1950.

Lazarsfeld, Paul F., Bernard Berelson, and Hazel Gaudet. *The People's Choice*. 2nd ed. New York: Columbia University Press, 1948.

Lijphart, Arend. "The Structure of Inference." *The Civic Culture Revisited*. Edited by G. Almond and S. Verba. Boston: Little Brown and Co., 1980.

Lindsay, A. D. *The Modern Democratic State*. Oxford: Oxford University Press, 1943.

Lipset, S. M. *Political Man*. Garden City, N.Y.: Doubleday, 1959.

Lowi, Theodore J. *The End of Liberalism: The Second Republic of the United States*. 2nd ed. New York: W. W. Norton and Co., 1969.

———. "The Public Philosophy: Interest Group Liberalism." *The Bias of Pluralism*. Edited by William Connolly. New York: Atherton Press, 1969.

Lukes, Steven. *Power: A Radical View*. Bristol: British Sociological Association, 1974.

———. *Individualism*. Oxford: Basil Blackwell, 1973.

Macedo, Stephen. *Liberal Virtues: Citizenship, Virtue and Community in Liberal Constitutionalism*. Oxford: Clarendon Press, 1990.

MacIntyre, Alasdair. *After Virtue, A Study in Moral Theory*. 2nd ed. Notre Dame, Ind.: University of Notre Dame Press, 1984.

———. "Is Patriotism A Virtue?" *The Lindley Lecture*. Kansas: University of Kansas, 1984.

MacKinnon, Catharine. *Towards a Feminist Theory of the State*. Cambridge, Mass.: Harvard University Press, 1989.

Macpherson, C. B. *The Life and Times of Liberal Democracy*. Oxford: Oxford University Press, 1977.

Magid, H. M. *English Political Pluralism: The Problem of Freedom and Organization.* New York: Columbia University Press, 1941.

Maitland, F. W. "Moral Personality and Legal Personality." *Selected Essays.* Edited by H. D. Hazeltine, G. Lapsley, and R. H. Winfield. London: Cambridge University Press, 1936.

Mandelbaum, Maurice. "Societal Facts" (1955). Reprinted in *Philosophy, History and the Sciences: Selected Critical Essays.* Baltimore: Johns Hopkins University Press, 1984.

McBride, William Leon. "Voluntary Association: The Basis of an Ideal Model and the Democratic Failure." *Voluntary Associations,* vol. 11 of *Nomos.* Edited by J. W. Chapman and J. R. Pennock. New York: Atherton Press, 1969.

McCloskey, H. "Consensus and Ideology in American Politics." *American Political Science Review* 58:2 (1964).

McClure, Kirstie. "On the Subject of Rights: Pluralism, Plurality and Political Identity." In *Dimensions of Radical Democracy: Pluralism, Citizenship, Community.* Edited by Chantal Mouffe. London: Verso, 1992.

McConnell, Grant. "The Public Values of Private Association." *Voluntary Associations,* vol. 11 of Nomos. Edited by J. W. Chapman and J. R. Pennock. New York: New York University Press, 1969.

———. *Private Power and American Democracy.* New York: Alfred A. Knopf, 1966.

Meehan, Eugene. *Contemporary Political Thought.* Homewood, Ill.: Dorsey Press, 1967.

Metz, Joseph G. "Democracy and the Scientific Method in the Philosophy of John Dewey." *Review of Politics* 31:2 (April 1969).

Meyer, William J. *Public Good and Political Authority: A Pragmatic Proposal.* Port Washington, N.Y.: Kennikat Press, 1975.

Mill, John Stuart. *The Subjection of Women* (1869). In *Three Essays by John Stuart Mill.* Edited with introduction by M. G. Fawcett. London: Oxford University Press, 1971.

Miller, David. "In What Sense Must Socialism Be Communitarian?" *Social Philosophy and Policy* 6:2 (1989).

Miller, Richard. *Fact and Method.* Princeton: Princeton University Press, 1987.

———. *Analyzing Marx: Morality, Power and History.* Princeton: Princeton University Press, 1984.

Moore, E. C. *American Pragmatism: Pierce, James, Dewey.* New York: Columbia University Press, 1961.

Morgenbesser, Sidney, ed. *Dewey and His Critics.* New York: Journal of Philosophy Inc., 1977.

Mosca, Gaetano. *The Ruling Class*. Edited and revised, with introduction by A. Livingston. Translated by H. D. Kahn. New York: McGraw-Hill, 1939.

Myrdal, Gunnar. *An International Economy: Problems and Prospects* (1956). Reprinted in *Value in Social Theory*. Edited by Paul Steeten. New York: Harper, 1958.

Nederman, Cary. "Freedom, Community and Function: Communitarian Lessons of Medieval Political Theory." *American Political Science Review* 86:4 (1992).

Nicholls, D. *Three Varieties of Pluralism*. New York: St. Martin's Press, 1974.

Nisbet, Robert. *The Quest for Community*. New York: Oxford University Press, 1953.

Nordlinger, Eric A., Theodore J. Lowi, and Sergio Fabbrini. "The Return to the State: Critiques." *American Political Science Review* 82:3 (September 1988).

Odegard, P. *Pressure Politics*. New York: Columbia University Press, 1928.

Okin, Susan Moller. *Justice, Gender and the Family*. New York: Basic Books, 1989.

Pateman, Carole. "The Civic Culture: A Philosophic Critique." *The Civic Culture Revisited*. Edited by G. Almond and S. Verba. Boston: Little Brown and Co., 1980.

———. *Participation and Democratic Theory*. Cambridge: Cambridge University Press, 1970.

Perry, Ralph B. *The Thought and Character of William James*. Cambridge, Mass.: Harvard University Press, 1948.

Pranger, Robert J. *The Eclipse of Citizenship: Power and Participation in Contemporary Politics*. New York: Holt Rinehart and Winston Inc., 1968.

Prothro, J. W. and C. W. Grigg. "Fundamental Principles of Democracy." *Journal of Politics* 22 (1960).

Rawls, John. *Political Liberalism*. New York: Columbia University Press, 1993.

———. "Justice as Fairness: Political Not Metaphysical." *Philosophy and Public Affairs* 14:3 (1985).

———. *A Theory of Justice*. Cambridge, Mass.: The Belknap Press of Harvard University Press, 1971.

Ricci, David. *The Tragedy of Political Science: Politics, Scholarship and Democracy*. New Haven: Yale University Press, 1984.

Rorty, Richard. "Thugs and Theorists: A Reply to Bernstein." *Political Theory* 15:4 (November 1987).

———. "Post-Modernist Bourgeois Liberalism," *Journal of Philosophy* 80:10 (October 1983).

Rosenblum, Nancy. *Another Liberalism: Romanticism and the Reconstruction of Liberal Thought*. Cambridge, Mass.: Harvard University Press, 1987.

———. "Studying Authority: Keeping Pluralism in Mind." *Authority Revisited*, vol 29 of *Nomos*. Edited by J. Roland Pennock and John W. Chapman. New York: New York University Press, 1987.

———. "Pluralism and Self-Defense." In *Liberalism and the Moral Life*. Cambridge, Mass.: Harvard University Press, 1989.

Sabine, George. *A History of Political Theory*. Revised edition. New York: Henry Holt and Co., 1950.

———. "Beyond Ideology." *The Philosophical Review* 57 (1948).

———. "Pluralism: A Point of View." *American Political Science Review* 17:1 (1923).

Sandel, Michael. "Democrats and Community." *The New Republic*, February 22, 1988.

———. "The Procedural Republic and the Unencumbered Self." *Political Theory* 12:1 (1984).

———. *Liberalism and the Limits of Justice*. Cambridge: Cambridge University Press, 1982.

Scheffler, Israel. *Four Pragmatists: A Critical Introduction to Pierce, James, Mead and Dewey*. New York: Humanities Press, 1974.

Schumpeter, Joseph. *Capitalism, Socialism and Democracy*. New York: Harper and Row Publishers, 1942.

Seidelman, Raymond. *Disenchanted Realists: Political Science and the American Crisis 1884–1984*. Albany: State University of New York Press, 1985.

Sidorsky, David. "Commentary: Pluralism, Empiricism and the Secondary Association." *Voluntary Associations*, vol. 11 of *Nomos*. Edited by J. W. Chapman and J. R. Pennock. New York: Atherton Press, 1969.

Smith, T. V. *The Promise of American Politics*. 2nd ed. Chicago: University of Chicago Press, 1936.

Sperlich, Peter W. *Conflict and Harmony in Human Affairs: A Study of Cross Pressures and Political Behavior*. Chicago: Rand McNally, 1971.

Stephen, Leslie. *The English Utilitarians*, vol. 3. New York: G. P. Putnam's Sons, 1902.

Stevenson, C. L. *Ethics and Language*. New Haven: Yale University Press, 1944.

Stouffer, S. A. *Communism, Conformity and Civil Liberties*. Garden City, N.Y.: Doubleday, 1955.

Sullivan, William. *Reconstructing Public Philosophy.* Berkeley: University of California Press, 1982.

Sunstien, Cass. "Beyond the Republican Revival," *Yale Law Journal* 97 (1988).

Talmon, J. L. *The Rise of Totalitarian Democracy.* London: Secker Warburg, 1952.

Taylor, Charles. *Multiculturalism and "The Politics of Recognition."* Princeton, N.J.: Princeton University Press, 1992.

———. "Cross-Purposes: The Liberal Communitarian Debate." *Liberalism and the Moral Life.* Edited by Nancy L. Rosenblum. Cambridge, Mass.: Harvard University Press, 1989.

———. "Alternative Futures: Legitimacy, Identity, and Alienation in Late Twentieth-Century Canada." *Constitutionalism, Citizenship and Society in Canada.* Edited by A. Cairns and C. Williams. Toronto: University of Toronto Press, 1985.

———. *Philosophy and the Human Sciences: Philosophical Papers,* vol. 2. Cambridge: Cambridge University Press, 1985.

Truman, David. "The Impact on Political Science of the Revolution in the Behavioral Sciences." *Behavioralism in Political Science.* Edited by Heinz Eulau. New York: Atherton Press, 1969.

———. *The Governmental Process.* New York: Alfred A. Knopf Inc., 1951.

———. "The Implications of Political Behavior in Research." *Items* 5 (December 1951).

Tufts, James H. "The Community and Economic Groups," *The Philosophical Review* 28:6 (November 1919).

Urban, William M. "The Nature of the Community," *The Philosophical Review* 28:6 (November 1919).

Wahl, Jean. *The Pluralist Philosophies of England and America.* London: The Open Court Co., 1925.

Wain, Kenneth. "Strong Poets and Utopia: Rorty's Liberalism, Dewey's Democracy," *Political Studies* 41 (1993).

Waldron, Jeremy. "When Justice Replaces Affection: The Need for Rights." *Harvard Journal of Law and Public Policy* 11:3 (1988).

Walke, John. "Pre-Behavioralism in Political Science." *American Political Science Review* 73 (1979).

Walzer, Michael. "The Civil Society Argument." In *Dimensions of Radical Democracy: Pluralism, Citizenship and Democracy.* Edited by Chantal Mouffe. London: Verso, 1992.

———. "The Communitarian Critique of Liberalism." *Political Theory* 18:1 (1990).

———. *Spheres of Justice.* New York: Basic Books, 1983.

————. "Philosophy and Democracy." *Political Theory* 9:3 (August 1981).

————. *Obligations*. Cambridge, Mass.: Harvard University Press, 1970.

Ward, Cynthia. "The Limits of Liberal Republicanism: Why Group-Based Remedies and Republican Citizenship Don't Mix." *Columbia Law Journal* 91 (1991).

Watkins, J. W. N. "Methodological Individualism: A Reply." *Philosophy of Science* 22 (1955).

Webb, L. C., ed. *Legal Personality and Political Pluralism*. Melbourne: Melbourne University Press, 1958.

Weinstein, Leo. "The Group Approach: Arthur F. Bentley." *Essays on the Scientific Study of Politics*. Edited by H. J. Storing. New York: Holt Rinehart and Winston, 1962.

Westbrook, Robert B. *John Dewey and American Democracy*. Ithaca, N.Y.: Cornell University Press, 1991.

Wilson, R. Jackson. *In Quest of Community: Social Philosophy in the United States 1860–1920*. Oxford: Oxford University Press, 1968.

Young, Iris Marion. *Justice and the Politics of Difference*. Princeton, N.J.: Princeton University Press, 1990.

Zylstra, B. *From Pluralism to Collectivism*. The Netherlands: Van Gorcomt Co., 1968.

Index